The Endless Country

The Endless Country

*A Personal Journey Through Turkey's
First Hundred Years*

SAMI KENT

PICADOR

First published 2024 by Picador
an imprint of Pan Macmillan
The Smithson, 6 Briset Street, London EC1M 5NR
EU representative: Macmillan Publishers Ireland Ltd, 1st Floor,
The Liffey Trust Centre, 117–126 Sheriff Street Upper,
Dublin 1, D01 YC43
Associated companies throughout the world
www.panmacmillan.com

ISBN 978-1-5290-9926-3

Copyright © Sami Kent 2024

The right of Sami Kent to be identified as the
author of this work has been asserted by him in accordance
with the Copyright, Designs and Patents Act 1988.

1 3 5 7 9 8 6 4 2

A CIP catalogue record for this book is available from the British Library.

Typeset by Palimpsest Book Production Ltd, Falkirk, Stirlingshire
Printed and bound by CPI Group (UK) Ltd, Croydon, CR0 4YY

Visit **www.picador.com** to read more about all our books
and to buy them. You will also find features, author interviews and
news of any author events, and you can sign up for e-newsletters
so that you're always first to hear about our new releases.

To Michi, who made this possible,
and to Tommaso, who, frankly, didn't help at all.

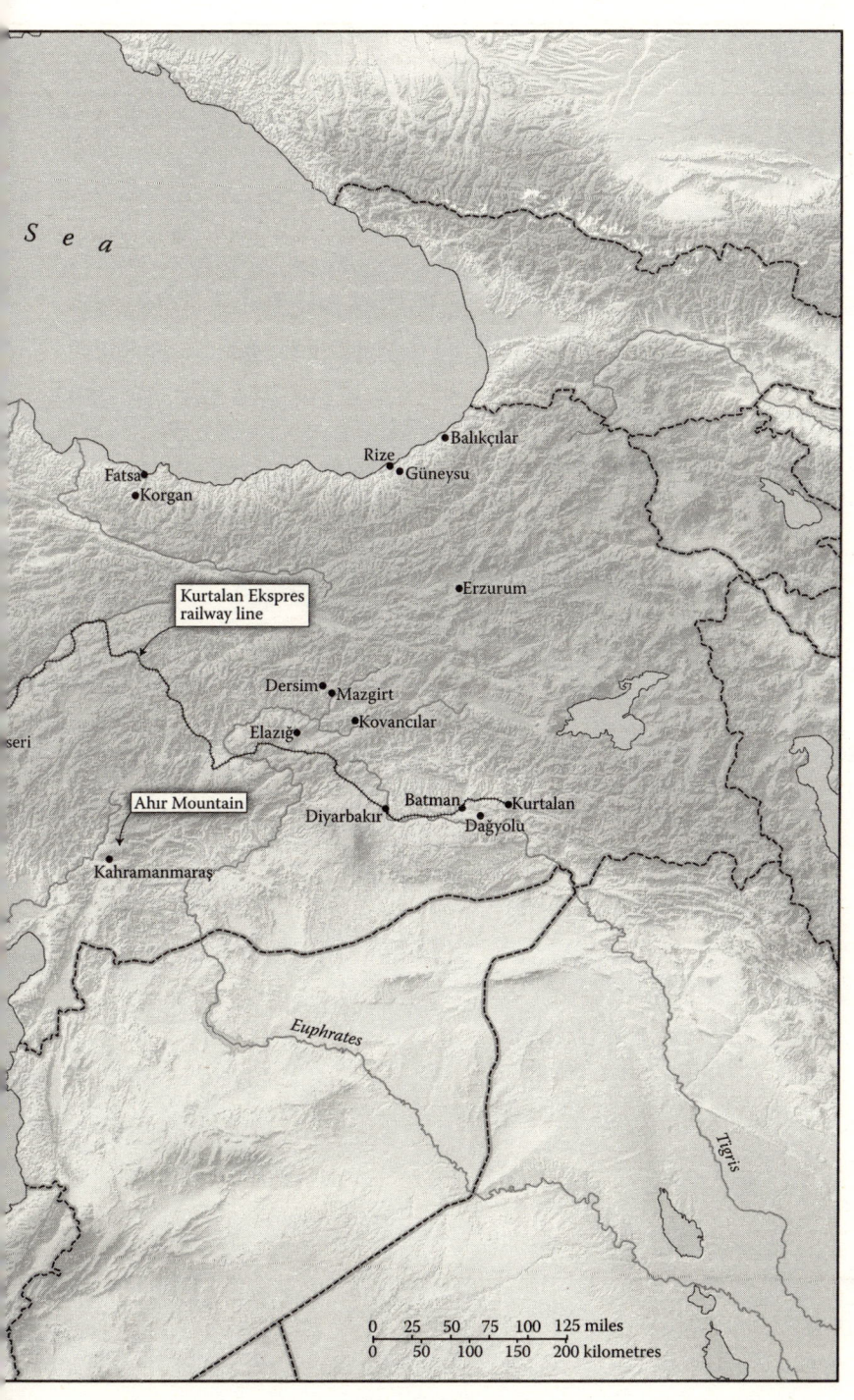

S e a

Balıkçılar

Rize
Güneysu

Fatsa
Korgan

Erzurum

Kurtalan Ekspres
railway line

Dersim
Mazgirt

Elazığ
Kovancılar

seri

Ahır Mountain

Batman
Kurtalan

Diyarbakır
Dağyolu

Kahramanmaraş

Euphrates

Tigris

| 0 | 25 | 50 | 75 | 100 | 125 miles |
| 0 | 50 | 100 | 150 | 200 kilometres |

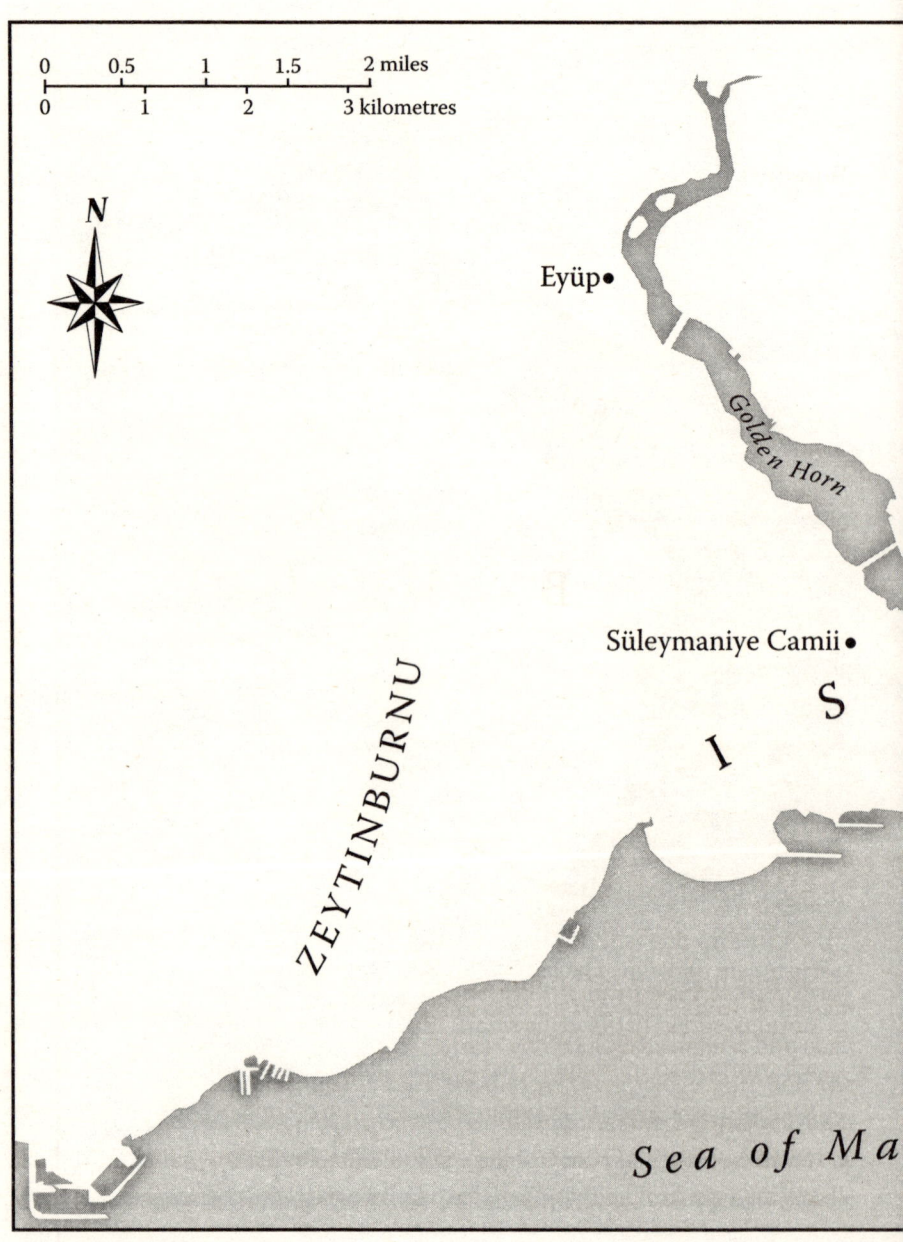

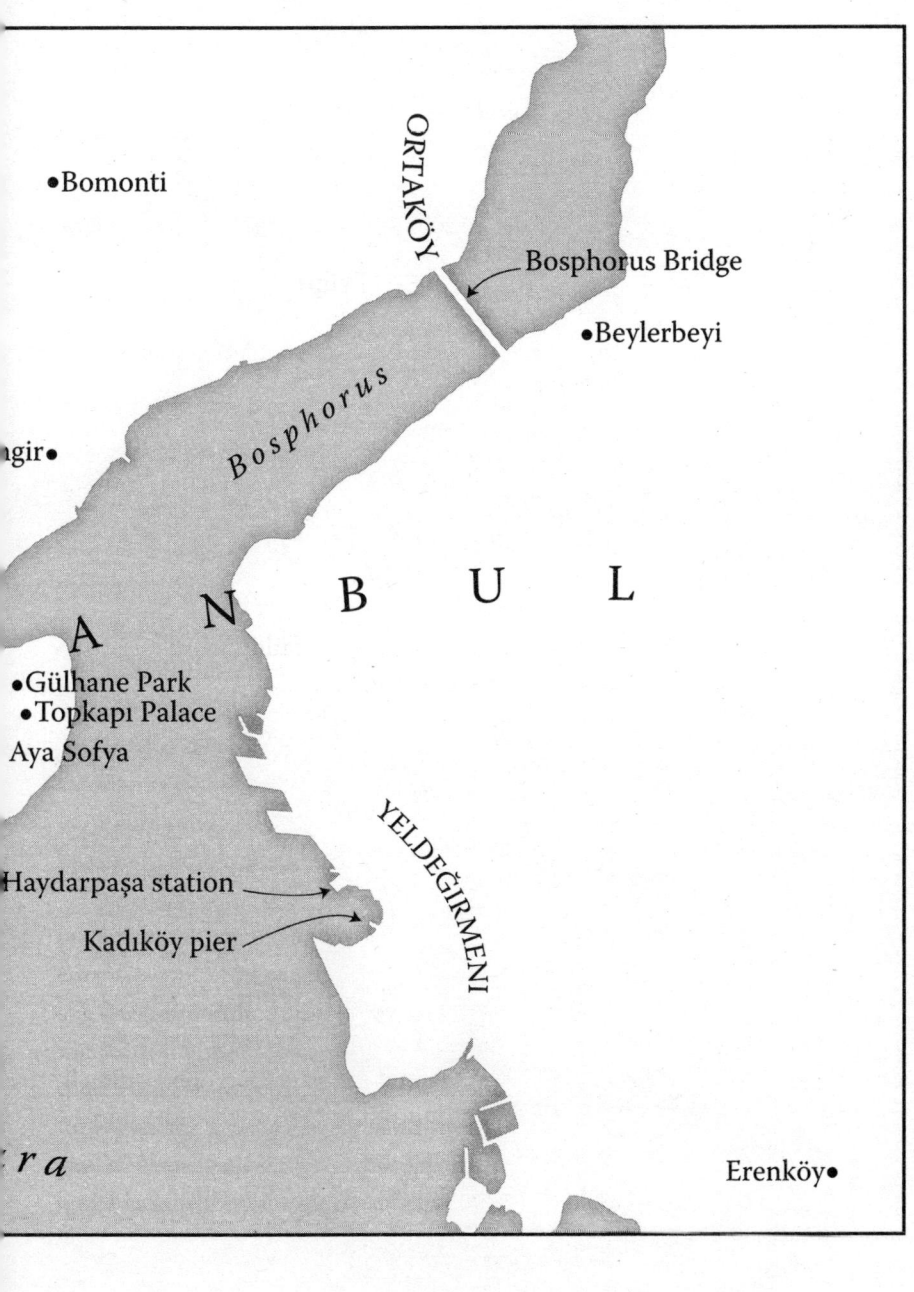

•Bomonti

ORTAKÖY

Bosphorus Bridge

•Beylerbeyi

Bosphorus

ıgir•

A   N   B   U   L

•Gülhane Park
•Topkapı Palace
Aya Sofya

YELDEĞIRMENI

Haydarpaşa station

Kadıköy pier

ra

Erenköy•

Contents

1. Introduction

1920s onwards: Rize, London,
Ankara, İstanbul

I AM SAT ALONE, THE ONLY PASSENGER IN A SEVENTEEN-seat minibus, and yet still somehow uncomfortable. It is late afternoon as we leave Rize, deep in the north-east corner of Turkey, and we are heading further east still, along the highway that lines the Black Sea coast. It is a tough and hardy region, of big hills and bigger noses. The *dolmuş*, the shared taxi, slowly fills up with them, and I watch the sea to our left, calm but unwelcoming: a wintry blueish grey. After half an hour, the driver catches my eye in the rear-view mirror – remembering our agreement – and lifts his considerable black eyebrows, as if to say, 'Here it is, this is Balıkçılar.'

I step off the bus, stood, backpack on, the road behind me and the hills in front, 'our' village rising up ahead. Balıkçılar, 'Fishermen'. Approaching the teahouse nearby – and the men smoking in front of it – I rehearse the introduction in my head: 'I'm Sami Kent. My father is Turkish, his family is from here: the Aytaçs, the Murtezaoğlus.'

I reach the teahouse – the words *çay evi* written in faded paint on its front – and try my best. A few suspicious questions follow: 'Who were they?', 'What was their name?', 'When was this?' Their guards are slowly lowering. I follow my aunt's advice, texted the day before: 'Mention Abdi Aytaç when you can.' Abdi Aytaç: my great-grandfather, a small village celebrity, famous for leaving this

1

place, for making it all the way to France, for running unsuccessfully as a leftist candidate in this conservative, religious heartland. *That* Abdi Aytaç!

They accept. Smiling, grizzled men stream out of the *çay evi* like cartoon clowns. A tea slides in front of me. They begin to offer, to me and to each other, their amateur genealogies, their half-remembered histories of this village of five hundred people. Amidst their thick Black Sea Turkish, I think I catch words I've learnt from textbooks, the bewildering array of terms Turks have for various relatives: *baldız* – one's wife's sister; *bacanak* – one's wife's sister's husband; *dayı* – one's mother's brother.

After a few minutes the *muhtar* – the head of the village – arrives, offering to take me on a tour of where my family once lived. He's a driver by trade, and we jump into his car and shoot up the hill: squeezing up the road, haring round corners, U-turning where we can go no more. He has one hand on the wheel and one on the phone, making calls to various relatives of mine, asking whether they are in the village. I have one eye on the certain falls below and one on the scene in front: the January sun setting on the tea plantations all around, the occasional splash of an orange tree, the Black Sea stretching out beyond us. There's no one here, the *muhtar* explains. Many families leave for the winter months. I am, I must admit, slightly disappointed. And then one calls back.

Me, the *muhtar*, two middle-aged men and an old woman – who covered her head as I entered – are sat in a living room, curved around the fireplace. A tray of coffees comes in, as we try and work out who we are. Again, the back and forth, the pinning of certain words to certain names. The enthusiasm in the room rises. They start to shout with excitement, they shout over each other, they shout to their near-deaf mother.

We're all related. The old woman, past ninety and still sturdy, is my grandmother's cousin, Abdi Aytaç's niece. She asks if my grandmother is still alive. 'Yes,' I say, 'she lives in İstanbul.' She begins to cry. She hugs me. She's looking at my face, at my nose, the slight hook of it – the same hook on my brothers, my father, my grandmother. She hugs me again. 'You look just like us!' she says.

*

There is a question you're asked often and early in conversations in Turkey. *Nerelisin?*, 'Where are you from?' *Memleket?* 'Your home town?' they might add. It's asked not only to migrants from outside but within the country too – a friendly recognition, really, that almost every Turkish family has a story to tell: journeys from villages to cities, each with their own pioneer across Anatolia and beyond.

I used to answer honestly. 'London' – the place where I've spent nearly all my life – but this was invariably met with a shake of the head. My father was Turkish, so my *memleket* had to be too. I soon tried 'Ankara', where my *baba* had grown up, but still no. It didn't fit – you can't be *from* the city. 'Rize', I learnt to say. Yes! 'Ah, a Black Sea boy!' they would reply, as I slotted into a more familiar groove. That would explain my fair hair as well – Rize is only a day away from the blonde hair and blue eyes of Russia. Forget the fact my mum was from Peterborough, east England. People were far more interested in my dad, anyway – in the figure who left Turkey at nineteen. 'Where does he live?', 'What job does he do?', 'How long has he lived abroad?' No one ever asks why he went.

*

The stories of Turkey my *baba* told us when we were children have an odd effect. The further my *baba* gets from events, the more colourful they become in the telling. The further I get from when I first heard them, the blurrier they become in the remembering. Both vivid and unclear, like a kaleidoscope mid-twist. Did he *really* used to hang street cats for fun? Was he *really* the slated Eurovision candidate in 1976, only for Turkey to pull out in protest? Was he *really* near Taksim Square a year later, when police fired on demonstrators and left forty people dead?

In a sense, it didn't matter. This was the character arc we moulded for him and we loved him for it: the dad with the larger-than-life tales from his homeland. And the migrant success story: the student who came to England, met his future wife in his first week there, and never looked back.

This is how we learnt Turkey too, as anecdote, as a set of stories. And of course the place where we holidayed every year, beloved and a little bit dangerous: the queues at passport control, where my *baba* would tell us – though we didn't know he was joking – that the border guard would shoot anyone who crossed the yellow line before their turn, and me – with all the subtlety of a nine-year-old – trying not to look at the pistol in his holster, for I had never seen a gun before; then, the blast of the warm evening air outside the airport, with its smell of olive trees and lemon cologne. Followed by two weeks of the glittering Aegean, the site even of my first memory: tossed out of a boat at three years old, lifejacket on, bobbing in the waves.

It was two weeks of *baba* to ourselves, in his holiday mode of yellow Speedos and a pirate bandana. He was our guide, our translator, our inveterate over-orderer. Grilled liver, garlic yoghurt, fried aubergines. I longed for them, and the Turkish he spoke asking for them too, the way the sounds fell together, magic in the way that all dads are magic, summoning something inexplicable, inaccessible, in an instant. It was another world, and another version of him. He would tease us with it, with the endless cases, tenses and subjects you can stack on Turkish words, loading them up like a waiter's plates. *Avustralyalılaştıramadıklarımızdan mısınız?* Are you one-of-the-ones-who-we-have-failed-to-Australianize?

His Turkish was – must have been – rusty, but still some part of him seemed more at ease, slipping into the rhythms of conversation, and the cues that frame so much of it. I didn't know it at the time, but it was a place deeply familiar to him: as a boy himself, he had travelled around the same coast with my *babaanne* and *dede* in a green VW camper van. He can still remember the licence plate.

There's another memory I have of those holidays, one that speaks to who our family is, and what it believes. One morning, my *baba* gave me one of Turkey's million-lira purple banknotes – value, approximately, one pound sterling – and all I could think was, *I'm a millionaire!* But his excitement was different, looking at my fair hair, and then the portrait of Atatürk, stamped on all Turkish currency. *'You look just like him!'* he said.

*

There is a black-and-white photo of my *baba*, around eight years old, in Boy Scout khaki, with matching cap and scarf, a slight smirk – a slight pride – on his face. The 10th of November was always a big day. Lantern in hand, he would keep guard of the school bust of Atatürk, on the anniversaries of his death. For my *baba*, Atatürk was not just the country's founder and first president, not just a military hero, but an intellectual giant. His various reforms – changing Turkey's script, or giving Turks surnames – were celebrated in their textbooks. Excerpts of his speeches were read out in class, though the Turkish was incomprehensible and strange. His statues and sayings dominated the Ankara where he grew up. Looking back, he says, it was a little bit 'Muscovite'.

My *baba* and his peers were to be model Turks, the newest generation for an historic and evergreen mission: to transform the country top-down from something stagnant and religious to the resolutely modern, scientific and secular; from the bankrupt and backward Ottoman Empire to a Western-facing nation-state. To put it in my *baba*'s words, more bluntly, 'we despised religion'. They revered the army though, the ultimate defenders of that legacy. The cartoons and satire of his youth, he remembers, were ruthless and cruel about Turkey's politicians, but no one touched the military.

Our family were fully a part of that vanguard, if not in influence, then at least in enthusiasm. By my *baba*'s time, of course, that hot, live project under Atatürk and his successors forty years ago had congealed into legend, but it was given real and beating life at home, by the man he calls the 'intellectual stimulus' of his child-hood: Abdi Aytaç, his maternal grandfather, who would burst into poetry over an evening meal, our own pioneer whose journey out west would explain so much of how our family came to be.

Balıkçılar, 1918, was not a promising place: poor, and rural, and always raining. Its hills were too steep to farm, or even to access by road – the only way up and down was by horse, on narrow winding paths. So the village that Abdi Aytaç knew, and the family he came from, looked to the water: uncle sailors who died at sea; grandads who traded with Russian port cities to the east. Plus the otherworldly relative Imam Hacı Hasan who – as the story goes – correctly predicted to his family one morning both that there would be a storm and that it would be his last day on earth.

For an ambitious Abdi, it would simply not do. So at seventeen years old – in the dying days of the Ottoman Empire – he moved to post-war İstanbul, to work the boats of the Bosphorus. The Great War, though, had left the people exhausted and their leaders upended. And here, the details I have heard only from my *babaanne*, who heard it in turn first-hand on her father's knee. One day, she explains, soon after he arrived in İstanbul – 'green eyed, black haired, and very handsome' – he was approached on the street by a carriage, carrying an exiled Egyptian princess. Soon after, he left his job to work for her. Namely – and this part she tells me with a glint in her eye and an odd pride in her voice – he became her gigolo.

As the family saying goes, *yemin edebilirim ama ispatlayamam.*
I can swear on it but I can't prove it.

From there, her family sponsored Abdi's education as they
hopped around Europe – in Geneva, at a commercial school in
Dijon, until somehow, eventually, he was studying political science
at a university in 1930s Paris, where his life transformed again. In
his Paris 'milieu', as my *babaanne* says, were some of Turkey's finest
minds abroad: Sabahattin Eyüboğlu, the son of a governor and
MP, and a famed writer–translator himself; and his brother Bedri
Rahmi, abstract painter and poet.* They were artists and thinkers,
economists and visionaries: Turkish but Westward-looking; committed republicans; secular if not completely atheist. Though he
carried a certain leftist romance, Abdi emerged fully on board with
the politics that had animated his country all his adult life.

On Abdi's return from Paris, he worked as an economist at the
Turkish Central Bank in Ankara, the new capital and ground zero
of that nation-making programme. Then he moved to a state paper
factory – as my *babaanne* remembers, on the grounds where the
factory management lived, there were formal balls, tennis courts,
and full, modern plumbing. They bought a summer house in İstan-
bul. In the early fifties, as Turkey's one-party system made way for
democracy, he tried to run as a candidate for Atatürk's party, selling
all his tea plantations to fund it. He failed but regardless, their place
in Turkey's Westernizing, secular elite was secure.†

My *babaanne* carried on the torch, outward-looking and

---

* Years later, he offered our family one of his originals, all shapes and bold colours. To my aunt's eternal regret, Abdi and his wife – not quite understanding
what it was, or more pertinently, how valuable it would be – turned it down.

† The other side of my family's participation in Turkey's great nation-building
was less illustrious. My *baba*'s paternal grandfather, Zeki Kent, was working as a
contractor at the presidential mansion in Çankaya, Ankara, in the 1920s. During

committed to progress. Even now, she speaks three languages, and uses Instagram deep into her eighties. She went back to Balıkçılar only once – at twelve years old, she could only stay one night, for it was boring and dirty. Why return to the village after your family had advanced to the city?

Her own marriage was a slightly awkward fit – a rushed affair and a brief elopement to my *dede*, a dark-skinned boy from Ankara's squatter districts. He listened to arabesk music, she hated it. He ate döner kebab, she had never tried it before; she wore miniskirts, his conservative older sister pulled her skirts back down over her knees. But they did at least share an outlook: dismissive of religion, admiring of the West, stoutly republican. My *dede* had originally worked as a translator, taught himself English, before founding his own firm in imports and exports. As my *baba* remembers, the house of his childhood was one of wild cocktail parties.

It's a path that puts a different spin on that old Turkish question, *nerelisin* – 'where are you from' – and its underlying logic: that your hometown, even generations removed, shapes who you are. Drinkers are from Edirne; imams are from Konya, et cetera et cetera. Here, what matters is not so much Balıkçılar as the leaving of it. Just as the country Abdi lived in had progressed – from crumbling empire to new republic – so had he, and his daughter and grandson after him. How could he not link the two? What story could be more compelling?

*

The Turkey of my *baba*'s adolescence, though, was creaking. Already by the time he was twelve, he had lived through two military coups, as generals deemed the country's politicians unfit to govern. Things

---

one shift, he fell off a ladder in an empty ornamental pool, and cracked his head. He had a missing part of his skull, and severe epilepsy, for the rest of his life.

spiralled still. In the 1970s, a series of financial crises left the economy reeling. *Hazine yetmiş sente muhtaç*, as they used to say, 'a treasury in need of seventy cents.' There was constant, low-level violence between left and right. My *baba*'s communist uncle – an alluring, handsome figure who played guitar and passed him the banned poetry of Nazim Hikmet – joined sit-ins in universities across the city. By the end of the decade, daily pitched battles on the streets between militants had claimed thousands of lives.

Uninterested in politics though, it was more everyday scenes that disillusioned my *baba*. There was the ever-present, demeaning corruption. The head of his youth conservatoire in Ankara – he played piano – was a tuneless butcher from Sivas, the cousin of someone or other important. In the end, it tainted everyone: working as a gofer at his dad's firm in the summers, my *baba* was instructed to pay bribes to each export official, calculated by the weight of the packages. He followed his father's orders – how could he not? – but he hated it all the same. There were more teenage reasons too. Once, I asked him what pushed him away. 'Freedoms,' he replied, before a pause, 'sexual freedoms.' Turkey, despite all the changes in its first fifty years, was still a conservative place. And at seventeen, he remembers, a neighbour had brought home an English date, and 'she was the hottest girl I had ever seen.'

Increasingly, his heart – and other organs, no doubt – were set on the UK. At seventeen, he told my *dede* that if there were a war between Turkey and England, he would fight for the latter. My *dede* – a proud Turk with a famous temper – made a point so forcefully, jabbing his finger into the table, that it dislocated from the socket.

All across the country over that decade, there are lots of 'leaving Turkey' stories. They are tales of opportunity and of *gurbet* too, of something between homesickness and exile. This was the era when millions of Turks would pack up and go, to the production lines and shopfloors of Berlin, Frankfurt and Amsterdam. Even my road in London now is flanked on one side by a *pide* salon, and on the other by a social club filled with old Turkish men, seemingly the only place in the city where you can still smoke indoors.

Of course these stories, of Turkish migrants heading out West, might share the same shape, but they each have a different tone: my *baba* was not escaping the grind of Anatolia; nor was he going to work on the factory floor: he was studying computer engineering. In his case though it did expose an insecurity at the heart of our family thinking, its adherence to republican values, so in awe of the West. As my *baba* remembers my *babaanne* saying, whenever they went somewhere nice, 'This is so lovely . . . it's not like Turkey at all.' But why imitate the place, when you can just move there instead?

My *hala* – my *baba*'s sister, eighteen years his junior – told me the 'leaving story' I find most touching of all, of the years when he had left, and she was just a little girl. Every New Year's Eve – with the clock striking ever closer to midnight – *dede* would insist on staying home. Osman, he said, might just come and surprise us. And then what would he do if we had left to go elsewhere? But the minute hand would always catch up to the hour, pointing straight to the Ankara sky – up to the fireworks all over the city – and my *baba* was never there.

*

My *baba* rarely came back, for he was not just frustrated by Turkey but embarrassed by it, and by Turks too. If there was nothing wrong with the Atatürk principles – and that was the given of his upbringing – then there must have been something irreparable about the people themselves. In his new world – lost amongst the canals and Midlands accents of Birmingham, where he first moved – he would avoid telling people where he was from. Besides, he didn't want to be associated with what people thought Turkey was, all tents and camels.

Here then, the family story takes another turn, from Balıkçılar to Ankara to Britain. Our own relationship to Turkey changed with it: one step removed, as if seen through film, muffling the noise, deadening the pain. And a *baba* determined that that film should grow thicker. In truth, my *baba* fell in love with the UK as well – and the woman he met in his first week there. Bacon sandwiches; Christmasses with the in-laws; a country so orderly the local council trimmed roadside hedges.

When they married, and then had the three of us, our Turkishness would be lightly worn – not least as he never taught us the language, beyond the phrases for ordering food, or abusing football referees. One reason, I've always told myself, was political: that 1970s England can't have been the easiest place for a young brown man called 'Osman', and he wanted his own sons to be as English as possible. It was the choice, as the philosopher Isaiah Berlin said of Britain's Jews a generation before, to assimilate or to remain forever 'betwixt-and-between'. But the other reason he didn't teach us was personal, in the way that the personal is also political: that dads tend to be a lot less involved in raising their children. And that by the time he regretted it, it was already too late.

As I would find out years later, he would squirm on holiday, as we would approach that passport control, and the border officer would see us – Turkish names but utterly silent – and ask my *baba*, '*Neden Türkçe konuşmuyorlar?*' 'Why don't they speak Turkish?'

*

Things were shifting though. Over my teenage years, there was a new government in Turkey, and they were different. For one, it seemed competent and purposeful – those million-lira notes disappeared, and all of a sudden Turkish money seemed like any other, in sensible notes of fives and tens. But there was something more profound about them, and what they stood for: conservative, overtly religious, to put it bluntly, a threat to the secular establishment my family had known their whole lives.

Elections after elections, referendums, court cases, showdowns with the military, they just kept winning. Before I knew it, first my teens, and then nearly all my twenties had passed, but they were still there, as the stories coming out of Turkey were getting darker and darker still: a failed coup, hundreds of thousands imprisoned, the country with the highest number of journalists in jail anywhere in the world. More specifically, *he* was still there. As I found myself asked more and more – even by strangers – 'What do you think of Erdoğan?' If I bristled at the question, I understood it too. It wasn't just that he seemed everywhere – striking a deal with the EU over refugees, or launching another incursion into Syria– but that they sensed Turkey, what was happening to it, perhaps had some wider lessons for the rest of the world: how flawed democracies fail, how strong men rise, and whether anything can be done to stem the tide.

The weight of our Turkishness began to pull again. My *baba* would play 'Aldırma Gönül' on the piano – another bit of dad magic, how he could instantly fill the room with music. It was an old leftist anthem from the 1970s, but its lyrics were mournful all the same, written by an imprisoned dissident poet decades ago: *Gönül aldırma / Görecekler günler daha var*, 'Don't mind my heart / there are still more days to see'. Our visits to our family – all long since relocated to İstanbul – had a different texture too. I remember the warm summer nights of my childhood, the procession of relatives, and the two-kiss greetings with men with stubble like iron filings. But now those long conversations on the terrace – the lights of the city twinkling below us – had a slightly tragic air, like an aristocracy displaced: wealthy but uneasy, baffled, feeling like history was moving against them.

I felt it as well. My interest in Turkish politics had always come in waves, but now – a journalist myself – it had become impossible to ignore. I restarted my forever project, getting to grips with the Turkish language: the reversed word order; the lack of gender; the extendable words. *Neşe-len-mey-eceğ-ini*, 'that he/she would not become cheerful'. *Parmağ-ın-da-ki*, 'which was on his/her finger'. I read novels. Painfully slowly. I began to – if not exactly move – spend months at a time there. I was removing the film my *baba* had put over Turkey since I was a boy, to tell some stories of my own.

*

I was interested in the politics – covering the pandemic, economic crises, political dissidents – but I was drawn back as well, not least as so much of Turks' understanding of what was happening to them seemed to rest on a broader sweep of history, of their stories from the past. Was this merely the silent masses finally being given a voice? Or the erosion of values – and freedoms – that once made Turkey unique? Or its authoritarian tradition re-emerging in a different form? Or all three? Or none at all? Of course politics everywhere is about stories, about carving beginnings, middles and ends out of reality, but in few places did they seem to matter so much.

The stories that follow are not a chronology of Turkey. Crucial things will be missed, or skipped over, or merely alluded to – for this is more mosaic than textbook of Turkey's first hundred years. But if they share anything – from hats to communists, headscarves to bandits – it is those questions which perhaps come more naturally to someone half-in and half-out: what is Turkey, and who is it for? As such, many of them too will trace the history of that republican project – the one that bound my family for so many years – and its attempts to re-make a country in its image. It is, at points, a tale of the hard hand of the state, and its tensions with a rich and layered society beneath. There is therefore – in the finest tradition of Turkish melancholy – no shortage of tragic heroes either. But many stories too celebrate this place that I have loved, and known, as long as I have known anywhere.

I have travelled across the country and beyond, from the hills of the Black Sea in the north to the banks of the Euphrates down south, from my ancestral village to my second city of İstanbul, and pushing beyond Turkey's borders, to communities where Turks have lived for centuries. I have spoken to hundreds of people and interviewed dozens. Still, though, this can only ever be a sliver of it. As Nâzim Hikmet wrote – that banned poet whose works my *baba* used to secretly carry around in his schoolbag – Turkey is *bitmez, tükenmez*, The Endless Country.

2. On the Cusp of the Republic

1910s, 1920s – İstanbul

MY AUNT, MY *HALA*, IS CELEBRATING THE ONLY WAY SHE
knows how. She has excused herself from her diet for the day, and
the flat is full of pastries, of *simit*, of *peynirli poğaça* and sugar-coated
kurabiye. From the kitchen and our eleventh-floor window, I can
see flags draped over whole sides of buildings. Multi-storey flags.
The deep red, the white crescent, the white star. They are all over
the city, hanging off every available horizontal bar, at metro stations,
hospitals, municipal buildings, celebrating Cumhuriyet Bayramı,
Republic Day. Today is Turkey's ninety-ninth birthday.

Politicians tweet out their obligatory congratulations, and the government releases a video commemorating the war of independence
before a quick cut, suddenly in colour, to President Erdoğan and the

15

message that Turkey is still fighting against external enemies, now trying to sabotage its economy. Suffice to say, this stuff still matters.

We're in Erenköy, on the Asian side of İstanbul, as the city shoreline starts its south-east slide down the Sea of Marmara. It is a district of broad thoroughfares and yacht clubs, where retired admirals play bridge. Wealthy, and secular to its bones. And a place that clings particularly to the story told on this day of all days, of Atatürk, the founder-father of the nation. After a long breakfast, I walk with my *hala* towards the sea, past the fishmonger and the seagull he calls Murat, who he feeds spare bread and anchovies. We go to pick up my *babaanne*, who's in her mid-eighties but still enjoys a parade. Our pace slows to the rhythm of her walking stick – shuffle, clack, shuffle, clack – and we head all together towards the main road, and the smell of roasting chestnuts.

It looks, frankly, like a football match where only one team has shown up, their fans all in red and waving little plastic red flags. Some wear T-shirts with Atatürk's face embossed on the front. One small boy, slightly incongruously, is instead dressed head to toe as Captain America – shield, mask and all – but he seems excited nonetheless. Buskers play patriotic classics on old synthesizers; street hawkers sell flag balloons in big bunches, like huge scarlet honeycombs.

They have set up stages along the road – turned over, just for today, to pedestrians – and on them kids play out their choreo-graphed routines, tumbling over each other, before ending their performances with a salute to the crowd. It reminds me of my own *baba* sixty years ago. As he once told me, on Cumhuriyet Bayramı in Ankara, they would go to watch the military parades, in awe of them, so clean and organized. And warm in the knowledge that one day he too – as every young man must – would wear that olive green and march in step.

As we move towards the main stage in the late afternoon, the

DJ cycles through the old nationalist playbook. Revellers sing along to 'Sarı Saçlım Mavi Gözlüm', 'My Blond Haired Blue Eyed One', almost a love song to Atatürk, longing for his return. Above us, a suspended screen shows images of parades all over the city, then flicks to a soundless history documentary, of black-and-white images of soldiers going over the top, of cannons firing, of Atatürk looking stern.

My *babaanne* retells the history to me: that a decadent Ottoman Empire collapsed after World War One, and the Great Powers wanted to carve out what was left. 'The French, the Italians, and I'm sorry to say', she continues, with a nod to who I am, 'the English too.' It was only Atatürk, through the strength of arms and courage, who roused a nation back to life. In the background, the DJ shouts, 'We are with you, Atatürk!' His playlist resets, and plays the '10 Yıl Marşı', a military anthem set to a disco beat, and my *babaanne* dances along to it, rocking from side to side, twirling her cane in the air. Then she has had enough, and my *hala* takes her home.

It is a warm October evening, and the light fades quickly. In the dark, some teenagers set off a red flare in the crowd, and the balloons glint a deeper red. There is a chemical smell in the air, and the trace of sweat. At seven o'clock, the local mayor arrives and tells us we are all children of the same republic, ending his speech with '*Yaşasın Cumhuriyet!*' 'Long live the republic!' The crowd cheer, before a sudden, reverent quiet. A bugle plays, and there is a minute silence, followed by those first stirring bars of the 'İstiklal Marşı', the national anthem. All face the stage, hands on heart, and start to sing:

'*Korkma, sönmez bu şafak-*
larda yüzen al sancak...'

'Fear not, the red banner that ripples in this dawn shall not fade', it begins. And after a minute, we finish to applause. A woman to my left wipes away a few tears, and dries her mascara with a tissue.

My *hala* always cries too. I – honed elsewhere – cannot think of anything in my upbringing like this: militaristic, celebratory, so focused on one man. It feels a world away from the sombre Remembrance days and paper poppies of school . . . but I feel the shiver of goosebumps up my spine all the same.

*

My own neighbourhood in İstanbul tells a different story, or at least the same story in a different key. It is the next morning a little up the coast in Yeldeğirmeni, a district on a hill by Kadıköy pier, the last point where the Bosphorus seems constrained before it spreads wide into the Sea of Marmara. The pier sits across from the city's historic Golden Horn, but this is a rainy day in a foggy season. The ferries are cancelled and the Horn, and the rest of Europe just across the water, are invisible.

Yeldeğirmeni is an area of four-storey apartments in faded colours, and a few old wooden houses squeezed between them – falling down, their white slats turned a little ashy from years of street exhausts, like kitchen tiles around an oven. They still retain an old glory though, and purple bougainvillea hangs down from their little balconies. A street hawker sells lemons and garlic, his cart – heaped with yellow – rattling along the cobbled road. He passes walls stamped with graffiti in support of the opposition, in referendums long lost, for this is a district of students, artists, and activists. Later they will pour onto the pavement on the narrow main road – the tables are already waiting – a line of *çays* and coffees and cigarettes, to the sound of mopeds, plates clanking, and endless, endless chatter. And towards the northern end of all this, almost hidden, are the remains of the world that came before it.

Tucked behind a gate, Ayios Yeorgios is a small Greek Orthodox church, near the crest of Yeldeğirmeni's hill. I enter, escaping the rain, but it still feels damp and close inside. It is stuffed with golds and silvers, icons, and plastic chandeliers with cheap white lighting. And, this being a Sunday, in one corner by a wooden lectern stands a priest with a white ponytail and black robes, delivering a sermon to an empty room. It is a pauseless, incomprehensible Greek, with the occasional *Hallelujah* and *Maria*. He floats between prayer and song, and then a younger priest appears, and they chant a back-and-forth. Close your eyes, and it is as if someone has forgotten to switch off the radio as they've left the room.

Slowly, though, a few of the congregation come in, in ones and twos across the morning, until they number just under ten. The younger priest swings incense as he paces the room, and on cues beyond me, they cross their chests, kiss the Bible, and light candles. After hours on my feet, I find a chair to rest, and I am immediately told off for crossing my legs – by Fedon, as he turns out to be called. He has lived here since he was a boy. A small man with an air of mystery, after the service he tells me both that he is retired, and that his job is too confidential to disclose. He has a strong jaw, dark blue eyes, and a certain vanity. As we begin talking, out of nowhere he takes out an iPad to film our 'interview'. Later, he offers to personally baptize my son.

Though rebuilt in his lifetime, the church, Fedon claims, is on a site that Christians have used for over four hundred years. Now in his seventies, he grew up himself in a Greek-speaking home, and tells me memories of his father, who made icons for all the churches in the area. He remembers his house, full of paints imported from Russia, Romania, and beyond, and the vivid blues that would make the Virgin Mary. His grandad drove a horse-drawn cart owned by the church, ferrying priests around the local Patriarchate. The Christians of Asian İstanbul are a deep-rooted community, from the days that ancient Greeks settled in Chalcedon (now Kadıköy), 'The City of the Blind', over two thousand years ago.

But in Yeldeğirmeni, Fedon tells me, now there are no weddings and no baptisms. He couldn't find enough kids to form a church choir. 'The sea,' he explains, 'is drying up.' It is a decline that began a little over a century ago, in the years just before the Turkish republic came into being, and the rising of that red banner that will never fade.

*

Jobs in old Yeldeğirmeni, describes the late writer Adnan Giz, were a pretty fixed gig. As he recalls in his memoir, the coffee-shop owner, the confectioner, the helva-maker were all Turkish; the pharmacist and tavern-owner were Greek; the grocer and fisher-men were Jewish; an Albanian cooked liver; the stovemaker was Armenian. It was a cosmopolitan and at times tense neighbour-hood, but one he loved. He remembers 'fat David', whose shop sold the tassels on fezes, and a seventy-year-old Greek barber with a moustache like Kaiser Wilhelm. But his favourite was the Bulgarian milkman, and drinking *cacık* – yoghurt with cucumber – on warm summer evenings, with a view out to the sea from his marble counter.[1]

This was a neighbourhood known for its climes and its winds. As Giz writes, the roses climbing up its wooden houses swayed gently to the *poyraz*, the cool northern wind coming from over Çamlıca Hill, İstanbul's highest point. It's a memory that speaks to the deep history of the place, for Yeldeğirmeni *means* windmill. They had all long since been knocked down by Giz's time, but the area used to have several, pressed into use for the great Ottoman state. Starting nearly four hundred years ago, this is where the Sultan's armies and officials would station before heading out east, into Anatolia and beyond, deeper into the Middle East.[2] Indeed, at the district's north-eastern tip, facing out to a dual carriageway, is Ayrılık Çesmesi, the parting fountain, where soldiers left their families before their campaigns abroad. It was Yeldeğirmeni's mills that provided for the soldiers. Perhaps a legacy of this, walking down its main road now, in just a few hundred metres one passes no less than eight bakeries, the smell of bread rising and ovens firing.

But its more recent story is shaped not by windpower but by rail. For on the corner across from the fountain is a bit of neoclassical central Europe plonked on the Bosphorus shore. I follow the road from the church, even and flat before the hill quickly drops away. And only then, at the bottom of the street, and with Yeldeğirmeni behind you, does it come into view: Haydarpaşa station – a grand old building, the colour of sand, all wide arches and narrow windows. And up on the fifth floor of its facade, a clockface flanked by two turrets looks imposingly out to sea. In summer evenings, they will face down the sunset too, turning a rich orange, as the sun sinks into the Marmara.

First opened in the 1870s, Haydarpaşa was dramatically expanded after a few decades, built to serve as the first terminus in Asia, to take passengers way out east. And so Yeldeğirmeni housed first the station's builders – Italian and German stonemasons – and then its railway workers. And then all the people washed up by the war that broke out five years after Haydarpaşa was reopened.

*

When war spiralled out of Sarajevo in the summer of 1914, one Turkish writer – a child at the time – would remember his grandmother pointedly asking his father, 'Why should a war in Europe make any difference to our lives?'[3] It was a reasonable question, but the country was under new leadership. Though the Sultan remained ever-present, the Young Turk movement – modernists and soldiers – had seized his government the year before, and were determined to reverse the Empire's decline. The Ottomans had, after all, been more or less in retreat since 1683.

When the war broke out, they saw an opportunity to regain lost territory and throw off foreign control of the economy. This, they believed, was the only way to save the Empire – still a sprawling thing that stretched from the eastern Balkans, across Anatolia, down to Arabia and to the southern point of the Red Sea. And so they threw in their lot with Germany and Austria-Hungary, and rolled the dice once more.

Seferberlik, mobilization, began in August 1914. As the same writer remembers of his childhood, he first heard the drums of war as he tucked into a silver plate of ice and melon.[4] All over the country it was announced by town criers, posters, drums, and church bells. Cosmopolitan districts like Yeldeğirmeni were affected in two ways. Men between twenty-one and thirty were called to enlist, with patrols going house to house to ensure they did, and the threat of capital punishment for those who refused. Christians, meanwhile – and Armenians and Greeks probably made up over half of Yeldeğirmeni – could pay their way out. The exemption came at a heavy cost, and many were forced to sell expensive wares and jewellery to stay home.[5]

Though officially the Ottomans had mobilized to ensure their security and neutrality, the war machine was whirring. A month later, the government unilaterally abolished foreign concessions, long-hated grants that had given European, Christian traders privileged positions in the Empire. Then, at the end of October, and on the eve of the end of Ramadan, Turkish ships attacked the Russian navy in the Black Sea. The Empire had passed the point of no return. The poet Nâzim Hikmet, who knew Yeldeğirmeni well, describes the soldiers heading out from Haydarpaşa, on trains running by wood-powered engines, smelling of burnt pine, on a railway lined with cherry and olive trees. Out to fight their multi-front war, for an Empire that was vulnerable on nearly all sides. He describes too a character who would become part of Turkish mythology over the next four years, Memetçik, little Mehmet – the Turkish equivalent of the British Tommy, the American GI Joe.

Dört cephe içinde koptu kıyamet. Doomsday on four fronts . . .
Vagonların kırk kişilikse yapısı The cars are made for forty people each,
Seksen Mehmet, yüz Memet yüklü hepisi. But each holds eighty, a hundred Mehmets.
Kilitlenmiş vagoların kapısı. The doors of the cars are all locked.
Tirenler gidiyor Memetçik dolusu. The trains roll on, packed with Mehmets.
Memetçik, Memet, Mehmets, poor Mehmets
Memetçik, Memet. Mehmets, poor Mehmets.[6]

Memetçik Memet, Memetçik Memet. This is not just Hikmet describing the scene of mobilization, but recreating the sound of it, as troops are shuttled out on Haydarpaşa's trains. *Memetçik Mehmet*, as if the clank of wheels on track is calling out to the soldiers themselves. My *baba* still remembers this part off by heart.

The early signs were not good. In December, way out east, Ottoman troops in summer clothes and bad shoes were dying not just from enemy gunfire but from the cold. And soon Russia began its move deep into eastern Turkey, forcing eventually one million Anatolians to flee west. As Fedon, the Greek Orthodox, would tell me, one side of his own family was part of that wave. They arrived in carriages at Haydarpaşa in 1915, refugees received by the church. Other Christians felt a little more precarious. A suspicion was growing amongst Ottoman high command that Armenians in the east were abetting the Russian, Christian advance.

As winter stretched into the next year, Yeldeğirmeni and İstanbul would face a threat much closer to home: an Allied attack on Çanakkale, at the southern edge of the Marmara, the sea that led eventually right up to Yeldeğirmeni's shore. Rumours flew around that they would be in the capital soon. The Turkish defence on the beaches of Çanakkale was fierce, and ultimately successful – the beginnings of the fame of a commander, one Mustafa Kemal, and his reputation as the saviour of İstanbul. But it was a painful victory too. At the beautiful Tibbiye medical school just up the hill from Haydarpaşa, every student of the 1915 cohort had signed up to fight, and every one was killed. In 1921, it would have no graduation ceremony at all.[7] War was no longer something far away, especially for Yeldeğirmeni, the district on the station's edge. As Hikmet would famously write: *Dağ taş Memet dolu, dağ taş sevkiyat / Gidenler aç susuz, dönenler sakat.* Mehmets everywhere, everywhere on the move. / They leave hungry and thirsty, they come back crippled.[8]

Haydarpaşa would soon witness worse. As the winter of 1915 eased into spring, the season, Hikmet said, when the station smelled of fish and bedbugs.

*

On the night going into 24 April, İstanbul's Armenians were, according to Bishop Grigoris Balakian, exhausted by Easter celebrations that had ended just a few days earlier. They were, he wrote, 'snoring a calm sleep'. It was all soon to change. For on the 24th of April, Talat Paşa, one of the three senior leaders of the Young Turks, ordered the arrest of two hundred and fifty Armenian intellectuals, politicians, and men of the church, like Balakian himself.

It was a Sunday, one they would spend 'terrified and confused' in a prison in the centre of İstanbul, on the European side. After dusk – and after hearing the call to prayer from a nearby minaret – their names were read out to make sure they were all present. Twenty-four hours in, they were stripped of their belongings by military police, and bussed to the port on the Golden Horn. Amid sobs, they were loaded onto steamship no. 67 – 'its engines already fired' – and in thick blackness and on a stormy sea, they crossed the straits to the wharf at Haydarpaşa. There, they were 'marched out in pairs encircled by hundreds of bayonets.'

After a few hours, they were stuffed into special trains at the station, ready to take them east. As Balakian remembers, 'The lights went out, the car doors closed, and with the policemen and police soldiers around us, the train started. Slowly we left behind the places where we all had grieving and defenceless mothers, sisters, wives, children, as well as worldly goods.'[9]

For the rest of İstanbul's Armenians – for those in Yeldeğirmeni, just minutes away – they knew something momentous was happening, but it would be years until they found out exactly what.

*

For most of İstanbul, the war was felt more in the everyday. A blockade of the straits from early 1915 was beginning to bite, and the city was hungry for bread and for light. Both flour and coal were in short supply. Gasworks closed, the waterworks would only work three days a week, and the capital's famous steamships barely ferried across the Bosphorus.[10] But it was the shortage of food that strained the most. As one survivor put it, 'The whole world revolved around bread.' As a child, he was forced instead to resort to eating almond blossom, or the berries from gum trees.[11] Dozens of soup kitchens were set up across İstanbul. Adnan Giz, the memoirist from Yeldeğirmeni, recalls the neighbourhood rumour that Celal, a resident of the district and one-time head of the Red Crescent, was feeding İstanbullites not mutton or lamb but donkey.[12]

And İstanbul, in the absence of food, began to eat itself, a society curdling and embittered. There were fights at bakeries and food riots; ever-increasing prices of sugar, rent and more; and a growing hatred of stockpilers and black-marketeers, *harb zengini*, accused of profiting from it all. The very cityscape was changing as well.

Beykoz, the forest to its north, was chopped and chopped, as wood came to replace coal for fuel. But still İstanbul fell into darkness, and the decay continued. Later, even Haydarpaşa itself was disfigured, the site of a munitions explosion unexplained to this day, its roof aflame, its turrets obscured by smoke.

This was a state fighting an industrial war without industry, increasingly heavy-handed towards its subjects. By the middle of the war, in its desperate attempt to feed the Ottoman war machine – and the hundreds of thousands of Mehmets who made it – the government was squeezing society on an unprecedented scale. In the countryside, officials were forcing labour, seizing animals, requisitioning grain. But the cities were not immune either, and all manner of goods were confiscated to fund the war effort. As one novelist wrote of a requisitioning officer entering a warehouse, barrels of olive oil, bales of wool and cotton would vanish, as if in his hand 'were the wand of a magician.'[13] After Çanakkale, the net for conscription was widened, calling up men both younger and older, and even refugees who had fled war themselves. The losses, though, kept coming. In 1916, Russia would reach far along the Black Sea. By the year's end, the net would stretch once more, and all exemptions for conscription were lifted: a blow not only for the Christian subjects now called to arms, but the city trades they dominated.

Still, the army could not hold, and began to see deserters by the score. Divisions were often riven with disease, badly clothed, going months without pay, and they had simply had enough. Many too were leaving not because of conditions on the front, but what they heard back home. In villages across Anatolia, many families had lost not only their main breadwinner but their traditional guardian. In their absence, there was a common complaint from women in an increasingly lawless region – *ırzımızı paymal ettiler* – 'they trampled our honour'. Women were being raped by the men still left behind. It was a problem that became so widespread that the authorities even introduced a law targeted specifically against it – on pain of capital punishment – but still it continued.[14]

*

Ayrılık Çesmesi Street is lined with small maple trees, their leaves in October a rusty purple, ready to fall. Stretching up from the fountain at one corner of Yeldeğirmeni, it is the very border of the district. On one side, an inaccessible, ragged old cemetery; and on the other, a row of hundred or so one-, two-storey houses in blues and pastel shades. It seems an İstanbul on another scale, and the road is mostly turned over to stray cats and a few old men.

It is quiet now, but a hundred years ago, this was Paris Mahallesi, Yeldeğirmeni's very own red-light district. The war years had seen a spectacular rise in prostitution, as women were left destitute, or forced to flee violence. Indeed, the authorities were so worried about the spread of venereal disease amongst soldiers – *frengi*, as it was known, 'the French disease' – that they passed a law obliging the state itself to carry out health inspections of brothels.[15] An unusual responsibility, perhaps, for a caliphate. Over the course of the war, four brothels had grown up around the wider area encompassing Yeldeğirmeni, but the locals were not happy, worried about the influence on young daughters of good, honourable families. There was, they complained, the noise every night of the *saz*, of songs and fights, of shouting and gunshots. Even more scandalously, they said, the women 'did everything out in the open.'[16] So towards the war, the trade packed up and moved to Yeldeğirmeni instead, on the street by the graveyard, and the fountain once built for soldiers saying goodbye to their loved ones before a long campaign.

But the campaigns now were failing. Armies everywhere were losing men at an unsustainable rate, to desertion, disease, death and captivity. In 1917, way down in Ottoman Mesopotamia, was the fall of Baghdad and Tikrit. Despite the respite of the October revolution, and the ending of hostilities with the new Soviet Union, still the Ottomans were overwhelmed, and the British would take Jerusalem before the year was out. By the spring of 1918, Kirkuk had gone too. A vast, centuries-old empire was shrinking by the month. Recruitment became even more desperate. Commanders reported receiving new soldiers who were blind or crippled. Sixteen-year-olds were sent to the front; their mothers would weave *vay anam* rugs, carpets to mourn the departure of their teenage sons.[17]

At the start of the war, the Ottoman army boasted eight hundred thousand men; four years on, it was one eighth of that. When the Ottoman ally Bulgaria collapsed in late 1918, the Allies had İstanbul in their sights – they could attack both from the west and the east. *Boku yedik*, as one of the three leaders of the government reportedly said, 'We've eaten shit.'[18] All three of them would resign, a month before fleeing entirely. Their successors wearily would sue for peace, almost four years to the day that the war had started. It had been a devastating, criminal gamble. Nearly three million men had been conscripted to nine different fronts. Almost eight hundred thousand of them had died. And civilians had borne even more, killed and displaced in their millions. They had been impoverished too, in an economy that had shrunk by half. Far away from the trenches of the Western front – from the Somme and from Ypres – practically no country suffered more from the First World War than the peoples of Anatolia.

*

The western edge of Yeldeğirmeni is on the other side from its old red-light district – a ten minutes' walk over the railway line, past the cafes on the main road, and then down the slopes, almost pushing you on, towards the sea. This is where the neighbourhood meets Kadıköy pier, and the Bosphorus beyond it. A few luckless fishermen stand patiently at the water's edge, and teenagers hold hands and smoke cigarettes, admiring the view out in front. Across the straits, immediately ahead are the ochre shades of the Aya Sofya, and the delicate kiosks of Topkapı palace. On a clear day, they look like Ottoman miniatures, their lines clean, their size shrunken by the distance. Then, out to the left, is where the Bosphorus breaks free, sprawling out into the Marmara, a vast expanse of sea and sky.

It would have been from here then, in November 1918, that the locals of Yeldeğirmeni would first have seen them coming. A flotilla of fifty warships – British, French, Italian, and Greek – appearing over the horizon, slowly growing larger, coming unmistakeably towards the Bosphorus straits, a great show of steel entering not only the Ottoman capital but the centre of the Islamic world. The armistice had been signed by Ottoman ministers under the impression – though not written in law – that 'not a single enemy soldier will disembark in our İstanbul'.[19] Their objections were brushed away. Marines soon landed at the British Embassy, the central post office, the rail stations in Europe and at Haydarpaşa, and at the three major quays, including Kadıköy itself. They requisitioned buildings and apartments, enthusiastic to finally see this gem in the Orient – the ancient and storied Constantinople – and shocked by the state they found it in, 'sordid and squalid'.[20] This was a society thoroughly bowed and defeated. One memoirist recalls seeing famous Ottoman officers selling lemons on the street.[21]

And this – the first day of İstanbul's occupation – pulled at the city's fabric once more. Muslims stood, stunned and embarrassed. İstanbul's Christians cheered the Allied ships from the docks. As Giz writes, one resident in Yeldeğirmeni hung a Greek flag from his front door on Duatepe Street. It was, he says, a 'betrayal' of the neighbourhood, with fights and scuffles to come.[22] Cheap American flour soon returned, but a tense, seething peace had come to Yeldeğirmeni.

The Allies only inflamed divisions further, and not just the French General d'Espèrey riding into İstanbul on a white horse, mimicking – seemingly avenging – Ottoman Sultan Mehmet II and his conquest of the city from Christian Byzantium nearly five hundred years earlier. In early 1919, French and Italian troops arrived in southern Turkey, ready to consolidate their claims, their spheres of interest. In May, along the Aegean, Greek soldiers landed in İzmir. It was a violent declaration of intent – hundreds of Muslims were killed as they took the city.[23] More Greek flags were hung by İstanbul's Orthodox Christians, but Muslim Turkey was aflame, reignited after months of shame and quiet. Just beyond Yeldeğirmeni's southern border, at the Şehri Emanet municipal building, its cream and blue tiles were shrouded in mourning black. From the balcony, the nationalist Halide Edib Adıvar addressed an audience of twenty thousand in the pouring rain, urging them to resist. 'Governments are our enemy,' she said, 'the people are our friends.'[24] And in that resistance, two things were happening. More and more, there were calls to defend not the Ottoman state, but a Turkish, Muslim nation. Secondly, what was changing was a belief in who could rally that defence.

The Sultan, holed up in his palace, had been helpless to prevent the seizure of İstanbul, or the arrival of Allied troops elsewhere – part puppet, part prisoner. Power instead was slipping east, out of İstanbul entirely. A ragtag resistance was forming across Anatolia: old Ottoman commanders and their leftover soldiers, people's assemblies, bandits. And Mustafa Kemal – that hero of Çanakkale – would soon take his famous boat out of the city to join them.

The legitimacy of the Ottoman government was about to sink even lower. In March 1920, the Allies – despite their divisions – implemented a full military occupation of İstanbul. Hundreds of Turkish nationalists, still in the city, were arrested; more buildings were commandeered; and thousands more Allied troops flooded the capital. One old resident of Yeldeğirmeni shared with me stories handed down from his own grandfather, memories of playing football with colonial Indian soldiers at Haydarpaşa station, and of Scots handing out sweets to local kids. The Allied forces' general reputation was less wholesome: an increased demand in Paris Mahallesi, the red-light district; and across the straits, on the European side, reports of soldiers openly drinking, brawling, even pulling off the veils of local women.[25]

It was a humiliation about to be made concrete in law. The Sultan's representatives – though almost all their demands had been ignored – signed in Sèvres in the summer of 1920 a treaty so infamous that it has its own syndrome, Sevr Sendromu, the belief that foreign powers always have designs on stirring up the country's divisions, and splitting it into parts.* Thrace – all land west of İstanbul – would go to Greece, including Edirne, the former Ottoman capital, with its magnificent domes and spires. İzmir, the largest city on the Aegean, would vote after five years whether it wanted to join them. Out east, the new Armenia would be vastly expanded, and become home to the ancient Black Sea port of Trabzon. Below it, to the east of the Euphrates, the Kurds would have their own territory under British control. Further south still, all Ottoman Arabia – Aleppo, Mosul, Jerusalem – would be lost. The French and Italians would be given zones of interest all along the southern, Mediterranean coast. The remainder would be the new Turkey, the Ottoman successor state. It would be a nation, in the words of one contemporary commentator, left with the 'dry interior of a peninsula'[26]. İstanbul would be Turkish, but its straits were to

---

* Once, at a *hamam* on the Black Sea, I was talking to the bath attendant about a recent earthquake. I remember distinctly, amid the soap and bubbles and with his hands on my buttocks, him telling me how it had been caused by an American bombing of Turkey's tectonic plates.

be internationally managed; the army would be dramatically cut to size; the foreign concessions would be re-imposed; an international commission would have substantial control over Turkish debt and revenues.

When the news of the terms came through to the nationalists, now centred around Ankara way inland, they declared the signatories traitors.

In cosmopolitan neighbourhoods though, even minorities were unsure how to react. The Greek Orthodox of Kadıköy, for example, were notably less fervent in support of Greek expansion than those across the Bosphorus: uncertain that this new political ground was so steady, and unwilling to upset their Muslim neighbours if it wasn't.[27] But for one community, the prospect of a home, of a safe haven, was particularly powerful. Bolsahays, İstanbul's Armenians, had celebrated the founding of the state, their 'Infant Armenia', by hanging out the tricolor of red, blue, and orange. Tentative and defiant, for they felt now just to survive was to resist, as they were still learning – still coming to terms with – what had happened out east during the war.

*

I meet Arto outside his workshop up the hill in Yeldeğirmeni, we exchange the usual greetings and, on learning my family is from Rize, he immediately puts his hands – blackened with grease – up on my face, plants his thumbs by my cheekbones, his fingers on my eyebrows, prises my eyes wide open, and peers into them. To check if I'm really from the Black Sea, he says. '*Gözler her şeyi söyler*', The eyes tell you everything. He is a mechanic with the side of poet, and sprinkles his Turkish with old, playful rhyming doubles. *Kafe mafe*, 'café-schmafe'. *Sokak mokak*, 'street-schmeet'. We enter his shop, cramped and made even smaller by his things. We are surrounded by naked engines, spare parts, nails, screws, filling up from the floor, and up the walls too. I perch, increasingly uncomfortably, on a free armrest – the chair itself is stacked with boxes.

Arto is Armenian, 'softened by the sea', he says, not like the tough, mountain Armenians far to the east. As we talk, old friends in their sixties and seventies drop by and tell dirty jokes, but slowly he tells me his family story. I ask when they came here to Yeldeğirmeni. '1920', he replies, an instant one-word reply. At home, he has a censer, an incense carrier, that has the date stamped on its silver cross. His grandmother, he remembers, used to light it every Friday when she prayed. They arrived at Haydarpaşa as *darakirs*, refugees who came to the city after the war, to share what they had seen.

İstanbul's Armenians knew of course that *something* had happened in the depths of Anatolia near the beginning of the war. They knew that leaders like Bishop Balakian had been whisked away on a weekend soon after one Easter. But the press was censored, and ordinary Armenians could not leave or enter the city. So the scale, the brutality of that something was unknown, of the Medz Yeghern, the Great Crime.

They were beginning to find out. That the Young Turk leadership, terrified of losses on the eastern border – and increasingly paranoid about Armenian collaboration with the Russian advance – had decided on a genocidal solution to this 'Armenian Question'. In the winter of 1915, Armenian soldiers had been disarmed and placed in labour battalions instead to become, in the words of one historian, 'sitting ducks'.[28] Then the scope widened. In early March, where southern Anatolia meets the north-east corner of the Mediterranean sea, Armenians were emptied out of a small town called Dörtyol to little resistance. Soon after, the ancient Armenian communities of Erzurum, Bitlis, Van, and Cilicia were all ordered out, to march away from the front lines.

Before the summer had even begun, local army commanders

were then empowered to deport anyone they saw fit, and in provinces not just near the battlefields, but right across Anatolia. Though initially there was no real idea where to send them, gradually the direction was made clear. As Talat Paşa, one of the three leaders of the Young Turks, later said, they can live 'in the desert but nowhere else'. Many did indeed make it to the sands in the east, to the Syrian provinces of Mosul and Der Zor, only to starve there. Many more found the journey too much: the elderly, the exhausted, the sick, the children left alone on roadsides by heartbroken mothers. And countless convoys were massacred en route, by Teşkilat-ı Mahsusa, secret organizations of Kurdish tribesmen, irregular soldiers, released prisoners, and bandits.

It was doubtless a chaotic policy, but under central, party supervision too. Over a million Armenians were killed, and as many uprooted from their homes. It was a new, twentieth-century violence. By August, Talat could telegraph: 'The Armenian question in eastern provinces has been resolved.'[29]

It is not a story that has dominated Arto's life, but the facts of them he has always known. All the same, he is slightly hesitant to share them. *Yapacak hiçbir şey yok*, he says, 'There's nothing you can do.' His grandparents lived in Erzurum, far east on the Anatolian plains. His great-uncle was killed, but they managed to flee west, burying gold under a mulberry tree before they went. I ask how his own grandparents survived. 'I don't know,' he says after a pause, 'I think about that a lot.'

I think about my own *büyük anne*, my *baba*'s paternal grandmother. In his words, she was a tiny woman with a huge nose, who made fantastic *sucuk* sausage from scratch. But there is something else we know about her. At five she was found around the Black Sea, abandoned and alone, by the side of a road after the war, only to be adopted by a local governor. Looking back on it now – though no one said anything while she lived – we suspect she may have been one of Turkey's many *dönme*, Armenians who converted or were converted to survive. Arto's own grandparents, he says, saw such a child on their road to safety as well, but there was nothing they could do to save them.

By the end of the war, the story of the Great Crime was being heard across İstanbul, in tentative whispers and silences perhaps, as survivors poured into the city. Over a thousand of them spent the winter sleeping in Haydarpaşa station itself.[30] And thousands more came, each with their own traumas to share, and perhaps desperate for that Armenia, carved out on paper in black and white, to be made real.

But the Treaty of Sèvres – as one contemporary put it – was as fragile as the porcelain that that French town produced.[31] Drawing lines on a map was one thing, but in truth much of Anatolia was ungovernable, a land of gang wars and demobbed soldiers. Slowly, too, an unruly resistance was coalescing. A series of commanders – amongst the rump of the Young Turks – were determined to fight back. And they were increasingly dominated from Ankara by that hero from Çanakkale, Mustafa Kemal. First, one general led his army east, crossing into and defeating Armenia, and going as far as Azerbaijan. 'Infant Armenia' was swallowed up after less than two years in existence, as the Turkish nationalists agreed with the USSR a new eastern border. Then attacks on the French and Italians in the south sapped their spirit across 1920. By 1921, war-weary and far from home, the two powers gave up on their ambitions for Turkey's Mediterranean coast. Only Greece, with the encouragement of Britain, was willing to claim its territory promised by Sèvres . . . willing but unable.

After Sèvres, it pushed its troops, cavalry, and warplanes inland from İzmir, taking Bursa, Eskişehir, Afyon, and others, but the momentum was slipping, and its soldiers were tired. After a famous stand in September 1921 at Sakarya – almost at Ankara's door – the tide turned, and the Turkish nationalists pushed back.* The Greek retreat to the Aegean saw more misery for the people of Anatolia. They burnt down hundreds of homes, and killed thousands of civilians – a near-final spasm of inter-communal violence after almost a decade of war.[32]

In Yeldeğirmeni – still, as the rest of İstanbul, under occupation – the memoirist Giz remembers his schooldays as the Turkish army fought back, 'the breeze of victory in the air that even children could sense.' He describes drawing the King of Greece with his 'bald head and big ears', riding a donkey, fleeing a Turkish soldier.[33] But regardless of the swings in fortune – battles won here, armies fled there – in Yeldeğirmeni itself, the deprivations of daily life, of near-permanent conflict, continued. Paris Mahallesi, its red-light district, had gained a reputation for danger: violence and murders; red lanterns hanging by dilapidated tin-covered houses; the road turned to mud in the winter. Not a place, it was said, to wander at night.

Amidst the seediness, it would witness a more touching scene too, for the authorities were still responsible for medical checkups, and the effort to prevent the spread of *frengi*. The inspections would start, according to one observer, on Thursday mornings. High-class escorts would walk down the hill to the district municipal medical office, shaded by their white umbrellas. But most – the poor, the refugees – would go in large groups, arguing amongst themselves, the sound of their clogs on the cobblestones alerting all of Yeldeğirmeni to their parade. And so the locals would come to watch, leaning out of their windows, spectators with a 'mix of curiosity and sadness'.[34]

---

* This is the story of Turkish history I first knew. Aged ten, for an English class I wrote an essay – not a word of which I can remember, but that still makes me cringe – about two fictional soldiers Hasan and Mehmet, off to fight the Greeks.

It was a neighbourhood scarred in other ways too. As in much of İstanbul – crumbled and decaying – big fires would sweep across its wooden homes. In the summer of 1922, Yeldeğirmeni was hit by a *patlıcan yangını*, an aubergine fire. In the season for fried *patlıcan*, because of an unlucky wind or a jumpy open flame, a fire broke out from a Greek home, and burned down nearly three hundred houses. As one old Jewish resident told me, the fire reached all the way up to the walls of the synagogue, and then miraculously stopped there.

*

Near the old Paris Mahallesi, on Kır Kahvesi Street, is a little corner of decaying wooden houses. They are from the late nineteenth century, their big bay windows criss-crossed in mesh, in the old Ottoman style, preserving modesty, allowing only those from the inside to look out. Amongst them is possibly the oldest building in Yeldeğirmeni, whose only flaw might be that right at the end of its idyllic little garden are the tracks for an intercontinental railway. Conversation is interrupted every seven minutes by the roar of an engine, the clank of metal on metal, before it recedes into silence once more.

Here lives Osman, a retired officer born in this house nearly ninety years ago, who is not so much hunching as sinking into his body, as old men do. He offers me *çay* and biscuits, and tells me – and the several stray cats listening in – his family's part in Yeldeğirmeni's war story. His father was an officer, and his father before that – an old and upright family of military service, and one that speaks to Yeldeğirmeni's centuries-long tradition of housing soldiers and their families.

In the late summer of 1922, those pleasant months where the Turkish sun begins to ease, the nationalists had nearly run the Greeks out of Anatolia. In early September, in mosques across

Turkey, prayers were read for the success of their national army, before they entered the only city left: İzmir, the old trading hub on the Aegean. Their arrival saw little fightback. Instead, thousands of Greek soldiers and Ottoman Christians lined the docks, desperate for evacuation out to sea.

And here, Osman takes me up the stairs, as the wooden floors creak and groan underneath us. We turn left into his living room and he shows me a flag behind glass, so different from those draped all across the city this weekend. It is handstitched and amateur; its texture thick and heavy; and the star and crescent are a little off, too far to the right, as if made by memory. This, Osman explains, is the flag his grandad hung from this window the moment İzmir was taken. They had been forbidden from hanging Turkish flags during the occupation, but now the mood had decisively shifted. There were flags of red and white, he claims, 'all over İstanbul in an instant'. But really it was not all of İstanbul, for only around half of the city's population was Muslim. For the city's Christians, it was a deeply uneasy time. İzmir was not only a moment of glory and reconquest, but of lynchings, fires, and looting against the Ortho-dox population. Over two hundred thousand of them fled, in the trail of the defeated Greek army.[35]

The Turkish nationalists closed in on İstanbul, and began to negotiate with the British, who knew the game was up, about a handover. For the capital's Christian communities however, the future was unclear, in a city where violence was always possible but, for now, mostly only threatened. Still, something had snapped. İstanbul's minorities – Greeks, Armenians, and others – started to leave.* Papers were suddenly full of adverts for ferries to Palermo, New York, and elsewhere.[36] By March 1923, over three hundred

---

* Just as the Sultan himself would do – already stripped of his powers, he left for Malta on a British ship, allegedly taking his jewellery but not his wives.

thousand had left – İstanbul's forever bakers, fishermen, traders, and bar owners.[37] Thousand-year-old communities were gone.

When the Turkish military arrived in October – its *paşas* on horseback, as if to erase the humiliation of occupation – the Greeks and Armenians left were said to wear fezes in deference. It was just one sign of the reversal of things, a little flourish to the diplomatic victory of the summer: the Treaty of Lausanne, to supersede Sèvres, one hundred and forty-one articles that would dramatically expand Turkey's borders, from Edirne to Van, from the Black Sea to the Mediterranean, and remove almost all limitations, economic and political, on the sovereignty of the new Turkish state. This is the great story celebrated by those historical documentaries, suspended above the crowds on Cumhuriyet Bayramı, the one my *babaanne* repeats to me too: a post-war treaty overturned by force; Allied plans subverted by Turks, in the words of one observer, 'few and poor and very courageous.'[38]

But in truth, this story only looks like victory when told through maps, and the absurd phrase sometimes heard that World War One was lost by the Ottomans and won by Turkey. For the people that lived through it all, more than they ever felt Ottomans or Turks, they were Yeldeğirmenili, or İstanbullu, or İzmirli, or wherever, a part of communities that had been ripped to pieces. And their traumas over the last decade – of the prostitutes of Paris Mahallesi, the Armenian refugees from the east, the crippled soldiers selling lemons on the street – would not be so easily reset. This *was* how the Turkish nation was born, but it was a birth like any other: out into the light, crying and confused, tender and pink.

It was perhaps most obviously true for the city's Christians, shrunk to a tiny minority. Lausanne entailed one last seismic shake: an exchange of populations from over Turkey and Greece. One million Greek Orthodox left Anatolia (though İstanbul was exempt); five hundred thousand Muslims came the other way. But it held for the battered Muslim population too. As the poet Hikmet wrote – that famous chronicler of Haydarpaşa station, and the soldiers who shuttled in and out of it – after a decade of conflict, *Ha dayan hemşerim, sonuna vardık.* 'Hang in there, brother, the end's in sight.'[39]

There would be no great victory for liberated İstanbul either. For the newly empowered Turkish nationalists, the city was now too tainted by its association – its collaboration – with the Sultan and the occupation. 'A Byzantine whore', as it was called, insufficiently Turkish. For those *paşas* and state officials who had lived around Yeldeğirmeni for centuries, there was another uncertainty to come. In October, a resolution was laid down to move the capital four hundred kilometres inland to Ankara, a bleak town on the Anatolian steppes.

*

There is a sense, wandering around Yeldeğirmeni, that this hundred-year-old story feels not so much history as archaeology, buried deep beneath the earth, the changes it wrought so profound, so fundamental, they are now almost impossible to detect. It is partly a tale of who left back then: over that decade the neighbourhood was wrung out, and made unrecognizable from its old self. It was an experience replicated all over, as a cosmopolitan, multi-ethnic empire transformed into a nation-state, mostly Turkish and almost exclusively Muslim. And it is partly a tale of who has come in the generations since: the layers and layers of migrants from within Turkey who have made the district home – the baklava-maker from Gaziantep, the neighbourhood association from Bingöl – so many of their journeys ending at the train station at Yeldeğirmeni's edge.

But it has left its trace on the few that still live here, on Fedon and Arto, proud Turks who carry a sense of loss nonetheless. Both, in their own lifetimes, have seen the final trickle out of their communities, and point me to houses where their friends once lived: Agop, Daron, and Konstantine, names that speak to another era. 'Slowly, slowly,' says Arto, a little cryptically, 'they made the mothers of this country cry.' I ask if he celebrated Republic Day over the weekend, and he leaves me with one last rhyme. *Bayram mayram*, 'holiday schmoliday'. Nodding to a stack of unfixed machines, he is simply too busy.

Down the road, there is a little street party, and more flags hung off street corners. Some old boys from Yeldeğirmeni are having breakfast, and share some of the district's thousand baked goods. They are toasting once more to that October day, nearly a hundred years ago. For just weeks after the last Brits had left İstanbul – with a ceremony the Allied general described as 'a wonderful send-off.'[40] – the nationalists in Ankara were already looking ahead. Drafted almost in secret, an amendment was presented to the new assembly. The Turkish state, it declared, was to be a republic. The members voted, not a murmur of dissent, and rose to their feet, chanting, '*Yaşasın Cumhuriyet!*', the same cry that would be heard all over the city this weekend. Three times they said it, 'Long Live the Republic!', their shouts growing louder each time, echoing back and forth across the hall. And a new nation was announced to its people with the thunder of a hundred-and-one-gun salute.[41]

3. The Legacies of Hats

1920s – Rize

MEHMET HAS A MOUSTACHE I COULD ONLY DREAM OF, AND underneath it, he whispers *bismillah* as he starts the taxi, and we head out into the green. He has a heavy accent too, but we understand each other well enough, and he is curious why I'm here. I begin to explain, but before I can even complete the first line, he finishes off the rhyme, for he knows it well.

Hamidiye, Atma, Atma / 'Hamidiye, don't bomb us, don't bomb us!'

It sounds different when he sings it, his words collapsing into a harsh, guttural O. It was a song I first heard from my *hala* in İstanbul, but I am a long way away now, back in the north-east of Turkey. As Mehmet tells me, even the air here is different, cleaned by the daily rains, though this morning there is just the gentle October sun. After ten minutes, he drops me off in Gürgen, the village where this song and this story began. And I begin to walk down to another, Güneysu, as they did nearly one hundred years ago.

It's a paved one-lane road next to a river, at the foot of a valley that winds for hours until it meets the Black Sea to the north. All the way down, it's walled in by the hills – they don't roll here, they are sharper than that, like small green mountains, occasionally touching the clouds. The road eases me downwards, further north towards Güneysu, and every now and again I see houses perched improbably halfway up, like goats on a sheer cliff. Then, the minaret of a village mosque above a brow, catching the light of the sun behind me.

Atma Hamidiye / Don't bomb us, Hamidiye
Atma, atma! / Don't bomb, don't bomb!
Din kardeşiyiz / We are your brothers in faith.

It's a region of tea plantations and forests, and the tops of the trees are ever so slightly yellowing, the first sign of autumn. A few women on the side of the road, sat next to huge sacks of tea leaves, try to sell me the last of the *çay* harvest. I pass more river bends and tiny waterfalls, until the land briefly flattens out a little, and I know I am near Güneysu, and the story of a village that didn't want to wear hats, and had eight people hanged on a beach in the end.

Atma, Hamidiye, / Don't bomb us, Hamidiye,
Atma, atma! / Don't bomb, don't bomb!
Din kardeşiyiz. / We are your brothers in faith.
Şapka da giyeceğiz, / We'll wear our hats,
Vergi de vereceğiz! / And we'll pay our taxes!

*

Turkey had been founded, but now its new leadership needed to make Turks – to give meaning to this new country, and the people who found themselves in it. Heroes of the wars, lauded for bringing peace to Anatolia at last; this was the time, so they thought, to transform this place for ever. This was to be the era of the *devrims*, the revolutions my *baba* would learn at school years later, and the leadership of President Mustafa Kemal – Atatürk, as he would later be renamed, 'Father of the Turks'.

In truth, Atatürk had not always been so opposed to the political influence of Islam. He had toyed with the ideas of Islamic modernists, that it was a religion compatible with Western science and truth; he had had clerics bless meetings of his companions and followers early on in the liberation war; even after Turkey had been declared a republic, its 1924 constitution explicitly recognized Islam as the state religion.[1] Besides, after all the changes wrought by war, he had to tread carefully: Muslim refugees from the Caucasus and the Balkans had streamed into the country. Demographically, it was more Muslim than ever. But at heart, the modernist, positivist elites of the new Turkey were set on reform: if not hostile to religion per se, then at least to the political hold it had had for centuries, and the opaque teachings and conservatism of its clerics. For Atatürk and his radical supporters, it was simply not how countries progressed, how they took their place in the civilized Western world. In the words of one local, the government wanted to 'blow away the Arab winds'.

The opening of the new parliamentary year, March 1924, was dramatic. With a mere show of hands, the assembly passed a new education law, abolishing all *medreses* in the country, and putting all teaching in the hands of the state. The old Ottoman ministry that managed the affairs of religious foundations was eliminated.[2] And finally, a deputy from Urfa – the city known as the home of the prophet Abraham – was chosen to put forward a motion to abolish the caliphate, that five-hundred-year-old seat at the heart of the Islamic world. It too was voted through. All this in a single day – moves not so much to secularism, the separation of Islam and state, as towards the complete control of the latter over the former. All imams, henceforth, would be trained at special state-run schools for preachers, and employed by a new government ministry once they graduated. Sharia courts were no more. The caliph was handed an envelope of two thousand pounds and an entry visa to Switzerland, and told never to return. His relatives too were bundled out of the country, sent on the Orient Express to Bulgaria. A new Turkey was taking shape, and they would have no place in it.[3]

The revolution soon came to the Black Sea, as Atatürk toured around the country, a nation he said that was 'in a state of war with ignorance and conservatism.'[4] In the centre of Rize – the city down the valley from Güneysu – they have still preserved the house he stayed in during his visit, and the bed where he once spent the night. On Turkey's Children's Day, school students pay their respects there, and lay down little paper flowers. There is a picture of his trip too: standing upright on a kayak as he comes to shore. He had come to promote Turkey's new reforms, to open new state-run schools. But already, in this conservative region, there were signs of dissent: a gathering of imams and muftis – the area was famous for them – who implored him not to shut the *medreses* down.

The programme though pressed on. It had dealt with the institutions – the caliphate, the *medreses*, the foundations – but now it turned its attention on the people. The following year, it shut down Turkey's tombs and mausoleums, where ordinary Muslims had prayed for centuries, enlisting the aid of great holy figures long gone. It was a backward superstition, in the eyes of the government and the president at its helm: 'a disgrace for a civilized society to appeal for help to the dead.'[5] Then it sought to close down the *tarikats*: religious, mystical orders that bridged the theology of the clerics and the religion of the masses – networks of sheikhs and shrines, pilgrimages and collective prayers. But still it wasn't enough, for the new state did not just want to change what was in its citizens' souls, but what was on their heads.

There was a long history, in fact, of hat politics in Turkey, of conflicts over fezes and kalpaks, homburgs and Panamas. A century before, an Ottoman sultan had introduced the fez for all officials, civil and military. Up until then, the men of the empire's various religious groups had tended to wear different headwear – this was supposed to eliminate their difference, to make them all united Ottomans. A fez economy grew around it. In İstanbul still, on the banks of the Golden Horn, in beige and turquoise tiles stands the old *feshane* – the fez factory – though it serves as a conference hall now. But the sultan's reforms never quite worked as intended; increasingly, the fez was seen as a Muslim hat. Not least under the long-serving conservative Sultan Abdulhamit II – bête noir of the Young Turks – who wore a fez tall, broad, and barely caving inwards, like a red block on his royal head. The fez then was inescapably backward. It can't have helped either that Atatürk years ago – when only the young Mustafa Kemal – a soldier on tour in Libya, was mocked while wearing his by some passing children. Turkey's modernizers had spent years searching for a more suitable, modern alternative. They had experimented with the *kalpak*, a large and furry thing worn across the Balkans and Caucasus, but slowly they migrated to the European-style brimmed hat, to the *şapka*, as it was called.[6]

Off went Atatürk once more then, in the late summer of 1925, to spread the message to his people. He set off to towns across Turkey – to Bursa, Balıkesir, Afyon, and İnebolu – in the words of one newspaper, to 'save the masses from the fez'. It was a tour accompanied by a massive propaganda campaign. During one talk on the northern Black Sea coast, he exited his car – to the shock of the crowd – bare-headed, holding a Panama hat in his hand. 'Our most valuable nation is deserving of civilized and international attire,' he said, gesturing to the peaked thing in his hand. 'This I want to express most clearly . . . the name of this headgear is "hat"'.[7] He mocked people in the crowd still clinging to their old head-gear.* When he visited the extremely conservative town of Konya in October, right in the heart of Anatolia, authorities organized a 'fez-rending celebration' to mark it.[8]

All over the country, Muslims were unsure how to react. One cleric in Konya was said to proudly show off to guests his new Borsalino hat, urging them that it wasn't *haram* to wear clothes associated with Europeans, that it was good to be modern, and that what you wore on your head did not affect matters of the spirit.[9] Others though, were unconvinced. Most famously, the Islamist intellectual İskilipli Mehmed Atif Hoca had published a pamphlet a year earlier named 'Mimicry of the Frankish Hat'. He was not, he emphasized, opposed to modernity per se, against the benefits of Western science, technology, and all the rest. Instead, he argued against the mere 'imitation of infidels' for the sake of it, and the loss of identity it entailed.

But the *şapka* was coming regardless. As it was announced on one newspaper front page in late September 1925, 'All the members of the Assembly are obliged to wear a hat'. In fact, the new rule applied not only to deputies but to all civil servants. Its implementation was chaotic. There were simply not enough hats to go round. Those that were left became so expensive that civil servants were permitted to buy them in instalments. Italian manufacturers reportedly had a field day.[10] The revolution had to go on, though. On 16 November, a deputy from Konya – his head newly and appropriately covered, no doubt – introduced another bill, the Şapka İktisasi Hakkında Kanunu, The Law on the

---

* He deplored the full veiling of women too but it was not his priority.

Wearing of the Hat. 'The General Headdress for Turkish nation is the hat', it declared, seeking to ban 'the continuation of any habit in contradiction with this.' In other words, for every man in the new republic, when out of their homes, they could either go bare-headed – a social taboo – or they would have to wear a hat. One deputy spoke out against it, saying it was unconstitutional; but he was shouted down, told that freedom cannot be a toy in the hands of reactionaries, and that the law's opponents were troublemakers and liars. To near unanimous approval in the chamber, Law No. 671 was passed. Across the country, it was announced by village chiefs and town criers.[11]

Most senior clerics – it should be said – kept their head down. Was this really the battle to choose? But many were not so accommodating, were offended by what was being asked of them. How could Muslims properly worship, they asked, in a *şapka*? What about the concept of *secde* – in the cycle of Muslim prayer, after standing, then bending over, that stage of kneeling down, forehead to the floor, prostrated before Allah – the position, as an imam once put it to me, where we are 'closest to God, where we can talk to him one-on-one'? How could you do that in a hat with a peak?

There was something more primal too . . . a lot of Turks simply didn't want to look like Europeans.

In Erzurum, far out east on the Anatolian plains, shortly after the law was passed a local imam petitioned the governor to allow them their traditional headgear – better suited, he argued, to their long, harsh winters. Plus, the Western hats looked like chamber pots.[12] A crowd of nearly three thousand gathered around the governor's building, calling the authorities infidels. The local gendarme opened fire on the crowd. In Maraş down to the south – where the *şapka* looked suspiciously like what the French occupiers of the city had worn just a few years before after the war – a treatise against the hat was left on the door of the Grand Mosque. Afterwards, a cleric denounced the reforms in a speech to his followers, who reportedly proceeded to bring down the gates of the city prison. In Kayseri, central Turkey, rumours flew round that the government would ban the veil and the Koran. But the biggest reaction was here, in the villages amongst the hills off the Black Sea coast.[13]

*

Güneysu, and the surrounding region of Rize, is an unforgiving place. For the further east you go down the Black Sea in Turkey – all the way up to the Çoruh River on the Georgian border – the more the land is squeezed and squeezed between the hills and the sea. By the time you reach Rize, it is just a thin belt of coast, before it rises quickly – too steep for tractors today, and too steep for plough animals before them. The hills are all scored with *çay* plantations now, but a hundred years ago, tea had not even been introduced, so they were just left with the weather you need to produce it: buckets, and buckets, of rain. Beyond the hills, snow-peaked mountains wrap around the horizon. The Turkey to the south behind them – the high plateaus of Anatolia, the cities of Erzurum or Erzincan – are hard to reach even now; but in the 1920s there was no road to them at all. The people therefore ate what they could: yoghurt, cornbread, and anchovies.[14]

Even going east to west, parallel to the sea, was hard. Neighbouring villages were cut off from each other – the valleys between them were too steep, and the hills too high. As my host Zeynep explained to me, *this* village is famously conservative, *that* one is nationalist; you wouldn't eat *kuru fasulye* – white bean stew – in Rize, but in nearby Çayeli it's famous. The highway that runs along the coast now was not built until decades later. Until then, the villages were islands unto themselves.

And if the place is tough, the people are tougher, and particularly direct. As one supermarket assistant asked me in sequence, minutes into our conversation: 'Are you Muslim? Do you like Erdoğan? Have you been circumcised?' I just needed to lie to all three, and then I was in his embrace. That is the other thing known about the people here: their warmth, their humour, and their courage. For centuries, blessed with a land that gave them little, they turned migrants, out to go and make their fortunes, for the boat out west was always possible. They were troops and sailors, merchants and craftsmen, long the footsoldiers and servants of the Ottoman Empire. As Zeynep told me, given they traditionally spent so long away from home, their men are famously jealous too. They were not just laymen, but religious scholars. It was a region that was taken by the Ottomans – and so became Muslim – relatively late, but they approached their faith with all the enthusiasm of late converts. Some of its villages would become famous for their *medreses*, taking in students from all over to study the Koran, memorize its passages, and discuss theology.

They were devoted subjects then, but still a little unruly. All over the Black Sea, there were powerful families and bandits – ultimately loyal to the state, but still occasionally a little testy, keen to protect their little fiefdoms. It was, perhaps, an awkward fit for the new regime* – loose cannons you'd perhaps rather not provoke.

*

The previous day – before my walk down the valley to Güneysu – I was in Rize, the city on the coast, and the place where its river eventually empties out into the Black Sea. I was going to meet

---

* Indeed, much of the internal opposition to Atatürk's rule came from deputies based around the Black Sea, who were more conservative, and perhaps more sympathetic to the caliphate too. In 1924, one deputy from nearby Trabzon was killed in Ankara. In 1926, another member from the Black Sea was implicated in an attempt to assassinate Atatürk himself.

Recep, a full-time imam and part-time historian, in his third-floor office near the main square. His room was chaos, small and stacked with papers, and with walls decorated not by any windows but by black-and-white sketches of himself. As we began to talk, the electricity in the building cut out, and in the dark I could see only the small red light of my recorder, and the orange tip of his cigarette. In his earthy, calming voice, he tells me *bekle*, to wait for the power, for he has things he wants to show me.

After ten minutes, and some distant beeping down the hall, the lights come on again, and he has the documents ready in his hand. They are delicate little things – history you can touch – ripped and frayed, with sepia mugshots clipped to the top. On one side, they each carry a faded red stamp; and all over in blue ink is the Turkish of another world, the delicate dots and curved lines of Arabic script, as old Turkish used to be written. He bristles when I ask if he can read them. 'Of course!' It helps that he's an imam, and has spent years studying the Koran. They are court documents, he explains. They are how he has pieced together what really happened here. When he received them from an archive in Ankara, he says, he was too excited to even sleep.

When the hat law was passed, he starts, it was a difficult time for Rize and the villages dotted around the Black Sea coast. It had not even been a decade, after all, since it was occupied by the Russian army during the war: many people had fled; its economy was in tatters; and the full force of the law, of the state, wasn't quite felt all over. There were gangs everywhere. Indeed, just weeks before, a commander had already been shot at in Güneysu, the village up in the hills, though he escaped unscathed. It was an unrelated incident, but warning enough that, at the very least, this was not the easiest place to control.

You could forgive Captain Osman for being a little nervous then, when he was sent from the city up to Güneysu, on the day the bill was voted through. Though he was due to carry out some basic administrative work, he would have known, walking up the valley, that he came as a representative of the state. And known too that his superior had already been told days before – by elders of the villages – that they would not comply. The imam and village chief of Gürgen – the village one up from Güneysu – had made clear their refusal to wear hats; as had several figures from Güneysu. They had threatened him as well.

But on the 25th of November, as the captain was making his way there, the hills all bare apart from the pines, it escalated further still. A crowd had gathered in Güneysu: locals who had walked down the valley from Gürgen; others from villages all over; and the Güneysu faithful themselves. They had come to protest,* and their leaders had bigger plans besides. (As Recep says to me, leafing through the documents, he doesn't think most villagers had planned what came next.) On the road outside the village, they – the imam and village chief of Gürgen, and a gang of twenty-five armed men – intercepted Captain Osman, and took him under arrest. From there, they raided the local police station, capturing four further gendarmes. They found an emptied-out armoury in the building, and locked all five of them in.

As Captain Osman would later testify, he heard the rest from within the walls of his temporary cell: the collective chants and prayers of the crowd outside; a local imam reading out a fatwa against hats; another calling the government infidels; and one – moving into ever more dangerous territory – declaring that from some unknown event, the Prime Minister had been killed,

---

* Some would later say they had come to Güneysu not to oppose the hat law, but for something else entirely: that they had been falsely told that there was to be a celebration and prayer around Şakal-I Şerif, a strand of the beard of Prophet Muhammed that had been brought to the village.

that President Atatürk had been injured, and that it was the duty for more religious leaders to take their stead. As the day wore on, some grew uneasy with the imprisonment of the gendarmes, and the insurrectionist mood of the crowd. They would, by the evening, release Captain Osman and his peers. But the hard core were already on the march: a hundred and fifty of them, armed and heading for Rize, a five-hour walk away.

Despite some accounts that they would arrive at the city and raid its market, Recep assures me the 'rebellion' – though he shies away from the word – was much humbler than that. They reached a village halfway down, he says, before dispersing into the night. But the part afterwards, he admits, was a little more dramatic. After a call for aid, the *Hamidiye* warship, the biggest in the Turkish fleet, had left the Dolmabahçe Palace on the banks of the Bosphorus in İstanbul, the day the trouble started. After a few days running along the length of Turkey's Black Sea coast, it arrived on the shore of Rize, with the rebels still on the run. Then – after a couple of days' wait more – it fired its guns towards the hills. And now everyone knows the song . . .

Atma, Hamidiye, / Don't bomb us, Hamidiye,
Atma, atma! / Don't bomb, don't bomb!
Din kardeşiyiz. / We are your brothers in faith.
Şapka da giyeceğiz, / We'll wear our hats,
Vergi de vereceğiz! / And we'll pay our taxes!

In truth, it was probably just a warning shot, and no damage was ever done. Indeed, Recep even plays with the idea that there were empty shells. But regardless, if it was to intimidate, it had its effect. The runaways that were left gave up, came to the city, and offered their statements for what they had done – the torn and yellowed documents in Recep's hands as we speak.

The tribunal began in a cinema complex in central Rize, just over a week later in December. It lasted four days and tried one hundred and forty-three defendants – charged with armed rebellion, using religion as a tool, and seeking to overthrow the republic. In the eyes of the tribunal, those five imprisoned officers were the embodiment of the very state itself. The court was not headed by judges, but by a selection of deputies from the assembly, who were – to put it mildly – untrained in the art of blind justice. At one point, as an imam is denying he ever said the government's leaders had been injured or killed, he is interrupted by one of the officials, who tells him that Atatürk, his deputy, and the republic will not die – instead, they will 'crush the heads of apostates like you.'[15]

On the 14th of December, the tribunal finished its work. Over half of the defendants were set free; dozens were given prison terms of ten years or more; and eight – the imam and the village chief included – were sentenced to death, taken out to the beach that same night, and hanged. Just beyond them off shore, the *Hamidiye* warship – its work done, and its near two-week stay complete – started its long journey back west.

It's an episode that speaks, in part, to the extraordinary fragility of the early Turkish state. For 1925 was also the year of the Sheikh Sait Rebellion, the uprising in February that saw up to fifteen thousand Kurdish troops conquer swathes of the eastern countryside. Eighty thousand troops were mobilized to put it down, to repel its siege of Diyarbakır, and capture Sheikh Sait himself, before he too was hanged at dawn.[16] In the eyes of the Turkish leadership, in other words, it was a time of existential threats. After that rebellion, it passed a law that, for the 'Maintenance of Order', allowed it to shut down papers and close down opposition groups. It set up Independence Courts that would arrest and execute thousands – courts with no judges, no legal appeals, and which one official confessed to his diary were 'a terror'.[17] These were the same tribunals – to deal with perceived enemies of the state – that were used to try opponents of the hat law. And here a certain paranoia took hold, and perhaps a legacy of the Treaty of Sèvres as well. In the eyes of the tribunal, these various small rebellions against hats across Anatolia were not spontaneous, but coordinated by clerics in league with foreign powers. As one official overseeing the tribunal in Rize told a defendant, 'What you did is what the Armenians, the Greeks, and the English want to make you do.'[18] In total, 808 were arrested in the two months after the law was passed. Fifty-seven were executed. İskilipli Mehmed Atıf Hoca, who had published his pamphlet eighteen months before the law was passed – on hats, modernity, and the loss of identity – was amongst them.

But of course it feels like something more too, of an overbearing state trying to drastically engineer society from above – like the novelist Ahmet Hamdi Tanpınar satirized: a fictional Time Regulation Institute that checked the watches of all passing citizens, issuing fines for each one not synchronized to the municipal public clock. Walking around the region today – past the old men thumbing their prayer beads, and the occasional striking blue eyes of the Black Sea – it feels even more absurd now . . . no one wears hats any more. As Recep tells me as we part, things move on, 'we drive foreign cars and use mobile phones now too.'

*

There is one other aspect of this story, about the village where it happened. As I approach Güneysu, down the valley road lined with *çay* factories, things all of a sudden look very new. I pass the Kaptan Ahmet Erdoğan İmam Hatip, then the Güneysu Tenzile Erdoğan İlce Hastanesi – a school for imams named after President Erdoğan's father; a local hospital after his mother. Then the Physical Therapy and Rehabilitation School of the Recep Tayyip Erdoğan University. There is a shiny sports complex, and identical Ottoman-style apartments running all along the river.

For this is the President's ancestral village, his *memleket.*

Güneysu is where his disciplinarian father was born; where his grandfather practised as an imam; and where he spent his summers as a boy. Down by the coast, in Rize's main square, there are not one but two giant posters of Erdoğan, hung up at opposite ends, staring each other down. Erdoğan's favourite poet, the Islamist Necip Fazıl Kısakürek, would go on to write about these events in the 1960s, describing the hanged eight as martyrs. Viewed from here then, it seems like another story too, and one with a particularly long tail: secular overreach, and religious blowback decades later.

I have an appointment here with a local imam, who would like to talk but not to give his name. It is late afternoon as we sit down, and from the office window I can see over Güneysu, up to the hills that frame it on all sides. He shares *pepeçura* with me in an aluminium takeaway box, a local dessert made with grapes and maize flour – 'poverty food', he says. It has the kind of bright purple you normally see only in children's sweets. He is suited, bearded, and fond of his opinions, with a habit of answering questions with sermons that sprawl through history, tackling not just hats, but NATO, Zionism, and Turkey's litany of coups. It is a long conversation.

I had come to meet him, fully expecting him to agree that this was a tale of secular repression and religious heroics, but he is furious. For one, he says, the poet Kısakürek never even left İstanbul, never spoke to anyone here. The story takes on another aspect again: of local history spun out for a national debate. After he laughs at the notion that the executed were martyrs, I ask him about the notion of *secde* – about the impossibility of prostrating yourself before Allah in a peaked hat – and he dismisses that too. Just bow your head further, he suggests. He seems angered twice over: as an imam, by the use of Islam for political gain – the story was stirred up decades later, he claims, by politicians trying to court the religious vote; and as a loyal Turkish citizen, offended by the notion that his village ever rose up against the government. He is a man of the Koran, but the Turkish state is something sacred too.

He finishes, and says there is someone he wants me to meet. We walk down the stairs, out the office, and across the bridge, to the other side of Güneysu. The house is on the banks of the river, with *çay* bushels and cabbage leaves growing in the courtyard outside. A life-size poster of Atatürk hangs by the front door. And, after a few knocks, I am introduced to a man with a thin moustache and huge drooping earlobes. He is Mustafa Resit Tarakçı, born in 1940, and with an energy like he has not spoken for the last eighty-two years, winding all the way up to his moment. His voice is raspy and his accent thick – all the hard Gs of Turkish turned to soft Black Sea Js. We sit down over *çay*. I strain my ears to listen to his answers; he slaps my knee at the end of each question.

His grandad, he explains, was Sabit Tarakçıoğlu, one of the eight hanged on the beach nearly a century ago. I ask him to share what he knows, what he has learnt from his uncles and aunts over the years. He disappears from the living room, and returns – to my confusion – with a *tarak*, an enormous wooden comb. His grandad was a 'carder', he says, and this was used for combing out sheep's wool before it could be spun. I ask if his grandad was a religious man; he takes a slight beat and answers: 'Not particularly . . . because he was also a bandit'. Brave, but a bandit nonetheless. When the crowds started gathering on that day in November 1925, he was mostly just following the orders of the village chief and local imams, so he raided the police station with the rest.

Sabit, he thinks, did not really know what he was getting into. He was even offered the chance to take a boat out to escape to Batum – beyond the Turkish border – before he was called to the tribunal, but he refused, for he did not realize what he had done was so serious. To my slight surprise, he then starts mocking his grandad and all the others instead. 'Does it mean you've left your religion because you put a hat on your head?' he laughs, calling them 'ignorant'. He refills my tea and leaves again, returning with his phone in his hand. Again a surprise: he shows me a picture of his grandad, taken shortly before his death. One eye slightly higher than the other, a neat little side parting, a wispy moustache. His grandad was twenty-five when he was killed. Mustafa's own father was nine at the time. The family were left 'with just a few cows'.

Dinciler kışkırttı, devlet katletti, he concludes, rather philosophically. The religious provoked, and the state killed. Though he doesn't agree with what his grandad did, he does think the punishment was harsh, given that they had already surrendered, and that 'no blood was spilled or money taken.' I ask a little tentatively about the poster on his front door, of the president whose government hanged his *dede*. He shakes his head. It wasn't Atatürk's decision, he says, but those of the tribunal below him. He has his sights on more recent presidents anyway, and is gleefully scornful about Erdoğan – his fellow countryman – before it's suggested that it might be best if I turn my recorder off.

We leave his home together, and I notice mandarins and peppers in his garden too. The setting sun has left the valley, but its golden light still colours the tops of the hills above us, and the steam from the chimney of a nearby *çay* factory, wisps of orange floating towards an ever-darker sky. Mustafa wants to show me his grandfather's grave a few minutes away – modest and hidden beneath the weeds. As we walk there, he holds my hand, and starts on about the president again, and how much better things were in the past. The thought crosses my mind that here, in this religious, conservative region, in Erdoğan's very hometown, he might well be the only Kemalist in the village.

*

That night I am back in Rize, in an apartment overlooking the sea. My host Zeynep brings me linden tea, picked from the trees of her village, as a hard rain thumps against the windows, and I begin to read what Recep – the historian and imam – has given to me. It is a book of the Rize Hat Trials, with testimony after testimony of the one hundred and forty-three accused. It's transcribed into Turkish script, but still I linger over old Ottoman words: *vukuat, tevellüd.*

Each defendant is asked their job, their age, whether they can read and write, and their recollections of the day. And soon, Güneysu's hat rebellion seems touchingly small. For there are no grand statements or words of defiance; instead, you can almost feel them recoiling from the power of the state. Gürgen's imam denies ever saying that hats were for infidels, and that all he ever wanted was a delay to the law. If he was found with a gun, he says, it wasn't his. Gürgen's village chief said that rather than marching to Rize to carry on his rebellion, with a hundred and fifty armed companions in tow, he was in fact heading to the city *to buy a hat*. He claims he wasn't armed, and that he did not order the capture of the gendarmes; he is contradicted by other witnesses. There are evasions, denials, and disagreements. Many say they are but simple farmers, obeying the wishes of the village's educated men. Then I come across Sabit's testimony, the grandad of Mustafa back in Güneysu: married; aged twenty-five; previous convictions; says he was just following orders. *'Biz isyan nedir biliriz?'* he asks pleadingly, 'Us, what do we know of rebellion?'

In all this, something else emerges too: a changing of worlds. When Gürgen's imam introduces himself and his profession, the tribunal officials ask him if he has the certificate to prove it. In the new Turkey – and the education law passed a year before – all imams had to be approved by the religious ministry. But the imam belongs to a different time, armed with a different authority, of *medreses,* of networks of clerics and fellow village imams, of informal groups of Koranic study. In other words, an authority being pushed aside. 'I am ignorant,' he concedes, 'since I don't have the education, I could not come and take the exam to get the certificate.' He is corrected: he is an imam no more. Here perhaps – beyond hats – this humiliation, this loss of status, was what was really at stake for imams of this Black Sea valley.[19]

*

Across Turkey, the hat law was met more begrudgingly. Internal party reports complained of low compliance, or that people would wear scruffy home-made headgear, or caps instead of hats – turned backwards, they would at least still allow the forehead to touch the ground in prayer. In the words of one scholar, the ambiguities 'raised the question of what qualified as a hat', for the legislation was unclear and the people creative. Some though continued to resist in other ways: one man in Antalya province, down on Turkey's southern coast, reportedly did not leave his house for seventeen years, until his death in 1942, to avoid wearing a şapka; others wore them to visit the city – where the chance of seeing law enforcement was much greater – only to remove them once back home. For those who were caught, normally the police would simply remove the offending headwear, but they meted out fines and beatings too. Still, the fez did not disappear. For years, there were stories of raids, of the authorities discovering hundreds of underground fezes here and there, kept by traders just waiting for the ban to be rescinded.[20]

It never was, and the transformations would only continue. A month after the hat law, just after Christmas 1925, Turkey's modernizing, secularizing programme pushed on again, looking now not just at dress but at time itself. The twenty-four-hour clock was introduced; the old ways – how prayer times had been calculated, by shadows and sunlight – were sidelined. The Gregorian calendar was implemented too. New Year, for the first time, would be celebrated a week later. Over the next year, even more sweeping changes were to come: a new civil code was adopted, taken nearly wholesale from Switzerland; the penal code came from Italy. The influence of clerics was removed completely from family law. The *devrims* rolled on: in 1928 Turkish switched to Latin script and Western numerals; in 1932, the call to prayer was to be read not in Arabic but Turkish; in 1934 Turks were forced to take surnames; a year later, Sunday became the official day of rest. They were reforms that were liberatory and revolutionary and repressive all at once: polygamy had been banned; with the script changes, a literacy campaign taught millions to read, and thousands of villages – with their names in Kurdish, Armenian, and Greek – were Turkicized and reborn. Including that village up the valley from Rize: Potomya, from the old Greek for 'creek', became Güneysu, 'South water'.

It is a history still up for grabs. On my last morning in Rize, my host Zeynep's father – who gives nightly religious courses in a building downtown – tells me about the oppression of that time, how people were killed for not wanting to wear hats, about the lack of democracy, and the historic mistake of moving away from Arabic script. It is slightly heated, and he moves seamlessly from then to now, and the achievements of Erdoğan. It is now a democracy, he says, you can wear whatever you want. I'm reminded of a historian I once read, who wrote that we have to 'give the dead room to dance'[21] – to accept that we don't know everything about the past and those who lived there, and not impose ourselves on them too much if we can. But the dead don't dance here, they are soldiers made to march, in Turkey's ongoing arguments about its present. I thank Zeynep and her father, and leave into a wet morning. As I reach the main square, there is a driving rain – the pigeons are heavy with it. Nevertheless, it is prayer time and the mosque is full: dozens of men who could find no space inside roll out mats and flattened cardboard on the ground, lay down their shoes, and begin their prayers. Kneel down, heads to the floor, stand up, all in unison. The moment it ends, they pick up their things and run to somewhere dry.

I catch the bus from the city centre, and it begins to move westwards, towards Trabzon, where the land between the sea and the hills is given a little more room to breathe. Just as we start, we pass the spot where those executions took place nearly one hundred years ago. All eight were hanged till noon, and buried right there on the beach. After twenty-eight days, the families were allowed to claim them, to take their bodies back to the village, like the little grave Mustafa showed me of his grandad, overgrown with weeds. The gallows were on the shore then, but the land has long since been reclaimed from the sea. It's the site of a state-owned power plant now.

4. '38

1930s – Dersim

THE ROAD FROM ELAZIĞ TO DERSIM HEADS OUT EAST, keeping the Keban Dam to our left. It is a huge, lifeless body of water, holding the Euphrates up from its path. This morning, it is half-covered in mist, for we are nearly a thousand metres high. Clouds sit low on top of the mountains around us – here they are not so much jagged as crinkled, almost steppe-like, with a thin cut of yellow grass on top. The earth itself is a rugged brown, sparsely populated by trees. As one explorer described this area long ago, it is a region of 'stunted oaks' and hawthorns.[1] They are red and bare now, preparing for the brutal winter to come.

The minibus rolls up and down the slopes, crosses the dam, and soon we are at Kovancılar, where we veer a sharp left, heading north. The engine starts to sound different – higher pitched – as it gears up for more mountains ahead. As we move closer towards Dersim, it's like someone is squeezing the earth closer and closer together, and the mountains are more tightly packed. Between them, on the flats, there are few trees or houses – just a vast empty space. A heron stands in a field, upright in the distance, the only thing to break the rolling expanse.

In the 1930s, a teacher from Elazığ used to take this route, a passenger in a military jeep. She was going to recruit schoolgirls from Dersim, to take them to another world. As she went, over deep ravines, waterfalls, lakes, and caves, she would see below her abandoned vehicles that had toppled over the cliffs: horse carts, trucks, trailers, a bulldozer. To calm her nerves, she would count the mountain bends instead: a hundred and fifty-seven over nine miles.[2]

It's a little simpler now, and we fly around the mountain and its newly laid asphalt road. But still, there is a sense of unease. We cross a stream – a crystal blue, despite the grey skies – that marks the provincial boundary. There is a checkpoint, and concrete blocks on the road just in front. We stop, and a gendarme in military fatigues boards the bus, to check everyone's ID. There are nineteen men, and two women, almost all older than him. On his waist, a pistol sits in its holster – its grip carries a tiny badge of the Turkish flag.

We climb up again, until we enter Dersim itself, past another checkpoint guarded by an armoured truck. It's a journey that recalls its past, for this was once like crossing an internal border, where only those with special military permits could enter. But I've come to talk to those who were already there, to those who were caught inside.

*

The rain in Dersim sounds heavier than it is, drumming as it does on the corrugated-iron roofs. It is a tiny town, with a centre of a few streets that I walk in ten minutes. All along them lie huge *kangals*, Turkey's old cream-coloured sheepdogs. They are slightly muddied by the rain, curled up on the pavements, making pillows with their paws. Around Dersim – already high up – the town is ringed again by small and steep mountains, in a dark and snaggy limestone. They look almost like waves that never come to shore – each one in the distance rolling slightly bigger than the last, as the land swells ever more. We are in central, eastern Anatolia, but – nestled here in the mountains – the neighbouring cities feel very far away. The area is flanked by two branches of the Euphrates that meet at the dam at its south; to the north, the peaks rise even higher, to three thousand metres above the sea. But it is not just the landscape that makes Dersim feel cut off from its surroundings, and the conservative peoples that live there. For they are a little different here.

We find Hasan in an underground market, sitting in a café, drinking *çay* alone. I am with his grandson Ali, a handsome twenty-three-year-old with the letters A-Z-A-D-I tattooed across the knuckles of his right-hand. It is the Kurdish for 'freedom'. His *dede*, he had told me, is ninety-two – that is, just seven years younger than the country he lives in – and he might have a story to tell.

Hasan is in a flat cap, two waistcoats, two shirts, a cardigan, and coat, all in dark greys and whites. As we approach, I motion for him to stay seated, and he ignores me, gets up from his seat, and is suddenly my height, if not taller. His eyes are slightly reddening, with dark pupils at the heart of them. He has a full head of hair, and a wild and broad moustache – with a slight parting at the centre; under his nose, it looks like a white river gushing from each nostril. After barely a word, we head for the stairs to exit, he extends a walking stick, and tackles them no problem. His grandson looks at him, and then at me, with a certain pride, as if to say, 'Not bad, eh?'

As we emerge onto the square, I ask Hasan how he is still in such a good shape. 'Village life,' he answers, his voice quiet but clear, a little husky. 'Good water and good air.' He says he comes from a great family too, the eighth generation of a line that came from Khorasan, Iran, and he starts to reel off the names of his ancestors: Mehmet, Ibrahim, Mustafa, Ali Rıza. They were the leaders of the Hiran tribe – part of a holy lineage that stretches back centuries – as Hasan is too.

They were all tall, he continues, *ağaç gibi*. Like trees.

In the Turkish press there are breathlessly reported surveys every year. Dersim supposedly has the longest-living people in the country . . . and the most unhappy too.

*

The 1930s in Turkey saw a different mood. The instability of the wars – and of the first few years of the republic – had somewhat eased. Now the state was trying to consolidate its grip. Atatürk and his government were still in power, and seemingly ever less willing to let go. In 1930, a brief flirtation with allowing opposition political parties ended after just a year; institutions deemed overly independent – such as the Nationalist Hearths, which had hundreds of branches, or the Turkish Women's Union – were shut down. Then in 1937 the distinction between Atatürk's party and the state was lost altogether. The six principles of its political programme – Republicanism, Populism, Nationalism, Secularism, Statism, and Revolutionism – were enshrined in the constitution for good.

There was something else as well – moves not just to increase the government's power, but to push it into a new direction. The 1924 Constitution had been fairly vague about who exactly it was who lived within the country's borders. 'The people of Turkey,' it stipulated, at Article 88, 'regardless of religion and race are Turks as regards Turkish citizenship.' It was not a claim that everyone who lived in Turkey was ethnically, linguistically Turkish; only that, when it came to their rights and responsibilities, they were 'Turks as regards Turkish citizenship'. Whatever that meant.[3]

Gradually though, the authorities sought to impose something a little more stirring, a closer union – an insistence that the people living in Turkey were Turks, and that that was something to be proud of. So across the 1930s, emerged a more strident, top-down nationalism. It had of course its own origin story. As the thesis went: the Turks were in fact a great and ancient race who had lived in Central Asia thousands of years ago; as they moved across the world in all directions, they spread their civilization to all those fortunate enough to meet them – to China, India, Egypt, Greece, Italy, and to their new home, Anatolia.[4] The Sumerians were actually Turkish; the Hittites were actually Turkish; as my *baba* would remember of his schooling, 'we learnt that everything was really Turkish'. It was a thesis that found a cousin in linguistics too, and the propagation of the Sun Language Theory: the idea that all human languages were in fact descended from the same proto-Turkic primal tongue. The River Amazon was thus called, for example, from the Turkish *ama* – 'but' – and *uzun* – 'long' – and early Turks stumbling across the world's largest river, exclaiming, 'But it's Long!'[5] Turks were in essence the source not just of modern civilization, but of speech itself. Flawed and as absurd as these theories may have been, they did have at least two benefits: one, they linked 'The Turks' to all those who currently lived within Turkey's borders; and two, they dismissed the impor- tance of the Ottomans, who had just ruled over the same land for the past six hundred years – for what was a few centuries, compared to this rich and storied past? They were taught in Turkey's schools and universities from the 1930s on.

The problem, however, was that vast swathes of Anatolia were unconvinced. They did not see themselves as 'Turkish', nor did they speak this language, as glorious as its history may have been. There were of course various minorities across Turkey: remaining Greeks and Armenians; Circassians and Laz; Bosniaks and Tatars. But the most significant group was the country's Kurds, who made up perhaps one in every ten people in the new republic. And so indeed up to that point, the most significant challenges to state power had come from the east where they lived: the Sheikh Sait Rebellion around Diyarbakır in the south-east in 1925; and another uprising around Mount Ararat to its north five years later.

In part, the state response was merely to try to persuade the Kurds that they were mistaken, that they were really Turks after all. As the secretary-general of the ruling party once said, they accepted that some people 'had the idea that they are Kurds', and that it was their 'duty to correct these false assumptions.'[6] As part of those efforts, the Kurdish language was banned in the public sphere – all teaching was already only ever conducted in Turkish – and the very word 'Kurd' itself erased from official discourse. They were henceforth 'tribes of the east', 'Mountain Turks', or Turks corrupted by their proximity to Iran. But things hardened still. After the rebellion of 1930, a minister asserted that only the 'Turk is master of this country.' Non-Turks would 'only have one right in the Turkish homeland: the right to be servants, the right to be slaves.'[7]

If they couldn't be convinced that they were Turks, then perhaps they would just have to be moved instead. In the summer of 1934, the assembly passed the resettlement law, empowering the Interior Minister to redistribute Turkey's population 'in accordance with membership of Turkish culture.' While the purpose was to designate zones of the country that were to become more proportionally Turkish – Kurds were referred to as nomads, and therefore fit for relocation out of where they lived – there was a special category created as well. Zone 3 areas were to be completely closed to human habitation, for 'sanitary, economic, cultural, political, military, and security' reasons. As the Interior Minister justified the law, it was to create 'a country with one language, one mentality, and unity of feelings'.[8] And they had special plans for a place like Dersim.

*

Dersim had long been set apart. Indeed it still is. Just an hour and a half away from Elazığ – its conservative, neighbouring city – in Dersim town centre there are wine bars and off-licences; women's heads are mostly uncovered; men's moustaches are not neatly trimmed to the upper lip – as in most of Turkey – but vast, untamed things. The holy day is not Friday but Thursday, when locals light candles in their homes. Dersim even has the country's sole communist mayor. There is, simply put, a different atmosphere here. It is not just that Dersim is mostly Kurdish, or that its people speak Zaza – a minority Kurdish dialect – but it is Turkey's only Alevi majority town too.

Alevism in Dersim is hard to categorize. A syncretic faith, it is Muslim but differs from Turkey's mainstream Sunnis in several ways, not least in its practice: Alevis don't fast for Ramadan; don't genuflect to pray; don't take the pilgrimage to Mecca; some have even argued that Alevis don't believe the Koran is literally true. They are influenced by Shi'ism, in that they pray to Ali, and mourn the death of his son Hüseyin at Kerbala. It has a strong streak of Turkey's old Sufi strain too, and its focus on the spirit and love – they pray facing each other, it is said, because Allah is in each of us, and best reached through loving one another. Then there are elements of pre-Islamic, Zoroastrian, and Christian beliefs. It's a faith passed on by hereditary holy figures – *seyits* – who each claim descent from Ali, and the secrets he revealed to their lines over a thousand years ago, taught not so much in sermon as in songs, poetry and ritual. Finally, it sees the divine in Dersim itself: in the Munzur River that feeds into the Euphrates, said to have erupted when a holy figure long gone spilt milk on the ground; or in the mountain goats that roam the national park to its north, purportedly the property of saints. In Alevism here, Dersim the place is a sacred, living being, a landscape of mystic powers.[9,10,11]

Beautiful and inaccessible, unorthodox and strange, Alevism had long been persecuted in the Ottoman Empire, its adherents seen as heretics and traitors, as Shi'ite sympathizers with Persia to the east. While Alevis could be found all over Turkey – and in various different sects – many found sanctuary in Dersim over the centuries, in its caves, mountains, and creeks, far away from the reach of the Ottoman state. There had been twelve separate attempts to control it since the 1870s, but it was rugged, distant, and hard to contain. In 1915 it proved a refuge again – many Armenians escaped the violence by fleeing to the relative safety of its mountains.[12]

For the new republican state, determined to impose itself, Dersim's politics proved just as much a problem as its faith, for its daily life was not determined by governors or mayors, or the laws passed down in Ankara eight hundred kilometres west, but by tribal law. It was a poor region – mostly eking an existence out of the mountains, reliant on its livestock, producing little but carpets. And one split into sixty or so tribes as well, each with its own venerated ancestor, and his line ultimately back to Ali. As the seasons came and went, they would roam across the region, in search of better pastures. It could be less idyllic than that as well: tribes would raid each other for animals and wheat.

Though Dersim was nowhere near the border, it was the last bit of Turkey not under state control. Worse, it barely even knew anything about it. Official maps of Dersim at the time were mostly blank, save for a few major rivers and mountain peaks. When units ventured there, commanders lost men to accidents – to falls, to altitude sickness, to the kind of mistakes that happen when you don't know the terrain.[13] In snowy winters, they could barely even reach it. So inside Dersim itself, the state's presence was lightly felt: tax was barely paid; men avoided conscription. As Hasan remembers of his childhood, the tribes fought between themselves. And when the government wanted tax, it sent an officer every autumn, with a cavalry forty-strong, and negotiated what it could get.

Dersim caused more and more concern. In private, officials claimed that it was becoming increasingly anti-Kemalist over the twenties, stoked up by Kurdish nationalists. Into the next decade, internal reports called for its reform, and even its cleansing. By 1931, the Interior Minister called Dersim 'completely anarchic'; another official said that it was 'overrun by aggressive and plundering elements who wage continuous banditry'; they worried that it was well armed, desperately poor, and prone to insurgency, to exploitation by its leaders.[14] À la mode, ideologues tried to prove its Turkishness too. An anonymous military document argued that Dersimis had the same type of head as Turks, brakisefal – short and broad; it claimed too that, unlike the Kurds, its women were not masculine; others posited that the locals were merely Turks who had never converted to Islam.[15] With the right action, they hoped, it could be turned into a second Switzerland.

But there is one word from that official discourse that all the Dersimis I meet remember more than any other: çıban, an 'abscess' that had to be removed.

A year after the resettlement bill, Dersim got a law of its own, passed without opposition in parliament or in the press. In fact, it was barely debated at all. In 1935, Dersim was separated from Elazığ, carved into its own province, and put under a state of emergency overseen by a military governor, with powers of arrest and deportation without appeal. There was 'nothing abnormal here', said the Interior Minister as he justified the changes, citing the backwardness and lawlessness of the tribes, and the exploitative rule of their leaders. The legislation was called the Tunceli law, for Dersim was to be renamed and Turkicized too. Tunc-eli: 'Bronzeland', for Turks it was claimed had been there since the Bronze Age.[16]

Over the decade, the state began to build up its presence. It surveyed the area, launching reconnaissance flights over the mountains, producing manuals and reports about Dersim, trying to fill in those whites on its maps. The eastern rail line extended to neighbouring Elazığ in 1934, opening up the region to soldiers and officials from further west. In 1936, the government began a disarmament campaign, collecting thousands of guns from Dersimis. In 1937, it set up the Elazığ Girls' Institute, a boarding school with a separate section to educate – and 'civilize' – the 'wild and stubborn' daughters of the region. The teacher who travelled to Dersim on a military jeep – counting the mountain bends as she went – was recruiting the girls for that very school. Most concretely, the state was building military observation posts, roads, bridges, and police stations.[17] Local Kurdish officials were moved out of the region. The administration that was left – with staff who spoke no Kurdish, and rarely wanted to be there – felt more and more like a colonizing force.

Some tribes were untroubled by the state's expansion into Dersim, or the newly named Tunceli, and even supplied men to help construct its barracks. As Hasan told me, his tribe had always been loyal – his great-uncle Mehmet Ali had fought with great distinction against the Russians in the war – and offered the same support to the new republic too. But others were much less sure, and resented the interference in their affairs. As one Kurdish activist would later say from exile, Dersim was being 'prepared for the gallows'.[18] And so Seyit Rıza, a tribal leader in his seventies, with a long white beard and a face scored like the mountains, sought an alliance. Together with four other tribes, they began to oppose the encroachment. They gathered four thousand men between them, and a confrontation seemed inevitable once more.

*

The evening draws in in Dersim, and around the town street lamps going up the mountain glow a warm orange, like Christmas lights strung across the slopes. I meet Dilek in the bar of a central hotel. She is an academic and anthropologist, who has collected stories about the area for over a decade. Though she wasn't born in Dersim, she has Alevi roots that trace back to here – her tribe's spiritual leader lives in a village in the mountains. He is one hundred and four.

I ask her how it all started in 1937, for I had heard one version: that on the eve of Newroz, March 20th, Dersimis from two tribes destroyed a wooden bridge out east, on the road towards Erzincan – the spot now, of local picnics – and cut the phone lines. They then, according to some sources, raided a police station and killed thirty-two soldiers. She told me another. For years she had been collecting *ağıtlar*, songs passed down through generations, retelling the past as they go. 'This is an oral culture,' she explains, 'this is how you understand the history.' And all of them describe something prior to the bridge attack: that soldiers had raped a woman in a nearby town. These songs are laments, she says, *acısı haykırıyor*: 'their pain cries out.' We spend the rest of the evening discussing what came next.

In May, the government agreed on its response to the attack, issuing a secret memorandum about a 'Punitive Expedition' to the region. 'This time,' it had decided, 'the people in the rebellious districts will be rounded up and deported.' Furthermore, the army was ordered to 'render those who have used arms or are still using them, once and for all, harmless on the spot.'[19] Their villages were to be destroyed, and their families removed. On the same day, planes flew over Dersim, dropping pamphlets, calling for surrender. 'If not, entirely against our will,' it read, 'the forces will act and destroy you. One must obey the state.'[20]

The operation was known as a *tedip harekatı* – a 'disciplining campaign' – and it mobilized twenty-five thousand soldiers, far more than the insurgents could muster. The rebellious tribes were fighting a guerrilla campaign, targeting police stations, roads, and bridges, before withdrawing into the mountains. But against them, the government was able to deploy new weapons of the state: planes that would bomb the villages believed to shelter them. *Çelik kartallarımız*, as they were referred to in Turkey's jingoistic press, 'Our Steel Eagles'. There was another angle for their propaganda too: Atatürk's own adopted daughter Sabiha Gökçen flew reconnaissance missions during the campaign. He was said to have personally given her a loaded gun before she took off.* A source of pride for much of Turkey, the Steel Eagles were utterly terrifying for those beneath them, who had never seen aeroplanes before.[21]

As the spring moved into summer, the rebellious tribes suffered heavy losses and internal divisions. In June '37, the Prime Minister undertook a celebratory tour of the region, as the press reported the rebels were surrendering en masse, that the uprising was 'in the throes of death'. The leadership of the revolt was suffering too, captured or killed one by one. Seyit Rıza, the man at its helm, was increasingly alone. In July, his friend and comrade – a Kurdish nationalist who had himself escaped to Dersim years ago for refuge – was betrayed by his own people. Killed alongside his wife, their heads were sent to the military governor. Across the summer, Rıza sought some alternative way out. He wrote to the Prime

---

* In the early republic, women were often used as symbols of the new modern Turkey – as teachers, nurses, civil servants, and so on. 'Emancipated but unliberated', as one scholar put it, for they were still pressed into service for the state. Gökçen was the same logic stretched further: she was allowed to fly in Dersim, and celebrated for it; but neither she nor any woman was actually permitted to join the air force proper.

Minister, describing his opposition to state policies, and detailing the destruction the operation had wrought. He sent a desperate letter to the League of Nations, asking vainly for help. He tried the British Foreign Office too – its recipients were unmoved, noting internally that it would 'create a good impression if we could let the Turkish government know, unofficially, that no notice has been taken of it.'[22] Short of options, by the end of August Seyit Rıza was the only rebel leader left. On the night of 10 September, reportedly exhausted and in poor health, he rode a mule to the Erzincan gendarmerie and surrendered.[23]

He was tried in Elazığ two months later. As the security chief responsible for his detention later wrote, when the judge sentenced him, Seyit Rıza didn't understand the judgement he had been given – he didn't speak Turkish. But he found out soon enough. As it happened, President Atatürk was due to visit the city that day, travelling on the newly built rail line, celebrating the country's opening up of the east. The authorities didn't want to risk a scene – perhaps of crowds imploring him to intervene – so they rushed the execution through before his arrival. The mayor, the security chief describes, found at the last minute a 'gypsy executioner' who demanded ten lira per head, and they all drove together to the gallows. It was only then that Seyit Rıza understood, and asked the chief if he could pass on his watch to his son. He did not know that his son was to be executed too. In a cold, empty square, Rıza made a short address, walked steadily to its centre, 'pushed away the gypsy and slipped the rope around his own neck. He kicked the chair away, and executed himself.'[24] On the southern edge of Dersim now, sits a bronze statue: his long beard, a turban on his head, his hands on his knees. He is facing the town centre, the valley falls sharply behind him, and down below, runs the sacred Munzur River.

By the autumn of 1937, the Dersim rebellion seemed over. The troops were ordered back to their garrisons for the winter, and it remained quiet for months. But that wasn't the end of it, by any means.

*

I'm with a local trade unionist called Hüseyin – in honour of their fallen imam, it is the province's most popular male name – and we are driving north, deeper into inner Dersim. The Munzur holds to our left, and we pass Ama Fatma Diyaret – a sacred place where the river bends, and foams up against the rocks below it. We push further in, following the curves of the valley, until slowly we rise further up the mountains, leaving the river below.

After half an hour so we stop, Hüseyin pulls out two red picnic chairs, and points to the cliff face across from us. That, he says, is Halvori Kayalık. The sun is at our backs, its light hitting straight onto the rockface, turning it a pinkish-white. He goes on: in '38, the soldiers rounded up hundreds of villagers from all across this area, and they gathered them up on that cliff. I am already a bit sick, because I know what he is about to say – seeing the flatness of the clifftop, and the sheerness of its fall. With bullets and bayonets, he continues, they threw them off. And then, a conversation of mostly silence: the whush of the river, and an eagle flying soundlessly above. The Munzur, goes the legend, was red for two days.

The execution of Seyit Rıza did not put an end to the violence in Dersim. As the new year began, there were renewed sporadic attacks and ambushes on gendarmes, by tribesmen who still saw the state's presence in Dersim as an existential threat. For them, there was nothing left to do but resist. So, once again, the Turkish government sanctioned another military operation in response, in February 1938. As the Prime Minister who authorized it later said, they needed to 'eradicate this problem once and for all'.[25]

It was different this time. When it launched in June, units spread for the first time to the plains over in the north-west, and further besides, all over the region. Detachments were ordered not to speak to locals. They were about to begin a new phase: *tarama*, as they referred to it. The cleansing.

*

Hasan, his grandson Ali and I enter his house on the upper side of Dersim town centre, in Cumhuriyet Mahallesi, Republic Neighbourhood. It is a little concrete bungalow, with a raised balcony onto nothing. We sit down over *çay*: me on one sofa; Hasan on another, and Ali beside him, acting not so much as a translator as an amplifier, shouting my questions into the hearing aid of his ninety-two-year-old *dede*.

Hasan, he tells me, was born on a spring day in 1930, and spent the first years of his life in their village to the south. He remembers feeding horses and mules, and that village life, with all his family, was *şahane*. Wonderful. The son of a prestigious family – loyal to the state – by 1938 he had already done two years at school. His father, he says, was an educated man, and could read the Turkish script introduced a decade before. He still has the textbooks his father used to learn it at home.

One summer's day, a troop of soldiers came to the village. As Hasan describes, they tied their horses to the fields in front of their house, to graze on their grass and drink their water. Amongst them, a captain walked to their front door, and asked to be let in. 'Burhan bey', Hasan says, retaining his name after all these years, 'Mr Burhan'. His brother brought him coffee, but the captain refused. And then, an eight-year-old Hasan watched on as he talked to his grandad, dad, and big brother. As he left, he told Hasan's father he would have to go to a gathering in Mazgirt, the nearby town, the next day. So his father mounted his own horse and made his way.

At this point, the details become hazier, reliant as they are on an escapee.

After arriving in Mazgirt, Hasan's father was detained, and spent three days and three nights in an abandoned church. Seventy to eighty people had been rounded up in total, and the building was under armed guard from the outside. On the dawn of the fourth day, more soldiers arrived, surrounding the church with ropes in hand. They bound the detainees, lined them up, and machine-gunned them down. Hasan's father was thirty-three. He was killed, Hasan believes, because a neighbouring and rival tribe had denounced him to the state, and claimed he supported the rebellion. 'They took it blindly,' says Hasan.

He found out the same day, as news spread to the village that there had been a massacre. Three of Hasan's tribe, travelling to the village from that direction, had seen the dead piled high in the forest. On the second night, relatives came to identify the dead, by a boot, or a trouser leg, or a finger. And there was Hasan's father amongst them. His family brought his body back, to be washed and blessed by the elders. That was when Hasan saw him first: a single bullet wound to his neck. It is seared on his memory.

At the end of this answer, he slows right down and takes a long pause, feeling the weight of what he has just said, even eighty-five years on. And then, '*Yaa neler geldi neler geçti.*' Oh the things we had, and the things we lost.

I ask what his father was like, as a person. 'He was a good man,' he answers, 'not a trace of badness.' It is like a child's understanding of their father, frozen in time. For what could he really have known? He takes out a thumbnail photo of him – as a sharply dressed soldier – that he has carried in his pocket for the last seventy years. And then we sit mostly in silence, drinking *çay*. I am not sure what he has made of our conversation, as he keeps flicking his eyes towards me, then looking away. Was it perverse to want him to have this story retold, his pain exposed to a stranger? We stand up after another silent tea, and I make to leave. He holds both my cheeks in his hands, and kisses them softly, not with his own cheeks but with his lips. I can feel the bristles of his moustache, catching against my own stubble. 'Write, write,' he tells me, 'don't forget.'

That summer, similar atrocities played out all across Dersim. In June, soldiers came to villages armed with machine guns and a list of those pre-determined to be killed: prominent tribesmen and their families; holy men; and any remaining Armenians too. As happened with Hasan's *baba*, it was a process that turned Dersimis on each other, for soldiers paid some families to guide them through the landscape and to point out potential victims. And as June moved into July and August, the violence spiralled out even further. Once, it had been limited to those most associated with Seyit Rıza and his rebellion; now, it was targeted at almost the whole population, at anyone who got in the soldiers' way. In August, a seventeen-day killing spree saw the murder of hundreds and hundreds of villagers – or as the official reports would refer to it, the 'annihilation' of bandits. As veteran testimonies admitted decades later, soldiers locked villagers in buildings and set them alight, or closed them in caves and threw in poison gas. They were told by their superiors that these people had given shelter to bandits, that it was time for revenge, or that they were Alevi or Armenian, and therefore subhuman. Some escaped into the creeks and caves of Dersim – as they had done for centuries – but for thousands there was no escape. At least thirteen thousand were killed in the *tertele*, as it is called, though the real figure may never be known.[26,27]

The state acknowledged the rebellion, but the massacres went unmentioned, and untold in the official history. Instead, a year later in 1939, an MP released a book about the pacification campaign, entitled 'Tunceli is Made Accessible To Civilization', celebrating the end of banditry, and claiming Dersimis had finally 'been made into human beings'.[28] The year seems apposite, for this is the language of fascism.

*

After the killings came the deportations. As the government had decided by early August, around five to seven thousand Dersimis were moved from the prohibited zones of Dersim out west, and many more followed. They were exiled to some of the most conservative parts of Turkey – to Denizli, Manisa, and others – and, as per the settlement law of 1934, they were scattered all around, so in no one place could the Kurds exceed ten per cent of the population. As a result, many of the sprawling families of Dersim's tribes were split apart.

As Hasan remembers, three months after his father was killed, soldiers came again to his village. This time, they didn't say anything. They simply rounded everyone up, and loaded them onto five trucks waiting by the road. Their possessions, the animals that Hasan used to feed as a boy, were all left behind. At eight years old, he thought he was going to be killed.

Instead they were taken down that route south, and its one hundred and fifty-seven mountain bends, to Elazığ. There, they stayed in a camp for fifteen nights, with thirty or forty other families, until the day came. Onto the *kara wagon*, as it's known, the black carriage. They packed five families into each compartment – 'filled with exiles', says Hasan. Then the doors were shut from the outside, and all was dark. He was with his mum, four brothers, three sisters, and his grandad. The train set off. For nine days and nine nights – 'oh what we went through!' – with the smell of sweat and smoke. And fear too – especially, for Hasan, when the train passed through a tunnel, and the dark of the carriage became completely black.

After a thousand kilometres west, they arrived, at Uşak, a town right the other side of the country. For another fifteen days, they

– and forty-seven other people – were put up in an abandoned two-storey inn. They ate and drank what they were given, and waited. Until finally – more than a month after their exile had begun – they were allocated their new plot in their new village. For the first few months at school, Hasan remembers, the other children wouldn't go near him. They had been told by older kids that Kurds ate people for food; another common story was that they secretly all had tails. But gradually, barriers came down, Hasan made friends – helped by the Turkish he had already learnt in class back in Dersim – and he grew to like his new life. After two years, he left school, and went to work in a nearby sugar factory, and materially at least their lives in Uşak were not so bad. Not least because, according to Hasan, his grandad – a man of great lineage, after all – had managed to smuggle some gold with him on the journey there. Still, they missed their village, their real village. Hasan's teens were passing, and his grandad getting older, but still it was forbidden to enter. Until in 1947, the Tunceli law was repealed, and one year later the state of emergency was lifted too. While many families would never return, Hasan's packed up their things, and headed back across the country once more. The village was rundown and falling apart, Hasan remembers, but they were very, very happy to come home.

*

This is living memory in Dersim, but only just. Slowly, the lights of it are being put out. Even in the time I was in Dersim, it faded a little more. I had organized to talk to one survivor, Bego, famous both for writing a book of his experiences, and for his phenomenal moustache. At nine years old, he saw his mum and three siblings killed before his own eyes. Instead, on a beautiful autumn morning, overlooking the Munzur River, I attended his funeral. He had died that week at ninety-two. His coffin was brought out, covered in a green shroud, and mourners grieved not just for him but for the steady disappearance of his generation. Another survivor proved too unwell to interview as well – her blood pressure was just too high. She is ninety-two, her exasperated granddaughter explained to me, but she just refuses to stop eating oily, salty foods.

But even as the last witnesses leave Dersim, those years are still felt all over, in a town suffused with loss. One afternoon, Dilek the anthropologist took me to a cafe where she and her friends liked to pass the time, and drink golden grass tea. Once they were all out for a cigarette and I was left alone, the owner – who had overheard what I was researching – started tapping her foot, quietly singing behind me, first to her teapot, and then straight to me. The words I could not understand at all – for it was in Zaza – but by the tone, of course I knew exactly what it was about: loss, pain, and what happened here eighty years ago. It was a song she had learnt from her village, she explained, and I asked her to tell me what it meant.

> That village was ours
> One hundred houses, but no daughter, no brides, no young
> It's in ruins
> I fell in love with Zere there. Oh no, oh no!
> I went, and said girl let's escape
> But winter was coming
> There was snow, and the roads were closed.

She sings it again, with her soft voice and the slightly harsh, guttural consonants of Kurdish, and her eyes never leave mine. I remind her of her young brother, she tells me, and insists that next time I come stay with her, her husband and her kids. Before we leave, she shows me how Alevis say goodbye, holding each other's arms, and kissing their shoulders.

Out on the street, Dilek explains, the songs – *ağıtlar* – are

mostly how the massacres are remembered, if at all. For the generation that survived them did not speak – their trauma carried
mostly in silence. You can still see it, she says, that people here
even now are on edge, can be quick to lose their temper, because
they faced an injustice that they couldn't confront. As one activist
told me, 'People buried it deep within themselves, and closed it
off, as if it never happened.' Generally, people just refer vaguely to
otuz-sekiz, '38 – an unexplained, and unexpanded starting point for
their lives. When I first asked Hasan where he grew up, he simply
answered, 'In 1938 there was a massacre.'

At the same time, that generation made sure that their children
assimilated into the new Turkey too – that something like *otuz-sekiz*
could never happen again. That activist only found out her family
was Alevi when she went to boarding school as a teen. A local
lawyer told me her grandad forbade his family to speak Kurdish in
their home afterwards. As his own daughter didn't know Turkish,
they did not speak to each other for the three years it took her to
learn it. Today, there is a disconcerting part of wandering around
Dersim, and chatting to those that live here. The wider region, east
beyond the Euphrates, is one of heavy Kurdish accents. But here
the Turkish is clipped and clear, like listening to a permanent, live
state broadcast. It is the legacy of a place that sent its children to
school in record numbers, determined not only that they would
become Turks, but perfect Turks. Every five years, there is another
striking aspect to life here: Dersim votes overwhelmingly for the
party that oversaw '38.

Near my last morning in Dersim, at 09:05, all the sirens go off
and the *kangals* bark along to it. There is a minute's silence, and
then the national anthem. As happens every year, it is to mourn the
death of Atatürk, who passed at that precise minute, 10 November
1938, just a few months after the massacres here. Around the time,
indeed, that Hasan's family was being sent on its long journey west

to Uşak. And here, as in all of Turkey, people stop in the streets, motionless, to commemorate him. I pass a primary school, and around twenty nine-year-olds are standing on the school steps, shouting out patriotic songs, in that slightly chaotic way children sing together, wearing black T-shirts with Atatürk's face. Parents watch on, taking videos with their phones. For many believe, including Hasan himself, that Atatürk did not know what was happening here, that he was not responsible, and that he had been ill for months by the time the massacres began. Besides, they still hold firmly to one of his ideals. For a religious minority, a secular state still seems the safest place to be.

*

Hasan had insisted all week I come to his village. It is called Doğanlı now, but he knows it as Kurcik. We pile into a family friend's car – his grandson Ali and me in the back, the friend driving, and Hasan, in aviators, directing us all the way. Crossing a river, hanging a left, onto a country road, and up and up. It is half an hour, and he knows the route without thinking – he still spends his summers here.

We step out and the air is immediately changed: cold and crisp and clean. We must be a thousand metres high. He explains the family history to me again, and the great lineage he comes from: Mehmet, Ibrahim, Mustafa, Ali Rıza, and so on. His grandfather's grandfather first came to this village, and he shows me his stone house, and its foundations from three hundred years ago.

This is where Hasan was in '38, when his father was taken away, and where his body was brought back, a single bullet wound in his neck. He points me to the wall, and a black-and-white picture of them in exile, all ten of them squeezed into the frame: his grandad at the forefront, a bright white moustache and a trilby; his mother to the right, clutching her youngest daughter; and a teenage Hasan stood behind her, cleanshaven, handsome and serious.

This of course was the house they returned to a decade later. His grandad died just a few months after their arrival, happy at least to be home. Hasan himself married after two years, aged twenty, and went on to have six children, and many more grandchildren besides. He shows me a now empty granary next door. He came back, in his words, to be a model farmer. They had fields in five different villages, and planted beets and cotton. In the fifties, he bought a Ferguson tractor, and started producing bales and bales of wheat.

We duck outside. The sun is alone in the sky and we squint from it, as it curves towards the mountains across us. The valley far below is already dark. There is just the sound of our feet on the earth, and his walking stick. I can feel his pride, as he shows me the vegetable garden he's working on – its aubergines, peppers, and tomatoes. As I listen to him complaining about wild boars who have turned up the earth, a Nâzim Hikmet poem comes to mind:

> *Yani, öylesine ciddiye alacaksın ki yaşamayı,* / I mean, you must take living so seriously
> *yetmişinde bile, mesela, zeytin dikeceksin,* / that even at seventy, for example, you'll plant olive trees—
> *hem de öyle çocuklara falan kalır diye değil,* / and not for your children, either,
> *ölmekten korktuğun halde ölüme inanmadığın için.* / but because although you fear death you don't believe it.[29]

To our back behind the village is *ziyaret tepesi*, a hill where the villagers gather, make sacrifices and share *lokma*, food eaten after prayer. For in Alevi belief, it is not just that nature – Dersim's rivers, mountains, its very earth – is sacred, it is made more sacred still by all those that have lived there before. To be in those places is to be closer to the world of souls, prophets, and perhaps even to Allah himself. That hill, Hasan says, was always on their minds in exile. This is where his ancestors were born, and where their souls will stay. And where Hasan knows soon he will join them. 'Now life has finished,' he tells me, 'and we're counting the days.'

He shows me the apricot trees he planted on his return here, more than seventy years ago. They tower over us, in bright autumnal yellow, and he tells me how good their fruit is in the summer. Instinctively, I ask if he's had a happy life. 'Apart from exile, we were always here,' he replies, 'it was good in every way, no problem. We had very good days, thanks to God.'

As the sunset approaches, it falls golden on the hill in front of us, turning all the plants and trees – their reds and yellows and greens – a little honeyed. We look out across the valley, the sun still just about warming our faces, but we can feel its strength waning. The first snow will fall in just a few weeks. It dips behind the mountains, and the temperature starts to plummet. Time, we agree, to head back.

5. A Turkish Tina Turner

1940s, 1950s, 1960s – İstanbul

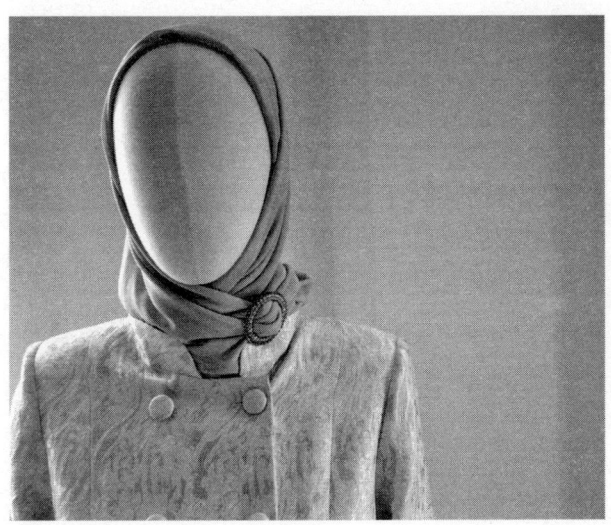

WHEN SHE WOULD TALK ABOUT IT LATER, THERE WAS ONE
detail about her appearance in court that seemed to offend Yüksel
Şenler more than any other: that before she was called to the dock
of İstanbul's 2nd Assize Court, she had to wait in the corridor outside, sharing a bench with murderers, thieves, and even 'traitorous
communists'. She was a writer of regard from a good family, after
all. Beneath the insult, however, she was scared as well. When she
was a child, nearly two decades earlier somewhere over another
part of the city, her mother would ask her to go and pick up food
from the grocers, and she would take the long route round just to
avoid the local courthouse. They were fearful places, full of bad
people and bad deeds. And yet here she was herself – after months

of legal process, of accusations and defence, of journalists and their cameras – about to hear her own verdict. And as she entered, she prayed not necessarily to be set free, but asked God instead not to let her cry, whatever the judgement might be, not to let her show weakness in front of the hundreds who were waiting for here there. And then she went in.[1]

In the picture distributed to the press, she is composed. Sitting in the dock, her hands on her knees, her covered head tilted slightly to the side – patient, as if waiting for a bus. She looks curiously alone, as either side of her on this dark wooden bench, with space perhaps for five or six more, sits no one at all. Curious, because then immediately to her back are stood dozens and dozens of men, all suited, stern, and tightly packed. One of them – with a huge walrus moustache – even grips the bench from behind her, his hands almost possessively on the spot where her head would be were she not leaning ever so slightly forward. And all are straining their necks to see her, this small, singular figure, sitting and awaiting her fate, in the warmth of this late September day. She is accused of undermining the secularism of the Turkish state. Şule Yüksel Şenler, as they know her, the woman who tells other women to wear a headscarf on their heads.

*

She wasn't always like this, Şule Yüksel Şenler. I'm back in İstanbul, the city that made her, on one of the city's strangely warm and wet November days. The seasons here are measured less by the trees – there are none left – than by the winds, and we are nearing the peak of *lodos*, coming not from the north as İstanbul's normal breeze does, but from the south-west, over the seas and the Sahara before it. Ferries across the straits are cancelled from its gusts; İstanbullus complain of migraines and sore throats from its dust. In the evening, the air is so thick you can even see it, swirling around in clouds beneath orange streetlights.

This is a story about an *İstanbul çocuğu*, a child of İstanbul, and so I find myself hopping from various wealthy, conservative parts of the city, trying to learn who she was – in the districts of the old city mostly, the historic peninsula at its southern edge, lodged between the waters of the Marmara Sea and the Golden Horn. I am in Eyüp, a neighbourhood with its eastern shore running up the Haliç, as the Horn – an inlet of the Bosphorus – is known. Eyüp is a holy place, where Ebu Eyyub el Ensari, a companion of the Prophet Mohammed, was buried. I pass his tomb – there are hundreds queuing to enter – and the mosque complex that contains it, all stone alleyways and gardens. Heading south, I pass by smaller mosques – medieval things striped in orange and white – and the plane trees that rise above them. Until, after fifteen minutes or so, I am there: at an elegant three-storey cream building with marble steps.

I am here to meet Demet Tezcan, who knew Yüksel Şenler for a long time. She is covered in black from head to toe, and we greet each other from a distance. Only her face and hands are exposed, and I notice a gold-coloured watch around her wrist. 'It's a Swatch,' she tells me, half-laughing at herself, 'I love watches.' Like her hero, Demet is a writer, and speaks in almost complete sentences, expressing ideas fully-formed in her head. And like Şule Yüksel Şenler too, she was born in Kayseri, seven hundred kilometres inland. 'It is a unique Anatolian city,' she tells me, with its waterfall and famous sour fruits. She moved to İstanbul thirty-five years ago at sixteen. Organizing a conference four years later, they thought to invite the famous Şule Yüksel Şenler. As she came up to the stage, though now she was nearing her sixties, they had never seen a crowd like it. And when the two met afterwards, Şule suggested to a young Demet that she become a writer. 'It was like a magic wand,' says Demet. Over the years, Demet went on to author several books. None would be more painful to write than the one that has brought me here today: *Bir Çığır Öyküsü*, 'A Pioneer's Tale', her biography of her friend and mentor. It was researched in the knowledge that Şule's health was failing, and that there might not be too much time left. An assistant comes in with a tray of black sugary coffees, and we begin.

*

Yüksel Şenler was born on 29 May 1938, a meaningful date in a meaningful year. 1938 was after all when Atatürk – Turkey's founder and president – died, six months after Yüksel was born. While 29 May had a deeper history still – the day that in 1453 the Turks finally took İstanbul, their Sultan heading to the Aya Sofya in victory to pray. And it was just a couple of kilometres away from that storied sixth-century building – once a church, then a mosque, and then again a museum – where Yüksel Şenler grew up. Her father was a civil servant, posted all over the country at the state's leisure. So while Yüksel was born in Kayseri, when he worked at a factory there, the family was soon relocated to İstanbul, where they would stay.

It was the mid-forties, and the city was beginning to see its first trickles of immigration from the country, little shanty cottages on its slopes and outside the city walls. But the Şenlers were a different sort – Turkish Cypriots in origin, from a family of status in Nicosia, who had moved to the mainland a few generations ago. Yüksel's grandfather had been a village chief and wore a felt hat; her father, a chemical technician, had studied in Russia; her mother – her father's cousin – owned not only books but pedicured feet; and she herself grew up with the help of a nanny at home. When they moved to İstanbul then, it was not to the outskirts but to its historic heart: to Süleymaniye, Laleli, and other districts up and down the old peninsula. Theirs were houses of large bay windows and open spaces, Demet tells me. As a local had explained to me the previous day, it was a neighbourhood of old wooden mansions of former Ottoman bureaucrats and generals, split into flats and rented out to middle-class families. Up on the hills of Süleymaniye, amongst its old stone walls and olive trees, is a green marble stone, placed by İstanbul's grand Ottoman architect Sinan to mark the literal centre of the old city.

It was that same Sinan who would so shape the district where Yüksel was raised. On its northern edge stands Süleymaniye Camii, perhaps the city's greatest mosque, with its famous bubble domes and views of the Bosphorus down below. It was – that old local told me – a religious quarter with 'big, fanatical families' and Turks who could speak Arabic like their mother tongue. The Şenlers were not one of them. While they may have been conservative, and culturally religious in a sense, they did not – as the family story goes – actively practise their faith. As one descendant told me, Yüksel's father would fast for Ramadan, but break it at the end of each day not with a date but with a glass of *rakı*, a Turkish aniseed spirit of considerable strength. In fact, according to Yüksel Şenler herself, they were a family of committed Kemalists: secular, Westernized, and modern. French culture infused their home, and her elder sisters went at the weekends to balls (still, they were only allowed to dance with male relatives). Every November 10th, she would say, Yüksel would cry along to the radio as they commemorated Atatürk's death, wishing it could have been her instead of him to go.[2]

She was a quiet child and gifted in class. She loved school, learning to write, and drawing tulips along the margins of her notebook. Even there, the family had its appearances to maintain, and Şenler would head to Ragıp Paşa Primary each day in a black satin apron with ribbons in her hair. Slowly, though, things were changing. Her father had left his safe public job for the private sector, to own a paint factory in İstanbul, but business was poor. Her school clothes were patched up more and more.[3]

*

Turkey itself was changing in those years. Throughout Şenler's early childhood, to put it simply, the economy was struggling and the government unpopular. The country had stayed neutral during the Second World War, but the conflict still left its effects: the cost of calling up huge numbers of soldiers, just in case; the loss of key trading partners; rationing and spiralling inflation. And after Atatürk's death, the space for politics grew just that little bit wider: a new party split from the old, and it had a serious chance of winning power. For there were vast groups of Turks – the rural poor, provincial businessman, the devout and religious – who were willing to hear its message.

So it was that in 1950, when Yüksel Şenler was just twelve, Turkey saw its first free and fair election, and voters came to the polls on a rainy day in May, faced with the choice of keeping in the only party it had ever known, or the Democrat Party that challenged it. It was – as one scholar put it – the first steps of Turkey's 'imperfect but real democratization'.[4] The Democrat Party, for its part, saw itself not as a repudiation of Atatürk, but as the party to finish off his work: to achieve not just independence and social reform, but democracy too. Indeed, the CHP, Atatürk's old party, had already begun to backtrack on some of its heavier-handed changes: the tombs and shrines were reopened; and religious education was again permitted in schools.

Regardless, it was not enough – the Democrat Party under its charismatic leader Adnan Menderes would sweep to power. As one Süleymaniye local told me, it was a Democrat Party supporting district, and you could feel the mood shift. Within a few months of coming to office, the party lifted the law mandating the

Turkish call to prayer – and the *ezans* from the minarets all over the neighbourhood, from Şehzade mosque and Beyazit, from Laleli and Süleymaniye itself, were heard in Arabic again. They did not enforce the veil or turn the script back to Arabic as some commentators feared, but doubtless the new government appealed to its religious base as time went on: boasting about the number of mosques it was opening across the country; increasing the number of schools to train preachers; and allowing religious literature, and the centuries-old sects, to come back out into the open. The Democrat Party weren't though looking back to some old and pious past; they were builders and modernists as well. They transformed the İstanbul that Yüksel Şenler had known. Across the historic peninsula, to make way for broad, six-lane thoroughfares, dozens of old neighbourhoods were bulldozed down.[5]

It was an exciting time, but the Şenlers were struggling through it – for both their father's finances and their mother's health were failing. Yüksel had graduated from her Ragıp Paşa Primary and was going to a local Kız Eğitim Enstitüsü, a girls' educational institute, where she was taught, alongside a normal, academic curriculum, how to cook and sew. Two years in, however, her mother had a heart attack that left her bedbound, and there was no one left to accompany Yüksel to school. To walk there alone was unthinkable. Young girls are like autumn leaves, her mother told her, they blow left and right with the breeze, and if a strong wind blows they fall off. So as Yüksel would put it later, she ended her schooling 'to protect her honour.'[6] When I ask Demet why she didn't return to the institute once her mother had recovered a couple of years later, she explains by that time Yüksel's body had transformed – puberty had come and gone, and left a young woman in its wake. She would be 'embarrassed' if she had to share a school desk with girls two years her junior. She was not just an honourable woman, she was a proud one.

Besides, she was happily educating herself. She came after all from a literate family, allowed to read novels if her mother approved. Her favourites, so she said, were the father of Russian literature Leo Tolstoy, the Turkish romance novelist Kerime Nadir, and the ultra-nationalist, self-identified racist Nihâl Atsız – the classic, eclectic list of an autodidact. After a while, at around fourteen, she started to write: short stories in the style of Nadir, playing around with Turkish's word order, using *devrik cümle*, 'broken phrases', to see how they might sound. As she would later explain, she didn't like these pieces at all, but still she kept writing. Within a year, she was published in *Yelpaze*, a children's magazine; after that, a youth column in *Yeni İstanbul*.

She had more primal interests too. Over these teenage years, unbeknownst to everyone but her sister, Yüksel had been exchanging letters with a local boy. Though she claims they never met in person or even spoke on the phone, they fell in love all the same. Once he had completed his military service and she had turned eighteen, they promised to marry. His family called when the time came, and together one evening in the Şenler living room the respective parents began to discuss the details. But the groom's family couldn't yet provide a home for prospective newlyweds, and even suggested the groom live with the wife's family until they could – *iç güveysi*, as they say, a shameful inversion of the expectation that the husband should provide for his wife. Angered and affronted, Yüksel's father called the whole thing off. Listening from the kitchen, Yüksel fainted there and then. Her period stopped for months.[7] As Demet tells me, she was convinced the shock left her unable to ever have children.

Keen to move her daughter on – to have her think of other things – her mother soon sent Yüksel to apprentice at an Armenian tailor's in Bakırköy, a district further west where they had moved. What better trade, she thought, for the teenager who filled her notebooks with sketches of the shirts she saw on French actresses each time she came back from the cinema. For in truth – between her aborted schooling and her abandoned love – Yüksel did seem a restless young woman, in search of something firm to hold. She had dabbled in the youth groups of Turkey's racist, nationalist right – falling into them after her beloved elder brother left home – but Demet says 'it didn't last for long'. She attended rallies in support of Turkish Cyprus in the mid-fifties – her body wrapped in the flag – but wasn't sure that it was for her either. While most of her family were pretty settled, if conservative, Kemalists, her own sense of herself seemed slightly less fixed.

They would all however soon be thrust into something new. For tensions over Cyprus were not the only source of instability in Turkey as the second half of the decade ran on. Though the Democrat Party was still popular in the countryside, things were starting to wear. Inflation returned, while the party grew more authoritarian. The press and universities were more tightly controlled. The atmosphere was growing tense. The army and the Atatürk establishment who had never trusted the Democrat Party were on alert. When in 1959 Menderes survived a plane crash at London's Gatwick Airport, some saw it as divinely ordained, proof of his historic mission. But others were less convinced. In the same year, the Democrat Party launched a commission into the crimes of the opposition, and banned all political activity apart from the National Assembly for its duration. It was, for some, too much.[8]

*

The coup – Turkey's first – was announced on the radio at 3 a.m., just two days short of Yüksel Şenler's twenty-second birthday. As it was conveyed to the nation on 27 May 1960, it was 'the end of one period in Turkish history, and to usher in a new one', and achieved without any loss of life too . . . at least at first. A curfew was imposed, and – as it would do many times over the next decades – the Turkish military took control. It was a shock for Yüksel's family, Democrat Party supporters themselves. Yet it paled in comparison with what came next, as Menderes and other leading figures were put on trial, on an island just off İstanbul. After nearly a year of proceedings under the watch of the junta – at once both serious and bizarre – the former Prime Minister and two of his cabinet ministers were found guilty of violating the constitution, and hanged. '*Nasıl halk ağlıyor*,' remembered Şenler once, 'How the people cried.'[9]

No sooner than Menderes had been executed, the generals were preparing to hand back power to the politicians again – elections followed after one month, and a new civilian government after two. It was a coup with a peculiar legacy: on the one hand, it let all future leaders know that the military was waiting in the wings; on the other, it left a new constitution more liberal than the one that had governed Turkey before. It introduced a second chamber, it gave more independence to the courts, and it expanded the rights of Turkish citizens, to come together, dissent, and debate.

The decade that followed, therefore, would be a very Turkish 1960s: an explosion of journals and magazines, student demos, and political groups appearing left and right. And it would be in the world of these new publications that Yüksel Şenler would properly launch her writing career. Scouring the archives, the oldest I find dates back to October 1962, in a magazine run by a conservative, Islamic circle of İstanbul. There on page eight – reserved for 'young pens' – in the bottom right hand corner, is a tepid twelve-line poem sent in by letter. 'I want a peaceful, quiet world', it begins, before ending with a prayer for Allah's grace.[10]

As Yüksel Şenler claimed later, she wasn't particularly religious at the time, calling this her *gaflet dönemi*, her blind period. Perhaps then, she was just doing what it takes to get published. The press amongst the religious right was flourishing, and in many ways a dynamic, exciting place to be. Turkish Islamism in particular had its own flavour. It was only in later decades that it would be influenced by global thinkers like Sayyid Qutb or Abul A'la Maududi and their more explicit calls for political action. Instead, in the fifties and sixties it was something more homegrown, and more mystic too: fiercely anti-communist, but focused also on the spiritual salvation of the nation, seen to be so cut off from its past.[11] Of course, in an environment where every shade of Turkish politics was printing pamphlets and magazines, it had a new intensity too. There is a new war, said one Islamist, and the 'weapons are press, propaganda, and education.'[12]

*

Few groups were so ready to thrive in this new atmosphere as the movement Yüksel's older brother – the family outcast – had joined nearly a decade before. Özer had become increasingly attracted to the works of Said Nursi, or Bediüzzaman, as he was known, 'Wonder of the Age'. A Kurdish scholar from eastern Turkey, Nursi had been in and out of prison and exile as far back as the 1920s, but still his movement had grown underground. Its members met in small groups, and distributed handwritten copies of his interpretations of the Koran across the country, follower to follower. As many as sixty thousand were produced. When Özer first met Nursi in 1952, he said he had a voice so compassionate it was like hearing your own mother, and he was soon visiting him frequently in his base in Turkey's south-west.[13]

To put it briefly, the Nur Movement aimed to revitalize Islamic thought in a modern Turkish society – by protecting the essentials of the faith, while clearing away the rest. Nursi had little time for abstract theological debates between scholars on epistemological truths. Instead, he turned to the Koran as a primary source, and sought to offer to his followers solutions for their current problems directly from it. Most acutely, as one scholar suggests, he observed a distinct absence in the emerging Turkey: a place of industry, towns and cities, newspapers and the radio, trains and even a few cars. This new society was deeply impersonal, argued Nursi, lacking not only in matters of the spirit but in the relationships that gave life meaning: between parents and children, masters and apprentices, preachers and believers, villagers and their neighbours. His goal then was to reintroduce these ties in a way that made sense in a mass, mid-century society. And he would do it using all the means that the era afforded to him: by the mid-fifties, his own text, *Risale i-Nur*, was translated from Arabic into Turkish, for many more to read; and it began to be printed by machine too – a lucky turn for those who used to write it out by hand, for it was 6,600 pages long.[14]

Though Nursi himself died aged eighty-two in 1960, his movement only spread in the decade to come. Özer, Yüksel's brother, became a particularly ardent follower, and an increasingly difficult presence in the family. He had moved out but his visits to the Şenler home were tense. He wanted them to read the *Risale i-Nur*, and live proper, devout lives; they found him joyless and a little strange. Once, as Demet explains, he came back to the house while the family were entertaining some guests. Yüksel was playing the *kanun*, a kind of flat Arabian harp, her father the *saz*, a long-necked Turkish lute, and their music teacher the violin. Her brother came in the room, spat on the dining table, and left. Another time, after Yüksel and her sisters returned from an evening ball, Özer slapped her, and called her a slut. It must have been for Yüksel a harder time than most. By all accounts she dearly loved her *abi*, her big brother, and his estrangement from them would have been deeply felt. So when he fell ill with hepatitis and was taken to hospital – when, as she would later say, they feared for the worst – he made one last plea for her to at least go to a meeting. Nursi supported female-only groups, and had even written a pamphlet, *Hanımlar Rehberi*, addressing specifically how pious women should behave. Özer was fine in the end, but his younger sister had already accepted, and would go to her first Nur meeting all the same.

As Yüksel described it, there were fifteen attendees, and fourteen of them were elderly women in long white headscarves, dressed 'like daises'.[15] She, instead, was a twenty-seven-year-old woman with a low-cut dress and manicured fingers. She asked the head of the group for a jacket to cover her arms, but there was none to lend; she tried to improvise a small piece of fabric over the big bun on her head, but it wouldn't stretch. It was, she says, deeply embarrassing. But there was something else about the meeting. The *Risale* – despite Nursi's belief in making the Koran accessible – was dense and difficult, full of Arabic and Persian words that characterized old Ottoman Turkish. Not only did many women in the group struggle to understand it, according to Yüksel, they couldn't even read it out loud either. She however had spent her life with books, and so she started to read. The group liked how it sounded out of her mouth, and perhaps so did she. For despite the *Risale*'s difficulty, it has its poetry too. There are three types of proof for spiritual truth, wrote Nursi once, 'some are like water, they can be seen and felt but cannot be seized. In this part it is necessary to dismiss thought and plunge into it . . . The second part is like rain. It is felt but cannot be seen or held. Turn against its forgiving breeze with your face, your mouth, your soul . . . The third part: it is like light. It is seen but cannot be felt or held. Therefore turn yourself towards it with the eye of your soul.'[16]

Despite the initial shame, then, maybe for Yüksel these meetings could have their appeal: in the form, of course, for she had loved language ever since she was a little girl; and yet also in the content

– maybe she recognized that absence Nursi observed in modern life, and yearned too to fill it, to turn her face towards the light. Intrigued, she started coming to the groups more and more – her sleeves longer, her skirts lower – and soon was organizing meetings herself. Her sister and mother were drawn in as well, until all the family were praying at home.[17]

For over a year, Yüksel barely wrote, instead going deeper and deeper into her faith. *Hidayete ermek*, as she would describe it, being guided to the truth.[18] Near the end of it, she took one of its most visible, tangible steps – she began to wear a veil over her head. It was both a rite of passage and a gift from Allah: for to be able to cover was a sign of the journey she had taken, of the inner distance she had travelled. I ask Demet about when she herself started wearing the veil, and why it meant so much. Like Yüksel, Demet didn't grow up in a religious family. Her father, she tells me, was a Kemalist teacher, posted to villages to spread the republican, secular message. He was a powerful, scary, and dominant figure in her life, and she used to hide from him to pray. Nevertheless, she first covered at fourteen. Islam teaches us the concept of *fitra*, she explains, that it is innate to human nature to recognize God – or, in other words, 'that all humanity without exception is born Muslim.' So for those raised in non-religious families, she continues, the search back to that original state is intense, and covering-up rich in meaning: like returning to the state women were supposed to be.

But it was not a return that was so readily welcomed. As Yüksel described it, when she first wore the headscarf – a white sheet tied loosely beneath her chin – her relatives told her she looked like a peasant. Worse, Yüksel agreed. As she said later, dripping with class contempt, the headscarf made her look like domestic help. And so – the girl who had drawn the dresses of French actresses in her notebook, and spent an apprenticeship at an Armenian tailor's – began to look for something a bit more modern. One day, standing in front of the mirror, she wrapped the cloth tight around her head and neck, pulled it back, and tied it instead by her nape. Thus, the Şulebaşı, the Şule head, was born. She had been inspired in part, by all things, by the silk scarf that Audrey Hepburn wore in *Roman Holiday*. Demet takes me to a room next door, and shows me a mannequin modelling it, clipped at the neck by a brooch with cream-coloured pearls. Her transformation complete, Şule Yüksel Şenler – as she would be known, adding the more feminine Şule to her name – was ready to be a writer once more, and a fashion icon too.[19]

*

She attacked her new life with all the enthusiasm of a convert. Indeed, she said her joining the Nur movement was like a 'rebirth', when her 'heart took wings and flew'.[20] Perhaps she was exaggerating how irreligious she had been before, but certainly she had new things to say. In her first column in January 1967, in the Islamist paper *Yeni İstiklal*, she wrote *İslam kadınına hitap*, her 'address to Muslim women'. She was obliged as a Muslim, she wrote, to point out injustice and sin, and she had observed a spiritual crisis: women who had lost their value in trying to live up to the republican, Westernized ideal. But there was hope: to cover up, she argued, was a beautiful and important command from God, to protect yourself – your arms, your legs, your skin – from the gaze of men beyond your husband and family. Most specifically, she urged her readers to cover their hair as well, for to throw away the veil had been to throw away their honour and chastity.[21]

She was already being noticed. The Turkish Women's Union was so offended at the notion that its members were 'lewd and dishonest' if they were uncovered that they filed a lawsuit against her. Regardless she seemed undeterred, and her writing continued furious both in volume and tone. When Pope Paul VI came to

Turkey in July, he visited the Aya Sofya, turned to Jerusalem, and discreetly prayed. Şule was insulted both as a Muslim and a nationalist – neither she nor any of her faith had been allowed to worship at the Aya Sofya since it was turned into a museum over thirty years earlier. In an open letter to the President, she said that when he and the Prime Minister had gone to meet the Pope at İstanbul's main airport, they had showed 'an inferiority complex', a 'Muslim nation bowing to a Christian leader.' Furthermore, she suspected a papal plot to recapture Constantinople and the once-cathedral at its heart – why else would the Pope also meet the city's Orthodox Patriarch on his trip? It was an article that both revealed her anger and the manners of a good middle-class girl, for all throughout it is addressed to *Sayın Başkan*, 'Dear President'. As her family would tell me, even at the height of her fury, the worst insult they ever heard Şule shout was 'donkey'.[22]

Still, she was beginning to walk on unsteady ground, and her first year back in public life was punctuated by appearances in court, as the case brought by the Turkish Women's Union took off. She was accused of undermining the secular basis of the Turkish state. And so she found herself – not yet thirty – entering the dock of İstanbul's 2nd Assize Court on a late September day, praying to God not to let her cry in front of all those present, and sitting down alone as a man with a huge walrus moustache gripped the bench behind her. She would describe the voice of the judge – 'noble and dignified' – and the typing of the scribes as she waited. It would be a test for the more liberal atmosphere of the decade, and where the limits to Turkey's strict secularism were to be found: what about the constitutional guarantees of free speech?; or to practise your religion?; but wasn't, on the other hand, to urge the veil precisely to *limit* the freedom of Turkey's women, and to send them back into another age? In the end, the judge found Şule not guilty: what she had done did not concern the affairs of the state, he concluded, it was not the *political* use of religion. She was emboldened like never before, and was about to take her message far beyond the readers of her Islamist papers, out all across Anatolia. With her fiery articles and legal controversies, her fame had been quietly growing all year. Now Şule had been acquitted, she would become a cause célèbre. The court case had barely finished, but she had already received an invitation to tour.

*

She was asked to come by an imam in Samsun, a Black Sea town seven hundred kilometres to the east of İstanbul, somewhere near the middle of the country's long, northern coast. He was part of an anti-communist association, and was curious to hear her speak. According to Şule, when they arrived at the conference hall the interest in her was so great that there were women spilling onto the streets. For the rest to hear her, they agreed to plug speakers outside, but only after she was assured by the imam that it wouldn't be *haram* if that meant men might inadvertently hear her too. And so she began to talk. The first conference lasted four to five hours, and she would barely stop after that: after Samsun, she was called back a little west to Karabük, and then on and on it went from there. It was the late sixties, and the country would witness a kind of Şulemania.

As Şule describes it, in the student town of Eskişehir, leftists 'with Stalinist moustaches' threw tomatoes at her in protest; there was a bomb threat in Bandırma to the west; authorities were often unwilling to give the go-ahead for meetings, and the lawsuits against her piled up. Still, her fans' excitement was at times wild and uncontained. Some covered up on the spot, in tears at their salvation. They pulled at her shoulders, turned her head, and kissed her cheeks.[23]

It was a strange atmosphere perhaps, given the nature of the speeches she was actually giving: conservative and moralizing, with titles like 'Spiritual Depression in Turkey', and 'The Place and Obligations of Women in Islam'. She railed against left-wing authors, miniskirts, and sex scenes in movies. She criticized Turkey's feminists, and their calls for jobs in the workforce, and equal rights and wages. Echoing Nursi, she saw a country severed from its spirit, and thought women in particular had fallen into moral decay, detached from their real worth. Their deliverance – and indeed the very liberation of the whole of society – depended on a return to honour and chastity. Central to this of course was their covering up, and she had participants repeat the Koranic verses on veiling three times. Each conference ended with the women praying together, and chanting '*Allahu Ekber*'.

In part, no doubt it was popular partly for the novelty. Turkey's speaking circuit was lively, but for a headscarfed woman to join it was unprecedented. What's more, because attendance was gender-segregated – and free – it allowed women from conservative families to go to events in a way they never would have otherwise. But certainly Şule was speaking to something more profound too. The republic and its early years of reforms had significantly changed the lives of women: co-education in schools was made compulsory as early as 1924 – as a result, hundreds of thousands of girls learned to read; the sharia courts were abolished soon after, and a new civil code introduced soon after gave women equal rights; by 1936 – though admittedly still under a single-party regime – they were given the right to vote. Of course the impact of all this was unevenly felt. Women in İstanbul, for example, were much more likely to go to school, even to university, and then maybe to work. By this time on average they had two children each; the average in the rest of Turkey was seven. But these were still real and substantive steps, and championed enthusiastically by the press, full of stories of the country's first female lawyer, its first surgeon, its first professional wrestler, and then finally – as the ultimate show of modern femininity – Turkey's first winner of Miss World, in 1932.[24]

Culturally, however, for many conservative and religious women, this felt a world apart. Particularly for a generation now born after the republic was founded, they may have wanted the schooling – and the comforts of mid-twentieth-century life – but did they have to dance at balls and go for luncheon dates, as they were being encouraged to do? It was, as one Turkish scholar put it, 'the forbidden modern' – for many felt the fruits of these gains would only be available to them if they embraced a Western, republican version of womanhood as well.[25] Here then Şule was showing a way between, of moving confidently through the city streets, its schools and town squares – and this was notably an urban phenomenon – while preserving your modesty, your Islamic self. Once you accepted the premise that women had to be protected from the gaze of men – and this was a given of Şule's and many others' lives – the headscarf wasn't a rejection of the modern world at all, it was the key to embracing it. In the long arc of her life, of course it made perfect sense: this was a girl who was denied her education because it was improper for her to walk to school alone.

Key to the message was Şule herself, and the brand new headscarf style she had designed. The Şulebaşı could be kept fresh and fashionable each week, with different patterns and colours, or accessorized with a buckle or brooch. Women could even style their hair wrapped tightly underneath it with pins and wires, giving their head a more elegant shape. As the story goes, often after Şule spoke, her followers copied her shoes, seeking out something like them at the local market. And seemingly the demand for her just kept coming. Travelling around the country on dusty Anatolian roads in her brother's old jeep, she often spoke to multiple venues a day, and wrote in the time between. Her brothers and father helped organize the venues, and accompanied her to them; her sisters helped reply to her vast amounts of fan mail. By this point – with her father's business failing – it was a family enterprise, dependent on the income from her writing. And as with fame anywhere, it began to take its toll. Şule barely ate on tour and became skinny. She fell ill: first with flu, then with appendicitis, until finally she was diagnosed and hospitalized with tuberculosis. Her doctor recommended she stay in a flat with central heating, but it wasn't possible: firstly, it was too expensive; secondly, the show had to go on. As Demet tells me, Şule was 'naive but with a heart of steel . . . like a one-woman army, a gendarme in armour'. A stubborn young woman with all the zeal of her new faith, she kept on going. Over two years, she crossed the length of Turkey three and a half times, addressing crowds in sixty-seven cities and six hundred towns.

*

Away from the tour, Şule's other work continued. She edited her own magazine from 1969, *Seher Vakti* – its first edition betraying the stern thirty-one-year-old she seemed to have become, bemoaning today's youth and their lack of fear in Allah and their parents. It is a striking publication. For the most part, it is full of the affirming language of teen magazines, and pictures of young and attractive models in Şulebaşı headscarves, here in polka dots, there in stripes. As the text reads underneath, the headcovers are superimposed onto photos of Western models. Yet in other parts, *Seher Vakti* is decidedly hateful. Above one article is a picture of a woman in a loose headscarf, with strings coming off each of her limbs, up to a giant puppet hand above. 'You are a puppet in the hands of a Jew,' it reads, 'you poor woman who's a prisoner of fashion.' Jews, it continues, are the enemies of Islam and humanity, and invented 'fashion' as a secret plan to destroy the notions of purity in women.[26] Here the traces perhaps of her own far-right past remain. Indeed not only was one of her favourite writers in childhood a self-identified racist, one of her main sponsors and editors throughout her adult life was a Holocaust-denier. I ask Demet about this piece, and she answers that Şule was not anti-Semitic, but anti-Zionist, and that this was just the language of the time. I am unconvinced: anti-Semitism may not have been central to this circle's worldview, but doubtless it was strongly felt.

It is a part of Şule's life that has mostly been forgotten: partly because it is inconvenient, and partly because her career and legacy were about to be overwhelmed by her next work. For at the same time as editing *Seher Vakti*, she had begun to write a novel. As Şule later said, the first pages were scribbled down as she was eating plums from their İstanbul garden on a summer's day. It was called *Huzur Sokağı*, 'Peace Street' – a sprawling, intergenerational love story between the pious and heroic Bilal and the party-loving, spiritually lost Feyza. It was a tribute as well to the historic İstanbul districts where she grew up: 'Peace Street' is full of neighbourliness, a little village within a corrupting city. Given her ties to journalism, it was not released all at once; rather, like a Dickens novel, it was serialized daily for over a year. Every morning, Şule's father delivered her writing to the paper on foot, while her mother boiled her coffee and made sure she ate. The family involvement in the book was wider than that: Bilal, whose faith never wavers, is based on her brother Özer, who managed to 'convert' her just a few years before.

And if Şule was breaking a taboo in her own circle – novels were a suspect, Western form – it was soon forgiven, for *Huzur Sokağı* was an enormous hit. Indeed, when they first met, Demet tells me the first thing she ever said to Şule was, 'Why did you have to kill Feyza?', the book's doomed romantic lead. She had read it in her teenage years, and had never come across anything like it, as it tackled a taboo even more thrilling to break. For the young conservative woman, what could be a more enticing part of the new world – of the 'forbidden modern' – than the love marriage yearned for across the five hundred pages of *Huzur Sokağı*. There was an assumption, Demet explains, that religious women didn't fall in love, that their marriages would always be arranged. But 'we are made of flesh and bones' too, 'why shouldn't we fall in love?' Perhaps even in this, one can gleam the influence of Said Nursi and the groups she attended so intensely: this was a work trying to reconfigure relationships – between man and woman, city resident and neighbour – for the modern age. And soon the book found an even larger audience still, as it was projected onto the big screen, with Türkan Şoray, 'The Sultan of Turkish Cinema', in the main role.

Şule was more famous than ever before, but soon she disappeared from view altogether, as the court cases against her finally caught up. She was found guilty of insulting the President for her article condemning the papal visit four years earlier. She had always denied the charge, citing her right to expression and her respectful tone, but this time her defence wasn't enough. She handed herself in at the prosecutor's office in Bursa – south-east of İstanbul – wearing a polka dot headscarf, and prepared herself for her thirteen-month sentence. She was, she admits, 'terrified' when she first entered prison: she shared her dormitory with 'murderers', 'thieves', and 'a woman who'd been with every man in Bursa.' And though her tuberculosis deteriorated inside – passing between hospital and prison – she still rejected the presidential pardon she was offered a few months in. To accept it, she felt, would be to admit she had done wrong. Instead, armed with her faith as always, she sought to convert the women she met, and persuade them to cover up.[27]

There is a picture of Şule as she turned herself in, in black and white, and walking beside her is a handsome, moustachioed man. It is Abdullah Kars, her husband. They had married at a modest ceremony a few months before she was imprisoned. She had, she said, turned down many offers over the years, but he was an Islamist and a playwright, and she liked the idea of being able to collaborate together. But on her release, her freedom was still curtailed. He was jealous, and did not want her out so much. He was violent too. At first, she would say, she was surprised by the beatings – they seemed to come so randomly – but things would get worse and worse. She told no one from the shame, and hid her bruises. Instead, she wrote a poem, begging Allah for advice, and Demet recites one of its couplets to me. . . .

Senden medet ister kalbim / My heart asks for your help
Bana bir yol göster Rabb'im / Show me the way my God.

Secretly, Şule wanted a divorce, but that was a taboo too far.

*

It's a story that reminds me of other conversations, still in İstanbul but in Kadıköy, on the other side of the water: sitting in the kitchen of a sixth-floor apartment with my *babaanne*, two glasses of *çay*, and the hundreds of pastries she buys for my visits. Sesame-covered *kandils*; mini-eclairs; tiny French tarts with raspberries on top. Eighty-six years old, she barely eats at all, but always insists I keep going. I oblige and she talks, her voice so soft and high, it almost floats in the air above me. Hers is a unique, old-fashioned English – with words like 'bumptious', 'nevertheless' – somehow both fluent and stilted.

She was born just a year before Şule Yüksel Şenler, but in some ways they could not have lived further apart. For one, my *babaanne* had never heard of Şule, despite her sixties-era fame. By that time, of course, they lived on other sides of Turkey's cultural divide: my *babaanne* was proudly secular, wore miniskirts, threw cocktail parties, and though her own grandmother and aunts tied cloths loosely over their head – in the traditional style – no one in her immediate family was covered. They differed in other ways too. Unlike Şule's tale of teenage heartbreak, when my *babaanne* met someone her parents disapproved of, she simply eloped with him down south. The family eventually reconciled, and she stayed with my *dede* – that boy from the other side of Ankara – until he died. But they had their similarities, not least because my *babaanne* wrote for a paper for months when she was nineteen, only to give it all up when she married. She needed, she says with regret, to concentrate on other matters, for she soon had a young family to raise. Then there are the things they shared that until recently I did not know, the things I wish weren't true.

I hadn't known my *babaanne* so well before I came to Turkey. She was the 'other' granny, the one I knew through my *baba*'s own distant relationship to her, as well as her slightly awkward visits to our London home: a mostly silent guest who ate not in large family meals but in regular tiny snacks, like a garden bird. Her clothes always smelled of naphthalene moth balls. She came alone, of course: the last time I met my *dede*, during a freezing Ankara winter, I was one and he was ill. But growing up I knew at least that he was our family favourite: a five foot three inch ladies' man who had a bottle of *rakı* and a cigar every night, until the habit killed him. From a distance, and in my childhood, this was a character – a family legend – I wished I had known. Of course I still do, but I learnt that some 'character' traits are not so easy up close, not least for the Turkish housewife bound up to them. As my *babaanne* let slip over our long conversations, 'characters' get drunk, cheat, and can beat their wives too. 'His tempers were out of this world,' she says, though she loved him nonetheless.

In Şule's case, there is a further tragic irony. On her speaking tours of Turkey – before her unhappy marriage – she had belittled domestic violence, defending the right of husbands to hit their wives when 'they had not fulfilled their duties', and condemning women complaining about it when they had barely left a mark. But perhaps the real tragedy is not that she could, in some way, be an accomplice in her abuse to come. Rather, it is in the dire choices presented to women in Turkey, regardless of where they are on the ideological spectrum: that this woman, strong in so many ways, who stood up to a president, was terrorized in her own home.

*

Şule later divorced, before another longer, but equally unhappy failed marriage. Her second husband was particularly conservative, and she moved from the Nur Movement to another sect, and disappeared again. She also repudiated the Şulebaşı style that made her so famous, regretting that the coats worn alongside it got tighter, and the scarfs smaller. She wore the much longer *çarşaf* – the long black shawl – thereafter.

In some senses, hers was a life of remarkable success. As Demet tells me, in every conference she hosts she comes across young women called Şule, in honour of their movement's 'pioneer'. And when she finally died – nearly half a century after her decade of fame – President Erdoğan carried her coffin. It was Şule who introduced him, then a young Islamist politician, to his future wife. She was laid to rest at Eyüp Sultan, the mosque just up the road from us, the holy site that holds the tomb of the companion of Prophet Muhammed.

For all that, there was something amiss. I ask Demet whether she was a happy person. 'Never,' she answers. And out of the blue, she compares her to Tina Turner: loved on stage, but deeply alone off it. She was satisfied, Demet says, by her professional work, by her conferences and articles, her books and their films, but away from it she was never content. It was almost as if there were two of her: Şule, the persona she adopted, and Yüksel Şenler, the woman she actually was, the one who prayed to God before a courtroom appearance not to let her cry, not to let the mask slip. 'Every young girl wants to marry', she once said, 'I didn't have that luxury.'[28] She had of course looked for love all her life – the romance novels she read as a teenager, the failed engagement that broke her heart, the book she wrote herself, and the two failed marriages that came later – but it had eluded her. As she grew more ill in later life, Demet says they became even closer, almost like an adopted mother. On spare evenings, she tells me, they would sing together, and I ask for her favourite song. '*Kimseye etmem şikayet*', she replies. 'I don't complain to anyone', go the lyrics, 'I cry to myself.'

It is a private grief mostly effaced from her story, for in its normal telling, Şule's life stands for something more historic: a journey from Kemalist origins to discovering her true, Islamic self. In the Islamist historiography, it could stand as a metaphor for the country itself over those first post-Atatürk years. And perhaps nothing symbolizes the shift in the decades since – the movement's journey from underground to establishment – than the very building we're in now: the almost-open Şule Yüksel Şenler Foundation. After I speak to Demet, I am taken on a tour: the President's wife, their patron, has donated twenty-four framed works of calligraphic art; it has a library with a capacity for ten thousand books; next to it, a cafe with a brand new coffee machine; on the ground floor, a lecture hall and a textile workshop full of silk. The assistant showing me round normally works for a deputy in the assembly. He has an enormous energy, and an Apple watch on his wrist.

Meanwhile, somewhere out in the sticks . . .

6. The Last of the Bandits

1940s, 1950s, 1960s – Batman

THERE IS AN ODD INTIMACY TO FOUR STRANGERS, FOUR men, making their beds at the same time. We are in the sleeper carriage on a fresh Ankara morning, and have just set off from the old station – a 1930s Bauhaus of brown walls and cream columns. As we started to roll east, the train creaked, groaned, and let out one note of its horn, and families and lovers ran along the marble platform to say goodbye. After twenty minutes, once we had passed the grand modernist buildings of the capital – big pyramids of glass, government departments, universities – and were out into the poorer concrete blocks on its outskirts, the conductor came by to check our tickets and hand us our bedding. And now we are pulling the sheets over our couchettes, plumping up our pillows.

Soon, we are wordlessly buying everything in four, and sharing them out between us.

The next carriage down is the *yemekli vagon*, the restaurant car, one of the many things my *baba* would claim that the Turks had invented. But we are far from the grandeur of the Orient Express. Here there are biscuits, toast, and *çay*, and a single plug where passengers take turns to charge their phones. As we sit down at one of its tables, a young dad shouts across the carriage, asking the staff if all the train's bathrooms are *allaturca* – squat toilets – on behalf of the mortified five-year-old boy between his legs.

We are on the Kurtalan Ekspres, a 1200 kilometre line from Ankara down to Turkey's south-east, opened on Republic Day, 29 October 1944. As we bend left, I see the length of the train ahead: the driver's carriage in deep red, and all the rest painted in white, with blue and red go-faster stripes across their side – designed, I assume, with a deep sense of irony. The Kurtalan Ekspres moves with all the speed of a lost suburban train. And there are still seventy stops to go.

After a while, we leave the city behind, into the steppe, and the towns that dot it up and down – sprawls of concrete, minarets spiralling above them, and the occasional outsized glass structure of a newly built mall. At some stops, without explanation, we are stationary for ten to fifteen minutes, before we trundle into the emptiness once more. If you look at a map of Turkey, this is at its heart: the green hills of the Black Sea to its north; the coasts of the Aegean to its west, of the Mediterranean to its south; and the rugged mountains in the east. Here in the middle lies this vast Anatolian plain, and its people: conservative, Sunni, and loyal. The land itself is not flat, but is at least more forgiving, and an endless dusty yellow under this morning's pale grey sky. It is the country's bread basket too. We pass fields and fields of wheat – though the land is resting, its crop cut ankle high – and the huge metal cylinders of granaries, huddled together in packs of six.

The day progresses – and the train, seemingly – and we talk over plastic cups of instant coffee. My cabinmates are construction workers, their fingers worn and faces weathered. They are taking advantage of a week's leave to head home. As the evening draws in, the colours darken, and the land turns a kind of mustard yellow. Soon, the only light around is the cheap white lamps of the restaurant car, as we edge through the night. We pass the city of Kayseri, and then loop back up again – the Kurtalan Ekspres is not just slow and delayed, but indirect too. Near midnight, as we wind round Sivas – nearly as far north as where we started, though five hundred kilometres to the east – I give up, and head to the bed I made twelve hours ago.

Around seven the next day, we are more decisively to the south. To our left, there are the first hints of colour to the sky, strips of airy orange between the horizon and the clouds. Slowly, the shape of the morning becomes clear, and peaks in the distance hint at the landscape to come. We spend the next few hours weaving in tunnels, through valleys, around mountain bends, as people filter back into the restaurant car for their meagre breakfast.

Slowly, all our number disembark – to Elazığ, Ergani, Diyarbakır – until I am left in our cabin alone, sitting, waiting, and waving every now and again to the children running alongside the track, in front of the wispy whites and browns of cotton fields. After twenty-six hours on board, gasping for breath, the train stops at Kurtalan, where the track runs no further. As a newspaper had it once, decades ago, 'Where the railroad ends, the rule of the outlaw begins.'[1]

*

How did Koçero become Koçero? Even this, his origin story, is a little unclear, told by everyone I asked with liberal use of the Turkish -mış – the tense you use to report things you haven't seen, that you don't know for sure. Even the sound of it is uncertain, the verbs ending in a fuzzy shhh.

No one really knows why, but there was a feud, in a village north of here, seventy years ago. It was a feud between two families, acted out by their sons: Halil and Koçero, though he wasn't Koçero yet. In one version, it just started with a slap, and the violence escalated from there. In others, it was about a trust betrayed. In another, it was seedier still: that Halil, the son of a local landowner, was harassing Koçero's young wife. Impossible, say others, Koçero, still in his early twenties, wasn't married then.

Regardless, as the story goes, Koçero fled to a nearby town, eager to avoid trouble. '*Gelme, öldürürüm seni,*' he said to his rival. 'Don't come, I'll kill you.'[2] He was not a man whose threats you'd ignore: well over six foot tall, broad shoulders, a long curved nose, and a thick black moustache. Made big, in the words of one writer, by inhaling mountain air into his chest.[3] Nevertheless, the threat wasn't enough. A month later – or was it three? – Halil was found dead in the town square, his body riddled with bullets. And then Koçero made off with 250 lira and a stash of gold coins . . . *mış.*

*

I am in Batman – between Kurtalan and Koçero's home village – in Turkey's south-east. It is a new city in an ancient region: Diyarbakır and its magnificent basalt inns lie to the west; Mardin and Midyat are to the south, old towns with perfect little stone mosques and churches, as if they are carved from the mountain themselves; and nearby, the Batman stream meets the Tigris, one of the area's two great rivers, which winds its way down south, forming the border of Turkey, Syria, and Iraq not far below. Batman has no such history, and, yes, an unfortunate name too – it comes from Batı Raman, West Raman, for it sits up on a plain by the Raman mountains. On my first day there, the wind comes down from over them, bringing a merciless rain to the city, and a cold that seeps into your toes.

It was in the 1940s a poor place in a poor country: of villages of mud-brick houses, with no electricity, running water, or even basic roads. Travellers instead came by longboats up the Tigris. It looked, in the words of one slightly partisan contemporary, like the ruins of a fallen civilization.[4] And it was in such a land that Koçero went on the run. He knew, after all, that he had to leave home. As one local author wrote, after he had killed Halil, it was simply too risky to stay – either the bereaved family would come to get him, or the gendarmes would instead. So early one spring morning, leaving his crying mother behind, Koçero set off with his father as far as Malabadi Köprüsü, the ancient stone bridge that gently arches over the local stream. And there, he parted from his father too, who left him with this final advice: go and find our relatives down south and don't come back.[5]

Thus his itinerant life began, wandering from village to village over the plains here, wherever his extended family might be, and trying to scrape by: selling odds and ends, perhaps a petty theft. But three things happened soon, in his early outlaw days, that shaped the rest of his life, as he gained a wife, a name, and a brother. Roaming around the districts to the east, he fell in love with a young woman called Saliha. He hit the road again soon, but not before marrying her first. It was while on the move too that he came across Şerifo, who had become an outlaw himself after shooting a dishonest moneylender back home. I've heard of you, said Şerifo, the boy who killed the son of a big family, and is now escaping the law. Both young and at large, they seemed to form an instant bond, about to be made real in flesh. They each cut a small incision in their arms, crossed them diagonally, and let their blood flow into each other. From now on, you're Koçero, Şerifo declared, a nomad – a *göçer* – in these parts.[6]

For the two outlaws, it would be too dangerous just to keep to the flats around Batman, they would have to head up into the ranges above as well. As it's told, in a village in the shadow of the Taurus mountains, they had one last meal prepared for them by Koçero's distant cousin, of yoghurt, figs, grapes, and cheese. She handed them her gold bracelets and coins, and wished them luck. And before the first call to prayer was even sung the next morning, they were making their way up to their new lives. In truth, they were about to become not just outlaws, but – armed with guns and horses – they would become bandits as well.[7]

*

It was at least a good time for it. Near the end of the decade, just before Koçero left home, this region was transformed. For somewhere up on Mount Raman, drilling 1,300 metres deep, Turkey's geologists had discovered something big. 'We didn't even know what oil was,' one local told me, 'and then all the outsiders came.' Hundreds of engineers and prospectors – far richer than locals could dream – relocated from all across Turkey. Offices, houses, schools, shops, bakeries were built for their families. There was even talk of a beach on the Tigris. A temporary refinery was set up; the first asphalt roads were laid down; and the famous Kurtalan Ekspres was diverted here too. A town was forming – Batman's population increased by ten times over the decade, bringing both oil workers and peasants looking to make good amongst them.[8] It is a history written large across the city today: I pass by locals enjoying coffee at branches of Café Petrol Firin, Café Petrol Oven; I find a bronze statue in its main square, expecting the usual scene of Atatürk or independence soldiers, only to see three workers in hard hats bent over a pump, now slightly shining in the rain; and down by the station, on the south side of the city, is Tüpraş Batman Rafinerisi, the Batman Refinery – a town unto itself, sealed off behind walls and barbed wire.

There was deep change outside the town as well. This was an area of the landed and the landless: near-feudal lords who owned the land, and the many peasants who worked it, and were taxed back in crops and livestock for the privilege. But something was happening. Far away, a government in Ankara had set Turkey on a different course. This would no longer be a country looking only to develop its industry in the cities; instead, it would become the granary of Europe as well. As the cold war began, Turkey embraced the capitalist camp – and its inevitable logic of supply and demand – to sell its food and raw materials to the West. It joined the IMF and – given its proximity to the USSR next door – benefitted from the Marshall Plan too. Aid and credit flooded its way. Turkey's agriculture was being launched into the twentieth century. In just six years, nearly forty thousand tractors arrived in the countryside; huge new areas of land were opened for cultivation; all across Turkey, the government rolled out thousands of kilometres of roads and highways as well.[9] But as *ağas* – as the landlords were known – bought subsidized tractors, they no longer had need for the peasants who worked there. Feudal lords became rural capitalists; peasants became seasonal workers, or even urban migrants. The small plot-holder who tried to stem the tide, maybe buying a tractor themselves, often ran into debt. Conflicts over land soared.[10]

In other words, as the oil world boomed, and the countryside seethed, it was a place marked by islands of wealth amongst a sea of the dispossessed. For a bandit, all of a sudden, there were roads to ambush, outsiders to rob, and thousands of poor villagers who might even cheer you on as you went.

*

It is a grey and rainy day, and I am in a taxi heading from the plains into the mountains, to Dağyolu, east of Batman. As we climb up, the patched-up asphalt cuts through pistachio fields, shorn of their nuts a month ago. Every now and again, the road fills up with hundreds of sheep walking the other way, their shepherd behind them, in a giant woollen traffic jam. My driver is a little confused, as we arrive at this tiny concrete village nearly 1,000 metres up, as to why I wanted to come. But here lives a man who knew not just Koçero, but the boy he was before. Koçero's older cousin is still alive.

Ali is sat on the carpeted floor in the warmest room of the house, underneath a wall-mounted heater, with a heavy green blanket over his legs. The rest of the home happens around him, bringing him *çay*, soup, and whatever else he asks for. He was born in 1924, or 1919. Neither he nor his family are sure. As I sit down across from him, he welcomes me in the little Turkish he knows – the smattering he remembers from his military service nearly eighty years ago – and then we get going. I ask questions about Koçero, he explains to me animatedly in Kurdish, and then sits back victoriously, and waits for his son Selim to calmly translate.

Koçero, Ali tells me, was his father's brother's son – that is, not some distant 'cousin' that links everyone to everyone else in Turkey, but something much warmer. And though they lived in different villages forty kilometres apart, they would see each other often enough. Not least at weddings – big family affairs that lasted a week, bringing relatives from all over – that Koçero enjoyed no end. Of course, he wasn't Koçero to Ali. His real name was Mehmet İhsan Kilit, born – depending on your sources – in 1921, 1925, or 1926. His grave says 1935, but Ali says that's wrong too. Though neither of Mehmet's parents could read, they did have some standing in the village, and his father would often assist the local *ağa* in his various affairs, for he was popular and empathetic, a trait he supposedly passed onto his son. Of course they were still poor. Though Ali says the family had small fields of wheat and barley, the father seemingly tended to sheep too. It would be fitting work, for they were part of the Alikan *aşireti* – a vast tribe that sprawls over south-east Turkey and beyond, down into Syria and out east into Iran, famous shepherds and goatherds, spending their summers up in the high plains, and their winters down below. According to one report, it was in young Mehmet's blood: he spent his afternoons catching mountain goats with his hands for fun, before releasing them back into the wild.[11] And though his course did not mirror his parents exactly – he went to primary school for three years and learnt Turkish – as he grew up he did take on the family work: helping out the local *ağa* if needed, and working as a shepherd. Until, of course, he killed Halil.

Ali remembers when Koçero came to stay in the village after-wards, and I ask if he seemed troubled, whether he felt any guilt. No, Ali says, he was obliged to do it. Besides, he continues, he was pretty busy those days. Batman was only growing – building a proper refinery, a hospital and a secondary school, electricity and sewerage facilities – and business was pretty good. With a rifle and a good threat, most workers would happily give you what they had. It was 'protection money', in a sense. After Koçero raided one oil camp nearby, Ali remembers the gendarme coming to Dağyolu trying to convince him, to convince his cousin in turn, to give him-self up. They were visiting more and more often.

As the pressure increased, Koçero decided to act again. He moved his wife and one-year-old daughter to Syria, and worked across the border from there. He stayed, so it is said, in a village of his Alikan tribe thirty kilometres from Turkey.[12] This, of course, was the great advantage of Kurdish bandits. Their ties down south were rich and personal, with families, clans, and tribes that spread well beyond the borders. '*Bu coğrafya*', as everyone here calls it – 'this geography' – this imagined Kurdish land, almost a character in itself, with a history far greater than the states that divided it. Deep too were their links to the trading hubs further below: to

Aleppo, Damascus, and Baghdad. The nation-states established a generation ago – Turkey, Iraq, and Syria – may have tried to sever them, but the movement of ideas, people, and goods continued. It carries on today. As I first entered the taxi to get here, it was full of a dark and filthy smoke. 'I prefer the smuggled tobacco,' explained the driver, 'it's stronger than the packet stuff.'

*

As all attest, Koçero and Şerifo preferred to travel in small bands of three and four. Big groups, they thought, attracted too much attention. Besides, Koçero was keen to stay mobile, and avoid conflict where he could. In the summer, they might stay up in the cooler mountains; in the winter, in Alikan villages, where they could be sure no one would turn them in. Still, they would never stay in a village for more than one night. Banditry was, for Koçero, as much about diplomacy as violence, and he would befriend all the riverboat captains and oil workers that he could.

But sometimes, of course, a bandit had to eat. As a magazine later claimed, once Koçero led a group of six armed men to ambush a series of highway buses, making off with the equivalent of twenty thousand dollars from two hundred terrified victims in a day.[13] Increasingly he smuggled goods across the border too. Turkey's closed economy made the black market in cheap imports a lucrative business. Koçero's work then was often hardly the stuff of Butch Cassidy, smuggling into Turkey anything from Ceylon tea and sugar to nylon and silk, watches and razors. Often, the other way, Koçero took into Syria and Iraq prized Turkish sheep. His skills at negotiation – learnt from his father – came in handy too. For this was a tense and dangerous world: *ağa*s vied for border territory, and 'taxed' imports through it; smugglers could be attacked by other bandits, fighting over their 'turf'. Let alone the actions of the Turkish state, desperate to stop the illicit trade – almost three hundred smugglers were killed by gendarmes in the late fifties. It even mined swathes of the Turkish–Syrian border. As the phrase went in one southern town, 'If you see a young man in Kilis with a limp, he's a smuggler; if you see an old man with a limp, he fought with Atatürk.'[14]

Though he is reluctant to talk too much about his past, I meet an old man in his seventies, who was a bandit around that time too. He describes his years under constant, tiring threat: moving only to friendly villages and trusting no one outside them. Territorial and primitive, 'it is like the life of an animal', let alone the actual wolves and bears that stalk the mountains too. It's scorchingly hot in the summer, punishingly cold in the winter; most people up there, he explains, are merely waiting for an amnesty to come home.

But Koçero seemed to thrive, and soon he and Şerifo had the gear to match: fine horses, rifles made in Austria, the latest binoculars, and as Ali remembers, a dagger with a silver-plated hilt. Koçero topped it off, supposedly, with a dark fedora hat.

*

Near Batman, I'm introduced to someone else who knew him, on another wet and misty day. 'Let it rain,' says Ali Mehmet, as we sit on plastic chairs by the side of the road. He is in his seventies – with a neat grey moustache and glasses – and a member of the Alikan tribe. Behind us is a large new apartment complex where he lives with his wife, but when he was a boy, he lived in a village far north of here. When Koçero crossed the border into Turkey, Ali Mehmet says – not with pride, but as if it were utterly banal – the bandit would stay in his family home, if not overnight, then at least for a couple of hours, chatting, resting, eating, and checking the whereabouts of the local gendarmerie. He remembers, as an eight-year-old boy, his mother killing one of their chickens whenever Koçero came. Sometimes, Ali Mehmet himself brought him pitchers of water to shave. He was handsome, he tells me, with thick facial hair and big black eyebrows. I ask if he was ever afraid to host a known outlaw in his home, but he is dismissive – no one in the village would ever tell the authorities. Besides, he was the king of the mountains. Once, Ali Mehmet continues – half in awe, half in delight – Koçero was confronted by the gendarmerie, and armed with only a cigarette lighter and a handkerchief, improvised a Molotov cocktail, launched it in their direction, and as they ducked in fear, escaped unharmed. He is laughing by the end of the story, as if he were the eight-year-old he was hearing it for the first time.

The longer Koçero and his band were in the mountains, the more his reputation grew. Here was a bandit of rare courage and wit . . . and utterly brazen too. He would walk into Batman city centre, transformed in a suit and tie; he would even go and watch a movie in its cinema; he would put on an officer's uniform and even receive salutes from his 'inferiors'. He was big and strong and 'faster than a horse'.[15] What's more, as one villager told a news reporter, he was *mazlumun babası, zalimin düşmanıdır*, father of the oppressed, and enemy of the oppressor.[16] As one story goes, once when he heard that a local gendarme captain – blond and clean shaven – was hounding villagers in his attempts to catch Koçero, threatening and beating them for information, he rode to his village hours away, stole into the captain's house at night, ordered him to stop at gunpoint, and left him tied up by his hands and feet.[17] Decades later, a former minister – who worked as a lowly engineer in the area at the time – described his own encounter. His team were spending days around oil wells in the mountains, and nights back in Batman, shuttling between them morning and night. Once, early in the day, Koçero stopped their car on the road out to camp. 'Empty your pockets,' he said, 'you are oil engineers. If you don't have money, who does?' Once they handed him their money, he called over some passing villagers and gave them everything he had just received. 'He was like Robin Hood.'[18]

Were any of these true? In a sense it didn't matter, Koçero's legend was becoming something else. As one local explained to me, he was 'the hero of our youth'. In an era without even the radio, guests would visit villages and spread the latest they had heard, 'and there are lots of good storytellers here'. And they had lots of reasons to want to believe, for they were being squeezed on all sides. With a police post in nearly every village, the state was present here, but it was distant as well. The majority of villagers spoke no Turkish; officials were forbidden to speak Kurdish. Worse – and perhaps almost as an inevitable consequence – the gendarmerie could be arbitrary and abusive too. Their nickname was *yumurtacı*, egg-stealer. The locals 'look at Ankara with awe', reported one journalist at the time, with a slight sense of understatement, 'but it does not lie in their hearts.'[19] The lure therefore of a bandit who could escape the gendarmerie time after time was irresistible. Of course, beneath that overarching authority was the layer that preceded it, the rule of the *ağa*s and their near-total control over the land. As one paper noted at the time, increasingly they were using bandits to do their work, collecting taxes, roughing up peasants, turfing them off their plots.[20] There were then good bandits and bad bandits, and Koçero famously never targeted those below. Finally, there was the rampant unfairness of any boomtown around Batman and beyond. Once Batman's refinery was finished in the mid-fifties, its new complex had not just houses and health clinics but swimming pools and restaurants. Soon, it would have not just its own football team – Batman Petrolspor – but its own orchestra too. Meanwhile, the Batman outside it, to the north of the railroad, was a sprawling, unserviced shanty town. As one musician visiting from İstanbul described it, on one side it was like a village, on the other it was like Paris.[21]

There was something more specific, more culturally attuned, about Koçero's fame. It wasn't that he gave from rich to poor; but that he was a man of honour. The killing of Halil, the smuggling, the highway robberies of the wealthy – these may have been illegal, but they weren't unethical. Most pertinently, Koçero didn't touch women either, as an armed and wandering bandit might. It would be honour that would excuse his second murder. On a hot summer's day in Syria, Koçero learned that something had happened to Şerifo, his blood brother of the mountains. Both he and another comrade, Alo, had fallen in love with the same woman, but she had chosen Şerifo to wed. And Alo, in a blind and jealous rage, had ambushed his old friend on the road, and shot Şerifo dead. So Koçero – in the brutal logic of blood and feuds – was obliged to take Alo's life too. He crossed the border, pursued him for months, and killed him in the night.[22] In my hotel in Batman, I happen across an old German-Kurd – who is back visiting for the week – with a moustache dyed as black as night. He remembers as a twelve-year-old hearing Alo had died a few kilometres from his village, and went immediately to the spot where he had been laid down, a solitary stone marking the spot. And he saw in the distance – and this I cannot quite believe – Koçero walking off in the distance, into the horizon, with 'a knife the length of your arm'.

Some stories, though, locals are keener to skip over altogether, those that speak directly to the primal violence of a bandit's life. One writer tells me something he was asked to leave out of his work entirely: that once, after stopping a bus heading down the highway to Siirt, Koçero saw a rival bandit amongst the passengers. He took him off the bus, sharpened his knife on a nearby stone, cut off his ears, and travelled back towards Batman with them in his front pocket.

*

Back in Dağyolu, sat on the floor with Ali, he tells me his cousin would still come back to the village every few months, with enough escape stories 'to fill ten books'. I ask how he seemed after so many years on the run. '*İçime doğmamış korku*', he remembers Koçero saying once, *fear wasn't born inside me*. Ali's daughter-in-law brings in bread she has baked in the village oven – flat, crispy, warm, and with black sesame seeds on top. As he reaches out to break it, I notice his hands, as big as planks. I imagine him in his youth – like his famous cousin, surely – broad and imposing, built to withstand mountain life. Koçero never complained about it, Ali continues, but he was tired nonetheless. Still, as he approached nearly a decade on the road – now well into his thirties – Koçero was expanding his trade, moving as far east as Van and the Iranian border beyond it, almost four hundred kilometres away. And it wasn't just his domain that was growing, he was smuggling new goods too. Once, a few days' walk from Batman, his band intercepted a haul of opium destined for Iran, and finished the job themselves.[23] Increasingly, there were Turkish products to sell more valuable than sheep and olive oil.

Inevitably, the national press was finally alerted to Koçero. He first appears in Turkey's paper of record, *Cumhuriyet* – its pages yellow, its title written in slightly dissonant red – on 13 November 1959. There on page five, it reports a robbery near Diyarbakır of nearly ten thousand lira from oil and animal traders, by an armed band in stolen military uniforms, covering their faces with handkerchiefs. One of them, it continues, is understood to be Koçero, 'wanted for murder and robbery.'[24] Soon, Ankara's newsmen are following more and more closely the efforts of Turkey's authorities to catch the country's most wanted – aware too, how popular the story is with their readers in the big cities, thrilled by the Western-inflected cliches and the frisson of real danger out east. No doubt, the state was increasing its efforts. A change in government a world away – after the 1960 coup – would have its own effects here: a fresh wave of operations carried out by gendarmes, and harsher reprisals on villagers suspected of hiding bandits when they failed.

The reports were full of wild rumour, for who really knew who Koçero was, or what he did? In one article in *Milliyet*, he is described as 'the murderer of twenty people'[25]; in other, he is accused of attempting to kidnap the fifteen-year-old daughter of a local trader.[26] If they were true, no locals believed it. Just as likely, others suggested, that every crime in the south-east was being attributed to the man that no one could stop to ask. One paper even carried the claim – later denied – that the state was bombing the mountains in the region in the outlaw's pursuit.[27]

But there was of course a barely hidden admiration for Koçero in these tales of daring-do. Here he was near Siirt, leaving behind just an army uniform, a razor, and an empty packet of cigarettes;[28] there he was near the border, escaping a manhunt dressed as a shepherd, crossing into Syria with two comrades and five hundred sheep;[29] now he was east near Tatvan, surrounded by five hundred gendarmes, and yet after a two-hour firefight, somehow still breaking free, killing a chief sergeant as he went. As the headline read a few days later, the 'martyred' soldier's widow would try to sue the governor who insisted on the ambush. The governor was too eager to catch Koçero, she claimed, and it was too dangerous to try, even with a force five hundred strong.[30] In truth, these reports were often more caper than Western, as the gendarmes are shown again and again to be inept. They are badly trained, inexperienced, and ignorant of the area; there are only a few of them stationed in each outpost; and often, as was once relayed to readers, the phone line didn't even work between them.[31] He, in contrast, had been catching goats in the mountains with his hands since he was a boy. A year into the goose chase, Turkey reached an agreement with Syria to help find Koçero. Finally, in late 1962, it seemed to bear fruit. 'We got him', as they might have said, extraditing him across the border to be detained in the Turkish city of Mardin. A special committee was gathered and sent there to confirm the good news. That's not him, they concluded, they don't even look alike.[32] As if to salt the wounds, on New Year's Day 1963, *Milliyet* newspaper awarded Koçero and the Prime Minister joint 'Man of the Year'. I ask Ali how the press attention – and Koçero's fame – made them feel. Proud, he replies. One of their own, their Mehmet, was standing firm in a 'time of cruelty and injustice'.

Of course, it couldn't last. It was a summer's day in 1964, and one everyone remembered well: 'how did it happen?', one local recalls asking around school, bereft, 'how was he shot?' The details of Koçero's life may have been unclear, but his death is a little bit sharper – the day when the legend was turned back into flesh and blood. The papers naturally had a different tone. As *Cumhuriyet's* front page had it, '*Mukadder Son*', *The Predestined End*. It would report the details over the following days. Koçero and his band had come to an oil camp on the night of 3 July, knowing its employees would have just been paid. They were told by the guard however that the payment was late, and they should come back the next day. But it was a trick. The guard warned the gendarmerie that Koçero would visit again. Sure enough, when they arrived the next night, a fight ensued. And Koçero – King of the Mountains, Nemesis of the Gendarmerie – was shot not by his adversaries, but accidentally, in the shoulder, by one of his comrades. As he had always managed to do, he escaped, but he was badly injured, stumbling away into the night. The next morning, his body was found, face up in a creek, kilometres away from the site. He would have been around just forty years old. On 7 July, the paper's front page carried a picture of Koçero as he was discovered: in a muddy ditch, his huge shoulders and head resting on the ground, his mouth slightly open, and his eyes looking up, not bloody but humiliated. 'Trapped and killed as he did to so many', runs the article underneath.[33] It would make the international press too: 'Turkey's most notorious bandit, Koçero, is dead after 14 years of terror', wrote the *Coventry Evening Telegraph* a month later, 'the country finds it difficult to believe the intense, thin-faced man is gone.'[34]

As Ali remembers, 'it was a very busy funeral' – while Koçero may have been born elsewhere, Dağyolu was their home village, where their ancestors had settled generations ago. People came from all over for three days, offering food and their respects, and noting too the length of Koçero's grave, impressive even in death. Still, some locals had trouble accepting it – as one journalist touring the region noted six months later, *Koçero'nun öldüğüne kimse inanmıyor*, No one here believes Koçero died.[35]

*

There are few left who knew Koçero, and fewer still who want to talk. After his death, Saliha and her children soon moved back from Syria: Nuri, Muazzez, Sırrı, Urfa, and – in a name that suggests that perhaps Koçero too was proud of his life's work – Eşkiya, 'bandit'. Their lives, though – Ali tells me – were not easy, left with little without their father. Saliha, a young widow, lived in a mud-house in the village for the rest of her life. Their children instead moved to the city looking for work. By the time I came to Batman, only two of the five of them still lived. His daughter Muazzez ended up marrying Mehmet Ali, the boy who had brought Koçero water to shave in the mountains. As he and I spoke on the side of the road, she was just fifty metres away in the apartment block behind us. But she was too ill to interview, Mehmet Ali told me, and was 'retiring from the world.' The other surviving sister, way out west in Antalya, was unwell too. The eldest son Nuri, who had lived a respectable life as an inter-city bus driver, had died a few months before. Anyway, he was seemingly always keen to downplay his background. 'My father earned his bread in the mountains', he once said to a journalist matter-of-factly, 'and I earn mine on the roads.'[36]

None of them – neither Saliha nor her children – ever spoke too publicly about the family's late father, Turkey's one-time person of the year. It wasn't shame of how he lived, explained one local, it was the fear of opening up old wounds. In a world where feuds could lie dormant for decades, to open up about what Koçero had done – who he had robbed, perhaps how many he had killed – was only to invite danger to all those who came after him. Besides, a part of me suspects the family are happy with Koçero-as-myth as well. Even talking to his cousin Ali, I find it hard to learn what he was really like. 'Like the Ahmet Kaya song', he tells me, referring to a song, based on a poem, written a decade after his death – where the life of Koçero, up against the government, the gendarmes, and all manners of injustice, becomes almost a fable. *Koçero bir oyundur yazılır bitmez*, a play that doesn't end by being written. As a journalist, I find it frustrating at times, not to be able to get to what is true, to a person of shades and textures, even from those who knew him. But maybe that is to misunderstand the point of legends themselves. I am trying to learn about Mehmet İhsan Kilit; they are telling me about Koçero.

It is a reputation that only grew after his death. In part, this was nothing new. Turkey has long had its celebrated bandits: Köroğlu, who fled to the mountains five hundred years ago, after a landlord cauterized his father's eyes; or the Zeybeks around the turn of the last century, the Robin Hoods of the Aegean. But no doubt, Koçero has his own meaning, out here in the south-east. For in the decades after him, the mountains around Batman would have new masters, ones the government would be keen to portray as criminal 'bandits' too: the PKK, and the thousands of militants, many of them from Batman, who would fight for a separate Kurdish state. As one local photojournalist put it, 'then people with degrees started going up there as well'. '*Bu coğrafya*', this geography, he continued, 'would suffer a lot'. So Koçero became a hero to a whole new generation. He had ruled over here – a bandit and outlaw, even sometime mediator of the *ağa*s – when Kurdish activism was in a quiet lull. But as the conflict reignited, he was recast. He was brave, just, and the scourge of the state. If you blurred around the edges of his story, he could be a Kurdish freedom fighter too. Indeed, that photojournalist's family history linked the two eras almost too neatly, and cruelly: his father was a bandit who had known Koçero; his son had joined the PKK, and was killed five years ago.

There were other profound changes in the years after Koçero that would seal his legend – he was one of the last bandits the region would see. It was, after all, transforming even as he lived. As peasants found themselves caught between landlords and the gendarmerie, hundreds of thousands moved to the cities, first to nearby Diyarbakır and Elazığ, and to the even larger ones to the west, to Ankara, İzmir, and İstanbul. The roads only recently laid out all over the country made it easier for them than ever to go. Indeed, they migrated not just from here, but from the fishing villages along the coast, the bread basket of Anatolia, the hills of the Black Sea – all across Turkey, for millions of different reasons, they packed up their bags and left. Few developments in Turkey over the century were so deeply felt. And here in the south-east, those journeys were marked with a particular sense of loss, for – as the conflict took off over the next decades – they were fleeing not just poverty but violence too. Koçero then was an honoured part of a disappearing world, before the land and the village were left behind.

*

I stand up and thank Ali – one hundred years old and still going strong after three hours – for his time. We have stopped talking about Koçero now. Instead, he and his son are trying to persuade me of the merits of village life and the healthiness of their yoghurt, and warning me about the dangers of technology in the decadent West. Not for the first time, I am struck by how conservative they are, the remaining relatives of the nation's most famous bandit. Before I go, they tell me to make the most of a break in the rain and visit his grave up behind the house.

It is a few minutes' walk, going higher up the mountain. I see clouds moving through neighbouring villages, like locals passing by. There is the sound only of the wind, and a few nearby goats and chickens. Behind a small fence there is a clump of white stone graves. And there he is, next to his wife Saliha. I realize only here, that in all I have read about him how little Koçero himself ever speaks. 'I am but a simple criminal,' he was supposed to have once told a journalist, bewildered by his fame, and the efforts the state was making to stop him. Was this true? Did he mean it? Did he ever even say it? I don't suppose I will ever find out. The mountains have their secrets, and they will keep them. 'Koçero Kilit', reads his grave, part real name, part legend.

7. Interlude – The First Bridge

1970s – İstanbul

It is early morning in late February, and it feels like we're leaving not just night but winter behind. It has been a long and hard few months, bringing snow all over the city, but now as my friend and I walk up towards the peak, the day is breaking to a pleasant chill. She is a nurse at a local hospital, and has just finished a twelve-hour shift. Meet me afterwards, she told me, and we'll go up to Çamlıca, but not before picking up some pastries first. We climb past the hill's pines and cypresses, straight and green, and its plane trees still bare. Their leaves will come soon enough. Over the last few days, İstanbul has had its surest sign yet of spring. The first of the *leylekler* have returned: the black and white storks who over the next few weeks will migrate here in their thousands, nesting

139

in its telephone poles and minarets, announcing their arrival with their unique *lak lak* call, the sound of their clattering beaks.

Slightly breathless, we reach the top, nearly three hundred metres up. This is the city's highest point, and a park to enjoy the view. Some families have already arrived to set up a picnic, and are sharing a *sahlep* between them, a hot milky drink made with orchids and cinnamon. Ahead of us by the park's edge, a group of school kids call to a cat just out of reach, beyond the railings, basking in the gentle sun. Wisely, she ignores them. A few of them give up, and return instead to the panorama in front, of İstanbul stretching out west. It is the Bosphorus in the foreground that draws the eye first: the bends of it, a blue ribbon winding through the city. It is deceptively calm from here: this famous strait of two currents – the one on top, from the Black Sea down south to the Marmara, and the one below slipping the other way. To our right out of view is Şeytan Akıntısı, 'the Devil's Current', the stream further north where the Bosphorus floor suddenly plunges down, stirring up the water, keeping the city's ferry captains on edge. Out to the left, I see container ships and tankers on the horizon, waiting in the Marmara for their turn to enter and continue north into the Black Sea.

Almost immediately ahead lies the bridge, seemingly so tightly strung above the water, linking this side of İstanbul to the other. Up here from Çamlıca, you can see the slight pinch of it, how it arcs upwards in the middle, and the shadow it casts on the Bosphorus beneath. And all across it, cars come either way, as İstanbullus head off to work, and the city wakes up to another day. We unwrap our cheese-filled *börek*, and watch them go.

*

The idea of building a bridge across the Bosphorus goes a long way back. As İstanbul tour guides like to recount, in the fifth century

BC the Persian King Xerxes, in his attempts to invade Greece, once strung one up in the Dardanelles straits further south, tying boats together from one end to the other with ropes made of flax, until it was destroyed in a storm. Attempts at something sturdier came later: da Vinci once wrote a letter to an Ottoman sultan, offering to design a bridge that would cross first the Golden Horn – the inlet that separates the two sides of the historic city in Europe – and then the entire Bosphorus if needed, uniting them with the Asian side that sits across the water. Though it was never taken up, the dream persisted, even as empires collapsed and nations came in their stead. In the 1930s in the new republic, a Turkish business magnate inspired by the Golden Gate Bridge aimed to build one in İstanbul. But his proposal to the government fell flat, for the city had neither the money nor the population to justify it.[1]

Things looked a little more optimistic twenty years later. Turkey in the 1950s sought to build itself anew, rolling out roads left and right, aiming – in the cold war parlance – to become Küçük Amerika, 'a little America': capitalist, developed and modern. It was a mindset that was hard to escape, and harder still to lose: my *baba* who grew up around this era is still thrilled by the sight of an electricity pylon – towering physical testaments to progress. The bridge became a popular topic in the press again, full of debates about what form it would take, where it would go, and whether the feet of its towers should be in the water or out. Among other discoveries, it turned out the mud and sediment on the Bosphorus bed were surprisingly thick.[2] The government commissioned a feasibility study, and signed off on a suspension-bridge design by a firm from New York. But the economy faltered, and within a few years a colonel was appearing on Turkish radio telling the nation that that government was no more.

The plan was shelved but the demand grew. As the sixties rolled on, more and more Turks were buying their own cars, and the city could barely keep up. To cross the straits with them, İstanbullus would have to take the *araba vapuru*, the car ferry: a kind of floating car park that took drivers and their vehicles between the two continents. It was, in the words of one newspaper at the time, 'a torture'.[3] There simply weren't enough car ferries to go round, and people could wait in line for up to three or four hours to board. The journey itself took twenty-five minutes on a good day. If it was foggy or stormy the ferry could be cancelled altogether, and the two sides of the city – as they had been for centuries – would be cut off from each other entirely.

So once again, the bridge idea sharpened a little. By the mid-sixties, Turkey was on a brief up once more: the country was richer and its government more popular. Prime Minister Demirel, once a civil engineer himself, set off another round of studies and tenders, bids and designs. By 1968, four firms were in the running, until an agreement was signed with Freeman Fox and Partners from the UK. They had designed a bridge over the Severn in Wales two years before, with a slightly new suspension model;[4] it gave them the edge over American competitors, whose bridges – and here I apologize, as I am no engineer – were thought to wobble too much. Finally, Turkey prepared itself for the Bosphorus bridge, though not to universal acclaim. The chamber of architects opposed the plan; academics said it would cause needless land speculation; as the economy began to struggle once more, the opposition criticized it too. Wasn't a bridge just for the rich and their cars?

Large stamps were issued for the opening ceremony, when the first stone would be put down. They showed a world map with the bridge overlaid on top of it, stretching from Spain at one end to China on the other, as if the 'bridging continents' metaphor wasn't heavy enough. When the day came, 20 February 1970, the Prime Minister and President together turned on the machine to start digging, deep into the Asian shore. Cannons were fired, and ship captains blew their whistles. And then Demirel addressed the crowd. Not only did he say the bridge would ease the city's traffic, he presented it as something far more profound as well: as almost the last step of the Turks' conquest of İstanbul more than five hundred years ago. For this would link the historic city to Anatolia for good.[5]

*

At the time, İstanbul was in many ways a city in between. On the one hand, it was a place lost in its own decline. It had been stripped of its capital status fifty years ago – 'I beg you', one deputy asked of the assembly before it voted, 'not to let İstanbul turn into ruins' – and its population had barely grown since.[6] As Orhan Pamuk described his İstanbul childhood of the fifties and sixties, it had the air of a poor, provincial city. He would described its *hüzün*, its shared melancholy, from an unarticulated sense of defeat, poverty and loss. Indeed, in the work of the photojournalist Ara Güler – the city's other great chronicler – İstanbul in those years is both full of life and in beautiful decay: horse-drawn carts and street kids, smog in the air and mud on the streets, workers in patched-up clothes. İstanbul may still have been the country's biggest commercial city, but perhaps it didn't *feel* that way to those that lived there. And perhaps it didn't look it either. Still by the 1970s, when the first work on the bridge was underway, the city had its medieval silhouette: a skyline of domes and minarets.

But something was happening too. In the Democrat Party years, the government had launched a programme to revive the city, knocking down old neighbourhoods, laying out wide boulevards, and giving İstanbul its first skyscraper – built in the 1950s, the Hilton Hotel was all clear-cut concrete and large glass walls. As a symbol of what could be achieved in the West, it was funded by the Marshall Plan.[7] Yet it was the less planned growth that would define the place, as Turks all over were starting to leave the village. İstanbul's population – stagnant for so long – was suddenly booming, from one million in 1950 to one and a half million just a decade later. They lived not in the city's old wooden houses or new apartments, but in *gecekondu* – 'put up overnight' shanty homes. Districts like Zeytinburnu, just to the west of the old city walls, grew and grew with them, with wells for water, primitive roads, and electricity, if at all, hijacked from the official grid. By the 1970s, half of those living in İstanbul had been born outside it. It had become a city of migrants, and hundreds of thousands of shanty homes.

Seemingly both growing and in decline, perhaps İstanbul was like the straits that ran through it, moving in two directions at once. This, then, was meant to thrust the city more decisively forward. What could be a bigger sign of progress, after all, than the world's first intercontinental bridge?

*

Construction started by boring holes deep, storeys down, into the ground. This was where the bridge's steel legs would stand, in Ortaköy in Europe, and in Beylerbeyi in Asia, both uptown districts that would never be the same again. Mounted with panels from Italy, they were finished by the summer of 1971, staring out at each other from across the water. As the British team overseeing the project later said, the builders – who came from towns and villagers all over Anatolia – were willing to work and learn. 'Welding is a skill that seems to do well in foreign parts,' they added.[8]

By early 1972, the towers had been completed, and the teams prepared the cable line to go between them, spooling out from huge steel bobbins fixed to the ground. So it was, on 11 January, that the first cable was pulled from one tower to the other, bringing the slightest, most fragile contact between the two continents for the first time since Xerxes, two and a half thousand years before. For months, once the two cables were fixed but before the road below was begun, that's how the bridge stood: two massive towers, linked together by a pair of drooping steel cords, like an empty washing line hung over the Bosphorus. In the final stage, they put together the road: sixty separate decks, each tied to the main lines above with their own cables going up from either side. The first one was brought by a boat adorned with Turkish flags into the middle of the straits, and lifted right up into the centre. The next decks spread outward from there, so this floating road in the middle of the Bosphorus got longer and longer, edging closer towards the land on either side. It was at times dangerous work, with strong winds and storms, as if the straits were resisting being tamed until the last. Still, by spring 1973, the final deck was hoisted up, fitting snugly in the last remaining gap. It was celebrated, as one paper reported, with champagne up on the completed platform, on the road that had been built sixty-four metres up from the sea. All that was left to do was to asphalt the decks.[9]

In total, the bridge was over a kilometre and a half in length, with six lanes for traffic and a pavement on each side. It had been the labour of four hundred workers and thirty-five engineers, who had managed it all in just over three years. And it had cost over twenty million dollars, financed through everything they could find. Besides, the government was confident the bridge 'would pay for itself inside two years', through the tolls it would charge for all cars that crossed it.[10] Anyway, some things went beyond dollars and cents. This was the fourth longest bridge in the world, and the largest outside the US. Perhaps Küçük Amerika was possible after all. It was good to hope at least. In the six years since it was commissioned, Turkey had seen four different prime ministers and a military coup. The one who was about to open it, a former banker, would only last nine months himself.

*

Fifty years and one day after the republic was declared, its biggest city would have its bridge. As the papers reported, on a sparkling blue morning on 30 October 1973, hundreds of thousands of İstanbullus, many in their finest clothes, attended the opening ceremony. Many more watched all over the country, for it was shown live on state TV – a novelty in itself, as it had only started broadcasting a few years before. Goats were sacrificed in the bridge's honour, dignitaries watched a troupe perform an old Turkish folk dance, and soldiers paraded at the start of the bridge, carrying a flag and a portrait of Atatürk. Then the President and Prime Minister cut a ribbon on the Asian side, and proceeded to walk. The plan was to cross to Europe – with assorted honoured guests in tow – but even this proved complicated. As one story had it, the crowd behind was too excited. One boy – never to be identified – raced ahead on his bike, arriving at the other side before all else. Thousands more were behind him on foot, ready to make the historic journey too. As the crowds followed, immediately at the back of the politicians, the bridge began to shake. The gendarmes pleaded for them to turn back, but they had lost control. With the steps of thousands of feet on suspended decks, perhaps a little shaking was to be expected, and regardless, the people would not be deterred, for there was a continent to reach.[11]

The press the next day mostly ignored the opening day chaos. '*Asayı Avrupaya Bağladık!*', declared *Milliyet*, 'We Have Connected Asia to Europe!' with instructions also for drivers on how to pay the toll, and for pedestrians how to get up and walk.[12] *Cumhuriyet* was a little more sober, but did inform readers that the bridge took fifty thousand lira on its first day, from nearly two thousand vehicles. It carried pictures of a deserted car ferry too – progress at last.[13] As the months passed, here at last seemed a point of pride for crumbling İstanbul. As one (unbearably upbeat) pop song would have it, '*Bogaz köprüsü inci gerdanlık / Altından geçtik, kahkaha attık*'.

'The Bosphorus Bridge, the pearl necklace / We passed underneath it and laughed.' By December, *Milliyet* was celebrating the millionth car to cross the bridge, with a photo of the lucky passengers in a classy old Ford.[14]

*

Up from Çamlıca hill it doesn't look so much the city's pearl necklace any more. Fifty years on, the bridge looks plain and grey, and even a little workaday, despite the night-time attempts to turn it into something more glamorous, lighting up its zigzag cables in whites and pinks. Noticeably, it no longer dominates the sky – seeming almost modest set against the hill behind it, and its dozens of high-rises of concrete and glass. This was one change in the years that immediately followed its opening, as the city's centuries-old skyline was dwarfed by skyscrapers and hotels: the Sheraton, the Intercontinental, a famous tall office block in Odaküle. But it wasn't so much the building upwards as outwards that would change İstanbul forever. As you look out from Çamlıca, in front and to the left sits the old city: the little kiosks of the Topkapı Palace, the dome of the Aya Sofya and its ochre walls, the minarets of Süleymaniye, but these are almost lost in the sprawl of the İstanbul beyond them – up and down the hills, a mottle of concrete until the horizon. This was the effect of the bridge, to decentre the city's historic heart to its south.

The bridge after all had opened up new parts of the city east and west. Jobs and businesses soon moved out of the centre, relocating closer to the road network it linked up, where rent was cheaper and there was space to park. Soon the migrants followed them too, putting up their *gecekondu* by the factories and building sites nearby. As the saying went at the time, *İstanbul'un taşı toprağı altın*, 'İstanbul's stone and earth is made of gold'. The city's population, one and a half million in 1960, more than tripled in the next two decades.

The newcomers changed not just the city's size but its character. Arriving from all over Anatolia, they were young and religious, unemployed and often uneducated – not, to put it mildly, to the taste of the classic, cosmopolitan İstanbullu. Not least in the music they brought to the city: arabesk, with its string orchestras and solo singers, longing for home, yearning for lost loves, a genre – as one writer put it – of 'rebellion without hope'.[15] It would be the classic music of the *dolmuş*, the cramped minibus taxi that came to serve the poorer districts: to take the men to the factories and markets, and the women to richer homes, to cook and clean.

'Our' İstanbul would also be remade, and the district where Abdi Aytaç had bought a summer home a generation before the bridge was built. For Kadıköy, sloping down the Marmara on the Asian side of the city, was once a very different neighbourhood: a place of old wooden mansions and vegetable gardens. As my *babaanne* tells me, she used to ride around its green and spacious roads on her red Raleigh bike; my *baba* remembers visiting the house in the winter, when their street was practically deserted. There were no shops either – a market caravan came periodically instead, to sell fruit and veg to whoever might be there. Yet the bridge, as one scholar put it, would be 'the affirmation of Anatolian İstanbul', as wealthy residents in the historic centre looked to move away to the suburbs. Kadıköy's timber houses became high-class apartments. As they packed tighter together, the old gardens too disappeared.[16] Looking down from my *babaanne*'s sixth-floor window, in her eleven-floor building, in this city of sixteen million people, it feels strange it could ever have been any other way.

*

Just after one o'clock, the *ezan* from a nearby mosque calls the faithful, and moments later we can hear prayers roll all around, up and down the hills, across the water, from mosques all over the city.

Soon more families arrive with picnics to enjoy the view, ordering *çay* from the park cafe, to warm themselves up on this winter's day. Later, even more will come to watch the sun set over the Marmara, turning the sky all bands of oranges and reds. This is still a city to enjoy – a place not just of *hüzün* but *keyif*, of quiet, deliberate moments of pleasure. Still, it is hard not to feel a sense of loss. As I find photos of the bridge being built, I'm drawn not to the structure itself but the fields behind it, green and empty. It is like looking at pictures of someone you know from fifty years ago: at once recognizable – the same shape, the same basic alignments – but at the same time utterly transformed. And with a similar sense of irrevocability: the sad knowledge that that beauty will never return.

Another thought strikes me too, as I watch the sun glint off the cars and taxis, moving slowly across the bridge, until they reach land again on the other side, bending left, then right, until they disappear from view. That perhaps it's better to think of it as a victory not of engineering but of the car. This was also Turkey's first motorway: the O-1, twenty-four kilometres of inner freeway that starts from Kadıköy in the south-east, crosses the Bosphorus somewhere near the middle, and ends in Eyüpsultan in Europe to the west. From there, it would join the famous Londra Asfaltı, the London Road, so called because it ran onto Edirne on the border, and then into Europe. It had been a city for centuries defined by its ties to the sea, by old steam ferries and rowing boats, by fishermen and seagulls – as Bedri Rahmi Eyüboğlu, that poet and friend of my great-grandfather, had once described them, 'half silver, half foam / half fish, half bird.' But the bridge spanning over the straits had made them less important than ever. It would be a city of the car now, of the *dolmuş* and the taxi. I watch a *metrobus* pass over the bridge – big public buses that move through İstanbul like high-speed convoys, one after the other, their own motorway lanes closed off with armco barriers and wire mesh. Of course, the bridge had been built to meet the age of the car – to ease the traffic – but it never worked out like that. The city grew bigger and its roads fuller. A second bridge was built fifteen years later, and then a third bridge, and then a tunnel too.

And it would seem like the triumph of the driver not least because soon they would be the only ones allowed on the bridge at all. It was a foggy week in January 1975, just over a year after the bridge had been opened. As it was reported on the front pages, at around noon, a twenty-four-year-old man and a twenty-year-old woman walked up the pavement from the Asian side, hand in hand. He was long haired and moustached, tall and in a navy shirt; she was in a red cardigan and a flowery dress, and had a scarf tied loosely on her head. After a few minutes, she climbed over the railings, and jumped into the sea, sixty-four metres down. He climbed over, paused for a moment, and followed her.[17] Who they were, why they did it, was never found out. But they would not be alone. There were hundreds of suicides and attempted suicides in the first years of the bridge. Disproportionately, they were young male migrants. As it turned out, the city's soil was not actually made of gold; nor could it be so easily launched into the future by building a bridge across its waters. After a few years, it was closed to pedestrians entirely. It was a fitting symbol perhaps for the country and the age. The 1970s, as Turkey passed its first fifty years, was not an easy time.

8. The End of the Left

1970s, 1980s – Fatsa

IN THE MAIN SQUARE OF FATSA, IT'S JUST WARM ENOUGH for the dogs to stretch out and feel the heat from the ground beneath. A few old men sit and chat, while young mothers watch their children play with pigeons, at times feeding them bread, at times chasing them until they scatter. The sting of winter is gone, but all are still wearing their coats, and linger by the warmth of a nearby bakery as they pass. There is a slight mist over the town and the sky is grey – as is the sea, on the other side of the highway, maybe fifty metres away. In the square, though the other trees are still leafless, a single magnolia has started to bloom, opening up its white petals with their undersides of soft pink. Perhaps it has felt the *cemre*.

In Turkish lore, this time of year is marked by the *cemre düşm-esi*, the falling of the embers, as little sparks drop down from the sun to warm the earth. The first comes to heat the skies; a week later, the second the water and the seas; the last, in these early days of March, scatters over the ground itself, finally breaking winter's resistance, and bringing on the spring. Soon, the plain trees around Fatsa will find their leaves once more, ready to shade its residents from the summer sun. Across the highway, out in the Black Sea, now warmer and stiller, the horse mackerel will return home, back from waters further south. But most importantly for this town, on millions of branches on millions of trees, in orchards all the way down the coast, the buds of hazelnuts will be coming out green, flanked by two small leaves either side, as if they are peeping out from a winter coat. They turned out a little early this year.

Slowly, as the *cemre* brings its warmth inland, the buds up the Black Sea hills will open out too, until in April the whole region is dressed in green. It is a nervous time for farmers all over. *Dumanlı Mart, fındık verimsiz*, as they say, 'If it's hazy in March, the hazel-nuts are no good.' For this is hazelnut country, not just for Turkey, but for the entire world. 'The hazelnut is everything for Fatsa,' once said its most famous mayor in court, trying to justify what he had done, 'a life without hazelnuts is unthinkable.' But still, it was no blessing. *Adeta kara yazgı*, as he described it, 'Almost a black fate.'[1]

*

The 1970s in Turkey started and ended with a coup: a decade of political turmoil and economic crises and, closer to home, the period where my *baba* came to consciousness, where my *babaanne* sat him down at an Ankara restaurant, all table linen and waiters in waist-coats, and told her teenage son, '*Lütfen git, ne yaparsan yap, buradan git.*' 'Please go, do whatever you have to do, just go from here.'

Already in the 1960s, it was an unstable place, straining as it grew: a young and booming population unable to find jobs; expanding cities unable to provide homes; a constitution that had granted new freedoms, but only under the watchful eye of the armed forces. In 1971, they performed – as they saw it – their 'constitutional duty' once more. The government was weak and unable to pass legislation; empowered trade unions were calling strikes; radical students were occupying campuses; inflation was running high. The military forced the Prime Minister to resign, and for a couple of years installed a series of technocrats in his place, before handing back power to the civilians again. But the fundamentals were unchanged, and the unfolding decade only saw the country's troubles deepen still. Few places would see it as dramatically as this sleepy town on the Black Sea coast.

*

Near the middle of Turkey's northern coast, Fatsa lies between two small rivers and the sea. The Elekçi creek runs down from the hills until it meets the sea to the town's west, a point marked by Fatsa's Lunapark, with its swinging ship and Ferris wheel. To the east rises the smoke of its industrial estate, on the bank of the Bolaman. The sea to the north is calm and almost completely without birds or boats – not so much a place that gives life to the coast, but like a vast, grey, endless border, hemming life in. It is supposedly an ancient town, once full of Greek and Armenian traders, but they have long gone, and no part of old Fatsa has survived. As I walk towards the older quarters, east and up the hill, the concrete is a little darkened, and the paint weathered, by decades and decades of rain. Hawkers work the streets with carts of fresh *hamsi*, anchovies, followed by hopeful, filthy ginger cats. It's an unlikely place, perhaps, to have moved so many, to have once inspired a banner hung off İstanbul's new bridge, proclaiming, *Güneş Fatsa'dan doğacak.*

'The sun will rise from Fatsa.' But forty years ago this was a very different town.

1970s Fatsa leant left. Long a stronghold for Atatürk's secularist, republican party, it had seen over the previous decade the beginnings of a politics in a deeper red, of socialists looking to make Fatsa their home. Trade union members, activists from Turkey's Workers' Party, university students, all emboldened by the course of the 1960s, had begun to come during the summers. Fatsa after all was easy enough to visit – the highway that ran along the coast brought buses from cities all over Turkey. They were a respectable type, as one local put it, 'in ties and ironed clothes.' And they found a receptive audience. Schools had expanded rapidly in Fatsa over the previous twenty years, and both their teachers and students were open to new ideas. Of course, the left were still a minority. Their high-brow discussions and literature would not even have touched outside the town centre, and the villages up and down the hills, where still around half the population could not read. Besides, even if they had, they might not have received the warmest welcome. Twice over the last century, Fatsa had received waves of Georgian migrants from the east – and those that fled the USSR would prove, understandably, a little hesitant to down their chains of oppression and unite.[2]

Leftism in Turkey however was changing, and Fatsa changed with it. The Workers' Party were parliamentarians, convinced of the possibility of changing Turkey's politics from within. But by the early seventies – after a couple of disappointing election results, and a squeeze on activists around the country – other leftists weren't so sure. What was needed, they argued, was something a little more direct. And while their different factions may have disagreed on certain points of Marxist-Leninist theory – the relative strength and consciousness of the peasantry versus the proletariat, who was the 'fundamental force' and who was the 'leading force', the role of the bourgeois vanguard, whether the model was Russian, Chinese, Vietnamese, Cuban, or Indian, etc. etc. – some basic shared arguments remained: that Turkey, a NATO member with sixteen bases within its borders, was under some sort of US imperialism; and that the only way of breaking free was through the strength of arms.[3]

These were not just abstract debates. In the years shortly before the 1971 coup, Deniz Gezmiş, a tall and handsome student leader – 'Turkey's Che Guevara' – was setting the revolutionary scene aflame first by robbing a bank in the capital, and then by abducting four American soldiers with his comrades, though they were released unharmed, while Gezmiş himself was arrested soon after. In the same year, the group of another radical, Mahir Çayan, captured the Israeli consul-general and killed him, once the authorities refused their demands and started searching for the militants instead. Çayan was arrested, only to escape from prison by digging a tunnel.[4]

These ideas had their appeal in Fatsa. It was a region of several NATO bases, long awash with guns, and full of hills to hide in. What better place for a guerrilla resistance? Indeed in 1970, Çayan had visited Fatsa, persuading many of the town's leftists to sign up to his violent interpretation of revolutionary change. By 1972, Fatsa was even more tightly bound to the radical left, and its history of heroes and victims. After his prison escape, and in a desperate attempt to secure the release of his fellow revolutionary Deniz Gezmiş – and save him from execution – Çayan kidnapped three technicians from a nearby NATO radar base for leverage, and took them inland. In the subsequent clash with Turkish soldiers, Çayan, his nine comrades, and all three hostages were killed.[5] In Fatsa, many followed the events on the radio, for three of the militants were from the town itself. They remember the funerals in the days that followed. According to one old activist, 'they were Fatsa heroes.'

*

Yusuf, I had been told, walks like his father: bearish, a little hunched, a cigarette always in his mouth. He is in a black leather coat, and we are heading towards one of the many empty tables in his favourite restaurant. We sit down by the window, overlooking the sea, as the colours of the day are starting to darken. He orders yoghurt with honey, a salad, a plate of meat, and a bottle of *rakı* between us. 'He drinks like his father too,' I remember being told, as he pours the *rakı* over the ice in my glass, turning it a milky white. As we speak, his answers get longer and longer, and – to be honest – I understand less and less. But this is what he said, at least according to my recorder placed by his knife and fork.

He was five years old, he remembers, when he looked out of his window early one morning and saw around three hundred soldiers, 'like an army', surrounding his old wooden house, just before the raid that took his father away. Fikri Sönmez was a member of Çayan's People's Liberation Party-Front of Turkey, and had helped, if only loosely, the doomed operation to liberate their comrades. Soon, Gezmiş and his two companions were hanged, and Fikri was sent to prison. Yusuf started school that year, and recalls that everyone knew him as the communist's son. He didn't know what it meant, but he understood the tone. 'It was like a big crime,' he says. He has a nervous habit of rubbing his belly clockwise as he talks.

His father, he explains, was almost the only leftist from his village, a conservative Georgian community not far inland – so Georgian, in fact, that his own father spoke only a broken, rusty Turkish, though the family had migrated generations before. While Fikri came from a line of farmers, after finishing primary school he went on to apprentice as a tailor, working under a Christian master on İstanbul's İstiklal Caddesi – perhaps the liveliest, trendiest street in all of Turkey, and perfect for a young Fikri, who was, as all attest, open, sociable and fun-loving. He brought a bit of İstanbul chic back to Fatsa town centre when he returned: Maltepe cigarettes, turtleneck jumpers, and fitted suits, walking the streets with his hair combed and moustache shaped.[6] But there was another side to him too. A thirty-something radical, he was a kind of self-taught intellectual. He had left school early but, as Yusuf remembers, he was always reading books at home. And the more he read – and the more time he spent with the literati from İstanbul, whiling away their summers in Fatsa – the more he too felt the need for something to be done. Did he believe in the use of violence, I ask, as I notice that outside suddenly it's pitch black. No, Yusuf insists, he just wanted to save Gezmiş from his fate.

After twenty months, the Turkish government announced a nationwide amnesty, releasing thousands of prisoners. As Yusuf remembers, he and his older brother were sent home while practising for the Children's Day parade, and there were dozens of people there waiting to greet his father. He was full of admiration, he says, because clearly it meant that he must have been someone important. And soon after his release, Fikri got to work again. So it was that Fatsa's hazelnut rallies would always be led by the town's famous tailor in his cream-coloured suit.

*

Hazelnuts are everywhere in Fatsa. As I walk through one district, I pass dozens of shops – their windows listing the price per kilo – and shelling and packaging warehouses, stacked with canvas bags filled with hazelnuts. In some depots, they are not even packed, just heaped in rooms in their thousands, like a ball pit. Outside one, a local trader sensing my curiosity explains the difference between the three varieties he's placed on his palm: the long and thin *çekildek*, he says, is like a Renault; the round and flat *palas* is a Mercedes; but the *yağlı*, looking like a tear drop about to burst, is the Ferrari. It is a temperamental nut, he says, but the only one that is good enough, sweet enough, to eat straight. The other two, he dismisses, are only for paste. Simply put, hazelnuts are so prevalent, he continues, because it is not wet enough here to grow *çay*, but too hilly for anything else. And they are well suited to the Black Sea coast, with its cool, rainy summers and mild winters. Indeed, Turkey is responsible for three-quarters of the world's crop, and the cheap and oily pastes are perfect for biscuits and chocolate spreads.[7]

It wasn't always like this. Only in the 1950s did the hazelnut spread over the region, as farmers uprooted wheat, maize, and everything else in the earth to make way for the *fındık*. As they did so of course, they were subtly changing their relationship to the land, and much more besides. Before, it provided their food – their cornbread and their vegetables, perhaps their yoghurt and milk one step removed as well; but now, it gave them a nut to sell, and cash to buy those things in turn. It was a richer existence perhaps, but a more capricious one, dependent as it was on buyers and exporters, shellers and packagers. 'Everything waits for it,' wrote a local columnist around that time, 'the education of the son, the trousseau of the daughter ... sickness, birth, and death.'[8] Still farmers struggled – their plots were small, and their fertilizers few. But more than anything else, they complained that the price they received from merchants – a price set by the state – was too low. As they only received one payment a year, after the harvest in September, for many the good times lasted only until late November. After that, if they had any need for upfront cash – an unexpected illness perhaps – farmers would promise middlemen next year's crop for an immediate but cut-price payment, or take out loans to bridge the gap. All over Fatsa, hazelnut farmers were in debt.[9] As one activist told me, when his father got back from the market one September, they discovered that their entire harvest had gone to paying off their interest from the previous year. 'Money merchants', 'usury', I hear the terms again and again – redolent not so much of Marx or

Lenin, but a more instinctive, almost biblical dislike of those who make money with money.

The people of Fatsa though were fighting back. As far back as the sixties, farmers had been protesting against poverty, high interest rates, and low hazelnut prices. They had barricaded the highway for thirteen hours and even stoned the governor's car. *70 lira hakkımız / söke söke alırız*, one local recalls of a banner, 'We have the right to 70 lira / and we'll take it by force.' It was a movement both of men who sold the nuts and women who gathered them. And there were protests not just in the countryside but in Fatsa centre – as many town-dwellers had houses and fields out in the villages. Not least Fikri Sönmez. 'His childhood was spent in hazelnut orchards,' his family told me.

*

Ahmet didn't want to speak in public when we met in a teahouse in the middle of town. Even decades on, he insisted, it's too risky. So instead we go back to his apartment, four storeys up, with a beautiful view of the sea to the north. As we begin to talk in his living room, he frees two pet budgies from their cage, who chirp along as he speaks. His is a clear and clipped Turkish, for he was a drama teacher by training. Born into a family of farmers over seventy years ago, he and his older brothers were the first from Kılıçlı to read, an Alevi village near hot springs, up in the hills close by.

He has a gentle presence, and white hair forming only a rim around his head, but his hardened, revolutionary past leaves its imprint on the way he talks even now. As with many old activists, when I ask them for their stories, they answer not with 'I' but with 'we', or speak instead to a different question entirely, about local, national, or global politics. As if their personal experience is a bourgeois distraction; but also, perhaps, because together they've constructed a version of those times that they want to protect.

Ahmet first met Fikri shortly after he had been released from his prison and opened his tailor's shop in the centre of town. He was a newly qualified teacher, posted to various schools in the area, but his wife came to work for Fikri himself. Both committed leftists, they began to spend more and more time at Fikri's shop – squeezed for space amongst its stacks of fabrics – or in the coffee-house next door. Indeed, Fikri's tailor's was known as 'The Academy', for it was always host to someone. As his son Yusuf had told me, it wasn't just at his shop either. 'He liked life and *rakı*', and perhaps four days a week would entertain family and friends at his home. Fatsa being a small town, most leftists in those days knew each other anyway – they were each other's husbands and wives, cousins and uncles, brothers and neighbours: one part socialist collective, one part traditional village ties. Over time, as Ahmet recalls, things were becoming more and more concrete. A cultural centre was set up in the mid-seventies, and increasingly teachers were recruited through the unions. But it wasn't just leftists that were grouping together. In Fatsa – as in the rest of Turkey – nationalists were organizing too. In martial arts schools and in far-right associations, The Grey Wolves, as they were known, were determined to fight back – to assist the state in its righteous battle against the godless, communist left. They had considerable resources to do so, tied as they were to Turkey's biggest far-right party, and its leader, a one-time colonel.

As Ahmet remembers, the violence started in 1975, with sticks, stones, and fists. Students from rival factions fought at high schools. But 'guns slowly found themselves on everyone's waist'. In nearby Korgan, a teacher suspected of being a Grey Wolf – a fascist, for the revolutionaries – was killed in the summer of 1976, though still Fatsa itself remained bloodless.[10] I ask Ahmet if he was scared at the time, a revolutionary in his mid-twenties. It was like 'riding a bike', he answers a little cryptically, 'you only fall if you don't know how to do it.' One of his two budgies, in sparkling turquoise, flutters past my ear and lands straight on his bald head, plucking at the few remaining hairs left.

Unlike the near-military discipline of the right, the Turkish left in those years was still fragmented. By one count, there were forty-eight different revolutionary factions.[11] But as the decade wore on, one group grew and grew: Dev Yol, 'The Revolutionary Path'. They put a new spin on the Marxist-Leninism of their earlier comrades: yes, they accepted, Turkey was under Western occupation, and could only liberate itself through armed struggle. But its focus for now should not be on the enemy abroad, but their manifestation here: on the fascists within the Turkish state, and organizing on its streets. It was a theory that soon became more popular than any other, and Dev Yol's literature had a circulation as high as a hundred and fifty thousand.[12] Perhaps, simply, it was a little more stirring, a bit closer to home, to square up to some fascists on your road. At the same time, Dev Yol was a fairly loosely organized front. Though there was a central committee at its top, it rarely controlled those below, its various units and branches across the country, who in turn had little contact with each other. It left each Dev Yol arm, then, with considerable room to move. Still, the basic logic had been set. 'We set out to create a resistance against fascism,' one leftist told me, arguing that they weren't an armed group, intent on kidnaps and assassinations, only that they carried weapons for their own defence, against attacks from the right. As Fikri's sons told me, their father walked around with a gun strapped to his waist, but he didn't really know how to use it.

Despite all this, it still seems a surprise when it actually happened, when the violence they talked about punctured their own lives, right on the corner of Fikri's tailor's shop. Kemal Kara was Fikri's apprentice, as well as the head of the cultural centre nearby. While Fikri was in prison, Kemal had paid the shop's rent by selling fish and lemons in the market, and bought his sons shoes and ice cream as well. A known leftist and Alevi, he was stabbed to death by a group of four or five, one summer's evening in 1977.[13,14] As Yusuf recalls, his father used to call Kemal 'his right arm', and spoke at his funeral in the days after. 'The atmosphere changed in an instant', one leftist told me; 'It could have been any one of us', said another. Fatsa's Dev Yol began to grow, and drive the nationalists out of town, combing through it street by street. Of course, this was part of the socialist theory, but perhaps there was something deeper underpinning it too: the pattern of the old Anatolian blood feud.

Through threats and beatings, by the following year most of the right had fled to neighbouring Samsun or Ordu along the coast. Some, of course, had been killed. I ask Ahmet whether he ever joined the clashes, and he laughs. 'That's a subjective question', he answers, 'to such a question you can say we joined when it was necessary, and we didn't when it wasn't.' A little unsatisfied, I ask if he ever shot anyone. 'I didn't clash with anyone, I didn't shoot anyone', he replies, as though he has said it dozens of times before, 'you're asking dangerous questions.' And the kinds of questions, he adds, that he was asked in court.

*

Of course, it was not just Fatsa that was tense; the whole country was spiralling out of control. It was in part a political malaise. Though Turkey had only two general elections across the decade it had more than ten governments, none of them single-party majorities. Instead, it was governed by awkward coalitions – for one brief spell, leftists together with Islamists – and fragile minorities. Ministers frequently contradicted each other in public; deputies, seemingly unable to pass any laws, ended up fighting each other in the assembly hall; and each time a new government was formed, they recolonized the state itself, replacing judges, policemen, teachers, and civil servants with their own.[15]

It was a politics singularly unable to deal with the crisis that faced it. For the Turkish economy was in trouble. The model until then had been for the state to foster Turkish industry: imported consumer goods were taxed heavily; homegrown enterprises received generous subsidies, if they weren't owned outright by the state; and the lira was kept high to help their factories bring in cheaper, heavy machines from abroad. 'The government sold everything,' as one Fatsa local put it, 'cigarettes and beer, sugar, it owned the factories and the land.' If it could produce impressive growth, it was also inefficient, and at times plain corrupt. State-run enterprises employed hundreds of thousands of workers – running huge losses – often only to hand out jobs to the right people. It was, all in all, an expensive business: inflationary, leaving the government in debt, and vulnerable to shocks across the world. And they kept coming across the decade: a painful string of oil crises and arms embargoes. Twice in two years, with the backing of international lenders, a left-wing government tried to solve a growing debt crisis by reducing state expenditure, increasing the prices charged by state-run enterprises, and devaluing the lira. But still the problems persisted. A late effort to reduce Turkish reliance on imports by rationing created not only bottlenecks in industry but a surging black market.[16]

It meant, to put it simply, real deprivation across the country. First imported goods like coffee and medicine disappeared, and then the daily basics: olive oil, margarine, sugar, and fuel. In the cities, people burnt their furniture for warmth, often sitting in the dark, for power cuts could last up to nine hours. Towards the end of the decade, inflation was running at over 100 per cent.[17] Fatsa suffered as everywhere else. Hazelnut farmers, now thoroughly integrated into the market, received the same pittance for their harvest, but found themselves struggling to buy what else they needed: soap, cigarettes, kerosene, and so on.

Amidst all of this, it seemed it was not so much the future of Turkey that was up for grabs, but its very territory, as all across the country youths from left and right fought over its streets, parcelling the nation into zones of control. They were normally young men, with frustrated aspirations: perhaps the first in their families to be educated, but jobless; or one of the five of every six students who took the university exam but were offered no place; or maybe simply those who came to the city and found it wasn't what they hoped. There were more political reasons for the violence too. When the far-right nationalists briefly entered government in 1977, for example, Grey Wolves all over boomed, and infiltrated the state – there were perhaps as many as a hundred thousand of them, and lots of them were weapons trained. Finally, there was a growing culture of martyrdom itself, of clashes and death not just as a means but ends in themselves. 'To die was to show courage to continue the struggle,' as one activist told me. Deaths led to funerals, which became rallies, which led to more clashes, and an endless cycle of violence.[18,19]

Slowly, Turkey was becoming a scarier place to be, even for those with no interest in politics whatsoever. My *baba* spent his teenage years not reading Marx but playing with circuit boards, convinced – he tells me with some pride – that it was computers not workers who would inherit the earth. Yet the atmosphere of Turkey in those years was hard to escape. He was accepted into İstanbul Technical University, but it was a place of student occupations and police raids, and always under threat of temporary closure. And before he could leave for good – to go to England and never return – much worse was to come. In May 1977, two hundred thousand people gathered for Workers' Day in İstanbul's Taksim Square. He wasn't at the rally, but he was nearby with friends, when mysterious gunmen opened fire from the rooftops around the square. 'We could hear it,' he tells me – the shots and the panic that followed – 'we had no idea what the fuck was going on.' Thirty-four people were killed.

These were years that still echoed in our home, decades on, as my *baba* played his piano, eyes closed, summoning them in an instant, filling the house with the mournful notes of 'Aldırma Gönül'. It was an old poem, transformed into a leftist anthem when he was young. Though he never sang, I could hear the words all the same – part beauty, part melancholy, part defiance – and what they must have meant to that nineteen-year-old boy. *Kurşun ata ata biter / Yollar gide gide biter / Mapus yata yata biter / Aldırma gönül aldırma.* The bullet that's been fired will end / the road you're travelling will end / the prison where you're sleeping will end / Don't mind, my heart, don't mind.

It wasn't just that the violence had grown larger, it had turned uglier too. For around its edges was a sectarian tension: nationalists tended to be Sunni; leftists were disproportionately from Turkey's Alevi minority. In late '78, in the southern city of Maraş, over a hundred Alevis were killed in far-right riots. The government responded by imposing martial law over much of the country. But few believed it could stop the descent.

*

In Fatsa meanwhile, amidst the turmoil, Dev Yol was growing. As the town was hit by long queues and shortages for goods at the official rate, and exorbitant prices for those on the black market, the revolutionaries hit on a simple, direct solution. They would raid the depots of stockpilers and 'hoarders', and – armed as they all were – tell the black-marketeers to hand out the goods at the legal price. In one raid, a queue of three thousand people turned up for margarine. In a region of heavily indebted hazelnut farmers, on some raids they tore up promissory notes. They led a series of hazelnut rallies, under banners against oligarchy and fascism, calling for *Fındıkta Sömürüye Son!*, 'An End to Exploitation in Hazelnuts!'. Adorned with red scarves, they walked across town to the pier, and met in their thousands in the square by the sea.[20]

They began to recruit more and more, holding solidarity nights and concerts with folk songs and worker-peasant anthems. It was 'like knitting a sweater', said one leftist – a healthcare worker here, a teacher there, a farmer there, until they had covered the whole region. In the countryside they began to organize after Friday prayers, discussing socialism in the courtyards of village mosques. They adapted in other ways. Dev Yol comrades agreed, for example, not to drink or gamble in public. Of course, there were still sporadic incidents of violence. Newspaper reports document, for example, the body of a religious student found decomposed in a hazelnut orchard, or a shooting at the beach house of a former far-right deputy – though in neither case were any suspects named.[21] But in truth, Dev Yol's success seemed to go beyond its threat of force; it was winning people over. It was, as one local explained, an exciting time: 'everyone had a book in their hand, everyone had a newspaper'. It was almost as if, in Fatsa at least, a class was bringing itself into being, forming its own consciousness – conservative, radical, and thoroughly suffused in the history of this place. Then came the election that would make it official.

*

Officially, across the country, Dev Yol was boycotting the senate and local elections that were due in October 1979. 'Why vote when the country is already ruled by the bosses and the IMF?' as one slogan had it. But it was a loosely organized thing, and in Fatsa they felt a little different. Didn't they have something special here? Couldn't they actually win? So when the incumbent mayor – a popular teacher from the CHP – fell seriously ill in the summer, and announced she would have to stand down, they decided to run an independent candidate of their own.

There was little question of who would do it, for everyone in town liked Fikri Sönmez. Of course, his revolutionary credentials were impeccable: he had been at the forefront of rallies and raids for years. But more importantly, he wasn't just for the people, he was of them. As one former comrade remembered, you'd see him raiding a warehouse one day, and cheering the local football team the next. He'd be at coffee-houses and circumcisions, weddings and funerals. And unlike his more educated peers, he spoke in more human tones: not of the proletariat and capital, but of workers and theft. He could be funny and sarcastic. 'Fikri could tell the same story twenty times,' recalled Ahmet, 'and you'd listen to the twenty-first.' It helped, as well, that he had a reputation across Fatsa for honest work, for handing back cash he found in suit pockets.

The campaign started in late summer, early autumn, the tail end of the season of heavy rains, fattening up the hazelnuts all across the region, turning their shells yellow. I find a video of him on the trail, giving his stump speech on a warm autumn day, dressed in an orange shirt and light jacket. It's a scratchy tape, and he can only be heard through a cheap microphone and the twang of feedback. But even so, beyond the Marxist theory, you can see he has a more primal authority: a deep chest and a deeper voice, a broad dark moustache and a heavy jaw. A man, as his family would tell me, with a weakness for his wife's Georgian cooking: for *mantı* dumplings and fried *kavurma*. Of course, it would be Fikri on the ballot, but all Dev Yol's activists would help run the campaign, directed from a central coffee-house. They split Fatsa into districts, each run by their own committee of four or five comrades, while women's committees would try and organize across the town too. And so they would go, knocking on doors and holding open-air meetings.[22] Those weeks, when the rains stopped and the sun reappeared, were always pregnant with hope in Fatsa – the time when farmers all across the Black Sea would pick up their ripe, fallen hazelnuts, or shake the trees for the remaining few, and lay them out to dry, almost ready to take to market. But for activists and those they were trying to persuade, if there was optimism in the air, it was a fragile thing.

Fikri survived three separate assassination attempts leading up to polling day. I walk to his old house by the highway, overlooking the sea – now falling apart, abandoned to graffiti, piles of rubbish, and two enormous stray dogs. It was here that saw the first and most serious attempt. As Fikri would later testify, as he got out of the car one evening, walked to his family home, and rang the doorbell, he was shot at from three different directions, leaving two wounds in his leg, before his assailants took off. Yusuf, twelve years old at the time, vaguely remembers him entering the house, and saying calmly that he'd been shot. He didn't understand enough to be afraid. For the rest of the campaign Fikri moved out of their home, but the risk remained. Just after he had left one meeting in a coffee-house, militants arrived to fire inside, killing two. Fikri felt abandoned by the authorities and, worse, he even recognized the first group who tried to take his life. They were local far-right nationalists, and fellow Georgians.[23,24] His opposition later complained of a 'different atmosphere' in the run-up to the election. Though there were no serious incidents against candidates from the other parties, their nerves were understandable. There were dozens of armed comrades organizing for Fikri. If they weren't explicitly threatening, they were surely intimidating. Nonetheless, the campaigns in all likelihood changed little . . . for everyone knew who was going to win. 'He was already the mayor,' Yusuf tells me of his father's reputation in the town, 'even when he wasn't the mayor.'

Demokrasi için sınav günü ran the headline of *Cumhuriyet* on 14 October 1979, 'exam day for democracy', alongside reports of the last day of campaigning across the country – stories that showed how frayed Turkish politics had become: a nationalist deputy was found travelling with an entourage with guns and dynamite in their car. There were local and senate elections in twenty-nine provinces, an electorate of eight million voters, and – as always – alcohol sales were banned while the polls were open.[25] In Fatsa, it was a landslide. Fikri received over half of the eight thousand votes cast, with none of the established parties even close. Perhaps, in those good months after the harvest and flush with cash, the locals had the courage to believe in something better. They felt they were on the brink of another world, one old comrade tells me, ready for 'the taste and pleasure of resistance.' In the main square, Fikri made a modest victory speech, lasting less than minute, promising that his struggle against exploitation 'will last for the rest of my life'. For all the young cadres, celebrations were muted. 'We were like priests,' one told me – they couldn't drink out in view.

The following day, *Cumhuriyet* reported that the opposition had now secured a majority – a new government was on its way. And buried amongst the other results was the tiny news that Fatsa, a little town up north, had been won by an independent.[26]

*

His team came to office inexperienced, but backed by the people and sure of their convictions. They had little time, therefore, for the bureaucratic procedures and niceties of local government, for the tedious division of power between the mayor, the municipal assembly, and the *muhtars*, the local district chiefs. As Fikri saw it, the members of the assembly – dominated by the traditional parties – were 'low quality and ignorant', representatives of a rotten system. The *muhtars* were even worse, arrogant and corrupt.[27]

Their revolutionary solution, therefore, was to sideline them entirely, and set up bodies to directly channel the popular will.

Ahmet – then twenty-nine, and one of the more senior members of the group – took up a position in the new public relations office, to hear from Fatsa locals face to face, and feed it back to the mayor's team. Meanwhile, they established People's Committees in districts across the town, ready to carry out municipal works. Elections to join the committees would be open to all, 'except for fascists'. Though as it happens they had to run the elections twice all the same. The first set of candidates, they claimed, were no good – aghast that one was a known prostitute. Still, the second round was not to everyone's liking either. 'A group of children,' said one disgruntled conservative, of the radical youth who seemed to be taking power all over town.[28]

After all the years of socialist discourse, it was through something a little earthier that the mayoral team would make their name: mud. Fatsa was full of it. The previous administration had launched a sewerage project but left it incomplete. Streets had been dug up and cobblestones turned over; when it rained, half-finished pits filled up with water; locals, as they waded through the streets, tried to avoid not only the mud but mosquitos and frogs too. And so – as the Dev Yol mythology goes – just one month into power, when Fikri was told it would take years to finish the works, he set the People's Committees on it instead. All over town, men were encouraged to pick up their wheelbarrows, pickaxes, and shovels, while women brought them food they had cooked at home. About one third of the town, they estimate, would take part in the Mud Campaign. It wasn't just Fatsa locals: Dev Yol cadres came from all across Turkey, from Kars in the east to İstanbul out west; local left-leaning municipalities lent their tractors and pick-up trucks. First they removed the mud, then they cobbled the roads, then they decided – while they were at it – to make the streets wider too. It was done in six days.[29]

Before we sat down in his apartment, Ahmet drove me around

Fatsa to show me what they had done – his revolutionary spirit apparently extending to traffic regulations: for half an hour we go the wrong way up one-way roads, driving on pavements, terrifying pedestrians. Even as we entered the car, he briefly stepped out to examine the pedals before bashing the clutch back in place with his fist. Satisfied, we drove on. On one road – Sevgi Caddesi – running parallel to the sea up the hill, he proudly explained it was laid down by the campaign. Other parts of that era, of its geography, still live on if only in his head. As we passed through one district, he told me this is where the 'fascists' lived, before Dev Yol chased them all away.

The mayoralty continued with its revolutionary programme, seeking to harness direct, people power to tackle petty municipal problems, even if without regard for formal, legal process. Permitless buildings, long allowed to stand because of their powerful owners, were demolished; new entrances to Fatsa from the highway were opened. Local authorities moved shop to shop, checking their prices were fair, and turned a blind eye to revolutionary raids where they weren't. At one point – and surely to their great delight – they uncovered a stockpile of over one hundred containers of oil, owned by an opposition member of the assembly. Beyond it all, they were trying to foster a new culture in Fatsa too: thousands turned up for anti-fascist protests; the town was covered in leftist graffiti; and, much to the displeasure of local traders, one day in March 1980 the revolutionaries forced them to close down their businesses for an hour, in honour of Mahir Çayan and the other nine revolutionaries who had been killed a decade before. It culminated in April, just as hazelnut buds had reappeared on green branches all over, with an event to mark Fatsa's own spring. Journalists and artists all across Turkey were invited to the People's Culture Festival, in an exhibition 'against the dominant bourgeois culture' of workshops, film screenings, concerts, dances, and panel discussions.[30] Ahmet – a creative arts teacher by training after all – ended up directing the Children's Choir. 'Çocuk İşçi Marşı', the Children's Worker March, they sang in their school uniforms, marching on the spot, left hands, in fists, in the air.

Fatsa, slowly, was drawing attention, and not all of it welcome. Twice in early 1980, security forces searched the municipality offices. For during a cold war, in a nation bordering the Soviet Union itself, to be so openly on the left was to court risk. But perhaps even more heretically, in such a statist nation, where the *devlet*, the state, is seen as almost something sacred, to set up these new, strange bodies of power was something else entirely. The raids were perhaps just warnings, but already – barely six months into office – Fikri seemed to be feeling the strain. It was a life of constant meetings, long public gatherings, and little sleep, and his health was suffering. As his family told me, he had bouts of breathlessness and chest pain. He seemed tired and out of energy. Perhaps he also missed his social life of old. As his son Yusuf reminded me, the revolutionary ban on drinking was still in place. So every night when he could – to the anger of his pious, upright wife – he sat at home, and nursed his double *rakı* over ice.

*

In Ankara, the mood was turning. The elections that brought Dev Yol to power in Fatsa also saw the end of Turkey's left-wing Prime Minister – a journalist and a poet – to be replaced by Süleyman Demirel, a burly, husky-voiced conservative. His was a minority government, with tacit support both from Islamists and the far right, but it was an administration permanently under threat from another power entirely: a military that was growing impatient with Turkey's politicians once again. As if to highlight their own impotence, in April 1980, when the assembly had to elect a new President, it took them over one hundred ballots before they could agree. Eager to rescue the economy once and for all, the new government instigated a programme that could not be further from the socialist haven envisioned up in Fatsa. A plan unveiled in January sought to roll back the state, remove price restrictions and subsidies, and devalue the currency again. Further measures were on their way – limiting the right to strike, and the number of employees on the state's book – but they were hard to implement. Turkey was still a country seething with strikes and occupations.

The violence did not stop, claiming by that point as many as twenty lives a day. Flicking through newspaper archives, by the spring they are reporting daily street battles and deaths, but they are more lists than stories, barely considered news at all: in Batman, Mardin, Konya, Sivas, Kayseri, Antakya, Ankara, İstanbul, Yozgat, İzmit. And still, the danger of sectarianism remained: in Çorum, central Anatolia, marches through Alevi neighbourhoods beginning in May left dozens dead. The government sent in three battalions of the army to try to restore the peace. Though Fatsa was quiet relative to most of Turkey, the government still seemed unnerved. In April, they appointed a new governor for Ordu, the wider province, who had previously moved from city to city as a police chief – known not only for his harsh methods, but for his links with the far-right too. 'The power of the government will be shown in Ordu,' he reportedly said on taking office;[31] 'We already knew he was a fascist,' recalled one old revolutionary.

*

In the new governor's eyes, Ordu province – and the districts around Fatsa in particular – were being run by *kızıl teröristler*, red terrorists. So he began to try to organize against them. Left-leaning mayors, even those from the established parties, began to complain of pressure and interference; far-right associations were set up, bringing in nationalists from all over the region; their sister newspapers started to open new offices. As nationalists were appointed to positions across Ordu, the tension was growing. Leftists – who had known this part of Turkey as a safe refuge for years – began to resist. The violence surged. While there had only been a handful of murders before April, there were nearly fifty in the three months after the governor's appointment.[32] For the state of course was not an innocent bystander in the conflict between left and right – how could it ever have been? Instead, it was a weapon to be used.

As Ahmet remembers that year, 'the demands for defence began to come from everywhere', for setting up village barricades or arming new recruits. And if there is one regret, one admission of fault from the revolutionaries forty years on – however difficult it is to prise out – it is this: they lost control of their own. 'We couldn't train enough people in the struggle,' says Ahmet diplomatically; 'There was a lumpen group,' another told me, 'and it got a bit messy.' A conservative relative of Fikri is more blunt: 'Thirty cadres became three thousand, and most of them were bastards.' As Dev Yol expanded in Fatsa – first after the election victory, and then to meet the challenge of the new governor – it became less and less disciplined. Some simply were spoiling for a fight with the fascist threat that was growing around them. Others were less ideological still. Young men, drunk on power, threatened citizens for money, or used their new positions to sort out family disputes. As the *Washington Post* claimed, they robbed the rich to buy weapons, commandeered cars, and beat people up in the street.[33] They were also playing right into the governor's hands.

The spark came in a village a few hours inland from Fatsa. In early July, a Dev Yol rally of a few thousand ended in a clash between revolutionaries and security forces: buildings were set alight, vehicles were burned, and three leftists and one junior officer were killed. At the soldier's funeral, the governor promised that those responsible would 'drown in a pool of blood.'[34] Turkey turned its attention to little Fatsa once more. In the press, it was described as 'Little Moscow' or a 'Liberated Zone', a place where Muslims couldn't pray. As Ahmet explained, 'black propaganda' had begun to spread against them, 'we knew we were being surrounded'. One week later, the Chief of the Armed Forces came to visit the new governor, inspecting troops before flying out again by helicopter. Mayor Fikri, meanwhile, denied to reporters the rumours that you needed a passport to enter Fatsa, that it was some kind of Paris Commune. He blamed the governor for the violence too.[35] But things were moving against him. As all remembered here, when Prime Minister Demirel was asked by a journalist about the months of sectarian violence that had just ended in Çorum, where dozens had been killed, he replied, '*Çorum'u bırakın, Fatsa'ya bakın.*' 'Forget about Çorum, look at Fatsa.'

The night before the end, they held a press conference in a central Fatsa hotel. It was warm and stuffy, and Ahmet tells me Fikri seemed a little off, mumbling and under pressure. Again, Fikri denied that Fatsa had separated from the republic. Meanwhile, the local branches of Fatsa's traditional parties – conservatives, Islamists, social democrats, republicans alike – released a statement that Fatsa was peaceful, and invited the Prime Minister to come and see for himself.[36] As the papers later reported, by nine o'clock almost everyone was in bed. They had heard the rumours that the city was surrounded. A few children scattered broken bottles at the town entrances, to impede whoever might come; while older revolutionaries improvised barricades with stones, branches, and cars. Then they slipped away into the orchards in the upper parts of the town, to watch what would enfold. Ahmet headed to a house up in the hills with Fikri and a few others. None of them slept.

*

The atmosphere in Ahmet's apartment changes slightly, as he talks about the Operation. It is stiller in his living room, and even his budgies have quietened. It was 4 a.m. on 11 July 1980, he remembers, and the first they heard was the tread of tanks, 'breaking through the darkness of the night'. They grew louder as they entered the town centre. They had expected maybe some armed fascist civilians to attack, but this was on a different scale. A mechanized infantry battalion, three gendarmerie commando squads, troops and police from other provinces as reinforcements, and three assault boats.[37] In that early light before the sun had risen, slightly stripped of colour, Ahmet could see them coming, he tells me, out on the Black Sea.

They had already decided not to resist, 'otherwise the place would be burnt down'. Besides, he laughs at himself, 'we only had fourteen guns between us.' The plan instead was to escape, out to villages beyond. As they watched from the hill, they could see the soldiers spreading out and searching homes. It was time. And then, Ahmet continues, a deep voice from somewhere in the room refused. *'Ben kalacağım,'* said Fikri, 'I'll stay.' A quiet followed. 'I am the elected mayor,' he went on, 'there is nothing they can accuse me of.' Though he surely knew – as they all did – that it wasn't true. Amongst his five comrades, it was a silence of shock, but perhaps of guilt too. They knew also that for Fikri – fifteen years older than them, and already struggling with his health – a life on the run would not be easy, yet they had no doubts they should escape either. 'For fifteen minutes, we couldn't convince him,' Ahmet remembers. As he speaks, he clears his throat and his eyes moisten, and after two hours of conversation – ideological and abstract – it is this moment that moves him more than any other. 'We hugged, tears in our eyes, and left . . . Even now it feels bitter, that we left him like that alone.' They jumped out of the window and went.

The operation was announced to the town centre through its

minarets, declaring a curfew, and calling on residents to denounce those in hiding. Locals, reported one newspaper, watched from behind their curtains, and for most of the day the only sound to be heard was the boots of soldiers and the tread of tanks on Fatsa's newly laid streets. On the outskirts, bulldozers came to take apart the barricades. The authorities moved from house to house, arresting hundreds, loading them onto trucks, to be taken away to the local fish and meat factory for interrogation. Ultimately, around three thousand – nearly one in three adults – were taken into custody. A sixteen-year-old boy complained to journalists he had been taken to the factory, where there was barely room to stand, and heard the sound of screaming; an old man, his white moustache made yellow by years of cigarettes, reported that he was detained merely for having a licensed gun in his home. It wasn't just people who were taken away either. As one report noted, soldiers confiscated books and the works of the communist poet Nâzım Hikmet.[38]

They took eight or nine sacks of books from Fikri's family home. Yusuf, then thirteen years old, watched on from a chicken coop out back, where he hid for three days. His abiding memory was of the two masked men leading the soldiers. They were informants, recognized by Yusuf and everyone else in town as local nationalists who had fled Fatsa a few years before. In all, there were about ten of them around town, pointing to houses without speaking. I come across a photo of one, and it is haunting, almost inhuman: a man, flanked by policemen, in a suit with slightly flared trousers, without a tie in the summer heat; and then, over his face, an improvised white cloth stretched across his brow, his nose, his mouth, with holes poked out at the eyes. It was confirmation – if any in Fatsa needed it – of how entwined the state and the far-right had become, and of how low the authorities could stoop: as it emerged in the following days, four of the ten informants had outstanding arrest warrants.[39]

One crisp Fatsa night, I speak to Gülin, her breath lit up against the dark by the streetlamps behind her. She agreed to an interview, she tells me, because I have a trustworthy face – she could almost be my grandmother, and it's hard to imagine that at the time all these protagonists were just past twenty. 'We grew up a little early,' she tells me, of her experience in the women's groups in Fatsa, 'we tried to assume responsibility for the country's future as well as our own.' Fleeing up to the hills during the operation, she was arrested in the end. 'How did the gendarmes treat you? I ask. 'Sizce?' she says with a smile, 'What do you think?', before adding 'Best not to ask that to anyone in Fatsa.' I ask whether she was tortured. 'Sizce?' she replies again. As we talk of Fikri's fate, she seems pained even now. 'He must have been like an uncle to you all,' I say, before she has one last correction, 'He was like a father.'

For forty days, Fikri could not be reached. He had been taken to the meat and fish factory on the outskirts of Fatsa, surrounded by marsh. As his lawyer later told me, they had turned the slaughter room into a torture workshop, beating him over the back and stomach with sandbags so it wouldn't leave a bruise. His internal organs, he says, never recovered. Other survivors left different testimonies of abuse: sleep deprivation, forced nudity, and stress positions for days. Towards the end of August, Fikri was moved to prison, his reign as mayor decisively over. It had lasted not even one hazelnut season.

Turkey though had already moved on. Within a week of the operation, Fatsa had fallen out of the news. For what was one small town, when all the country was in chaos? Besides, it would see something similar soon enough.

*

Again, the announcement came in the early hours. As it was relayed to the nation on TV and radios at four in the morning, 12

September, the military had 'taken the decision to take control of the country'. It came from the Chief of the Armed Forces, the same man who had inspected the troops around Fatsa the days before its own military intervention two months before. Across the country, he says, five thousand had been killed in the last two years, education had been disrupted, millions of workdays lost. Still, he reassures his audience, the newly established National Security Council believed in democracy, but for now, 'resistance to the junta will be punished heavily.'

Tanks and armoured personnel carriers moved onto the streets; checkpoints were set up on major roads; soldiers patrolled the streets, and the searches for the wanted got underway. The Prime Minister, his cabinet, the main opposition leaders, and a hundred other deputies were detained. The political parties and trade unions were shut down. And on that first Friday, an all-day curfew was put in place. My *hala*, my aunt, was five years old at the time, and it is one of her earliest memories: sent out to quickly buy bread on the deserted streets, for the family reasoned no soldier would stop a little girl.

There was little resistance. As one conservative paper described it, the coup was *kadife eldivenli*, 'velvet-gloved'; another claimed it had been met across the country with 'a sigh of relief'.[40] It was the most significant coup in the republic's history, aiming not just to take power but to fundamentally, brutally, reset the place for good. Over the next few years, activists and ordinary citizens were detained and tried in martial courts in their hundreds of thousands. Tens of thousands meanwhile lost their jobs, or fled the country. Scarcely a single political organization – from parties to unions to civil society associations – remained intact. The press and broadcasters were squeezed as never before: everything from *Time Magazine* to Tarzan was banned. It was an attempt, as one scholar put it, to create a new, passive citizen.[41] And of course to reaffirm the state's most basic power too – it confiscated eight hundred thousand weapons from its citizens.

*

In Fatsa, a few Dev Yol revolutionaries remaining at large launched a desperate and ill-fated guerrilla war, but most were now behind bars. Indeed even Yusuf – thirteen going on fourteen – was rounded up during the coup, and sent to adult prison for over six months. Of course, his father, and older brother, were already there, subject to interrogations, torture, and the more mundane procedures of a military court. 'If I had ruled like the others,' Fikri wrote in his testimony, 'with the latest car and a bottle of whisky in my hand, none of this would have happened. I chose to serve the people and not the powers.' When the trial came in 1983, a few hours west of Fatsa, nearly eight hundred defendants were present in the hall at once, charged with subverting the constitution by use of armed force, as well as a series of murders, thefts, and bombings across the last decade.[42] As Fikri's lawyer told me, of the hundreds on trial, perhaps only forty, or even just a handful, had really been violent, armed militants – the rest were just radicals under the umbrella of the same organization. Besides, he points out, most of the violence occurred *after* Fikri was removed from power.

Of course, the evidence against them was rarely watertight. Much of it was based on testimony from far-right nationalists, or confessions from fellow revolutionaries seeking lighter sentences – famously, even senior members of Dev Yol's Fatsa branch turned on their comrades. And obviously, many were desperate simply for the torture to stop. As one policeman later admitted, leftists were beaten and shocked with old phones;[43] an activist told me electric nodes were attached to fingers and penis, before adding, without wanting to elaborate, that he 'still can't sit down in a dentist's chair.' All in all, over four thousand Dev Yol activists were tried across the country, in cases that lasted for years. Fikri Sönmez never saw his to the end. As his lawyer told me, weakened by the beatings in prison, and increasingly troubled by his heart, he was deteriorating all the time. He was still a proud man, angered by the libel he read about Fatsa, and at times still revived by that old revolutionary spirit, seeking to organize amongst his comrades inside – but his health was failing all the same. By 1985, he was unable to eat, and could drink only milk, as if a new-born once more. He died of a heart attack. His wife once said they found it difficult even to find an imam to wash his body, at a funeral few were allowed to attend. As her son Yusuf tells me, in the new, cowed Turkey, they had been utterly cast out. Even close friends wouldn't stop to talk or say hello. He was on the cusp of adulthood now, but it was just like it had been thirteen years before, when all the other children in his first days of school called him the communist's son.

Of the hundreds on trial in Fatsa, fourteen others died before the verdict, finally delivered in 1989: around half were acquitted, over a dozen given life sentences, and eight the death penalty. Ahmet was one of them. After leaving Fikri alone in that house, the morning of the operation, he was arrested a few months later. As he repeated to me, he had always denied being directly involved in any violence, and successfully appealed his conviction. Indeed, none of the Dev Yol revolutionaries were executed, and by 1992 all had been released.[44] But they returned to a very different town.

*

Already, in the years immediately after their radical experiment, Fatsa seemed to be on the turn again. When the military junta put a new, more restrictive, constitution to a referendum in 1982 – before handing power back to civilians – it passed with 90 per cent approval across Turkey, though of course in conditions neither free nor fair. In Fatsa, 95 per cent of the electorate voted in favour.

If then the town was merely acting out of fear – still recovering from the trauma inflicted on it by the state just two years before – soon it was out more decisively on that same path. In elections ever since, Fatsa has voted solidly for conservatives and Islamists. As one old revolutionary told me, once they were all locked away, Fatsa filled with *tarikats*, religious sects offering courses in the Koran and dormitories for the local youth. Now, they complained, it's hard here to even get a drink. It's something in the Black Sea character, offers another: brave and stubborn, when they are on the left, they are the most committed leftists; when they are on the right, they are far to the right as well.

Fatsa took off in another direction too. For 1980 marked not only the end of the organized left in Turkey, but the beginning of its capitalist present. Even in June 1980 – a month before the Fatsa operation – the country received a $1.6 billion loan from the IMF, after its most savage currency devaluation yet. More restructuring was to come. On the eastern outskirts of town, on the industrial estate by the Bolaman stream, I go to meet one final former revolutionary. At the entrance of his factory, even on a Saturday morning, I see forklifts going back and forth, packaging and loading hazelnut spread – hundreds of neatly stacked jars ready to go. After I'm checked by security, an assistant takes me through to his office: a flatscreen TV on the wall, trophies on his desk. Another member of staff brings me tea. 'When did you become capitalists?' I ask him, and he laughs. 'We are still trying.' The firm is called DKC, named after the initials of the three founders' children. But it has another meaning too, he says. Devrim Komün Komitesi. 'The Revolutionary Commune Committee'. Perhaps the spirit lives on.

9. The Orchid Ice Cream

1980s – Maraş

WE ARE WALKING IN WHITE COATS AND HAIR NETS, WITH elastic blue covers over our shoes, down a long corridor to the turnstiles that only unlock once you've disinfected your hands in the automatic sanitizer above. It's 9 a.m. on a Saturday, but you'd be hard pressed to know the time or the day in here – almost windowless and forever busy – only that it is something resolutely of the twenty-first century: all steel pipes and workers scuttling around, head to toe in white, under a harsh white light.

It reflects off Mehmet's head, a bright spot on his scalp. He is in his seventies now, and his hair is long gone. In the *börek* room, I try to engage him in conversation, over the whirring of machines and the clanking of metal, but he has more important things to do. We enter another room, and around a table four headscarved women are making *kadayif*, their hands working away at the shredded dough, their fingers alert and dextrous. He tastes the powdered pistachios in heaps between them. I can almost feel his employees cowering, as he moves on elsewhere, and checks the apples for another dessert. Cheeses, breads, *kadayifs*, *böreks*, cakes – we walk from room to room, all warm with the smell of baking, stirring, stuffing, and sugaring. I have not had breakfast, but still I'm not tempted. For this place feels more spaceship than kitchen.

We step into another country – cold storage – and the temperature is suddenly biting. It's quieter here, and I can hear our footsteps: me, Mehmet, and his entourage. Again, I try and ask him, to reflect on how far he's come, but still nothing. And then we arrive at the heart of it, the food where it all began: *dondurma*. Ice cream. Steel pipes up the walls and over our heads pump goat's milk into giant cauldrons in the mixing rooms next door, where machines churn out ice cream in all colours. We pass the chocolate, oozing out in a never-ending, extremely unappetizing stream. Another machine prints out six perfect little white droplets at a time. Still, there are dozens of workers all in white on the move, working around the steel tables, packaging it all up, checking the equipment, or – perhaps – trying to avoid Mehmet's attention, the owner of this vast dessert campus.

*

Visit any tourist town along Turkey's southern coast – Bodrum, Fethiye, Antalya – and sooner or later you will find its famous ice creams, and the show of the peddlers who sell them: the velvet waistcoats, the shouts of *maşallah*, the ring of brass bells. He'll lure customers in with a cast-iron stick, scoops stuck at the end, only to pull it away as they try to grab them; perhaps he'll dab ice cream on their nose as they reach forward next; then finally handing it to the poor tourist, before another quick jerk of his stick leaves only an empty cone in their hand. It's called Maraş ice cream, after the city it comes from, a thousand kilometres inland.

Maraş – or Kahramanmaraş, as it's officially called – is on the country's southern edge too, but it is a different Turkey. If you follow the shore east, at a certain point, the coast marks the border no more. The sea dips down further south; Turkey's frontier heads resolutely east. And so, around the plains of the Euphrates are the regions whose southern borders touch not the Mediterranean but Syria instead. And they are not like the easy, secular, wealthy regions to their west, but something a little more conservative, a little more Anatolian at heart.

Inescapably, it is a strange time to visit. The first thing you notice is the wind, bitterly cold and loud, blowing through spaces where buildings should be, and whipping up against the canvas of the tents. Even now – months later – people are still afraid to sleep indoors again. Not long ago, in this city and a dozen others near it, two earthquakes in a single February day left tens of thousands dead. In one district, I see a crane – they are all over – by a building not yet collapsed but not safe either, slowly picking it apart to a low rumble: the creaks of its boom, the whirrs of its engine, and the surprisingly soft sound of apartment floors falling to the ground. A cloud of dust covers the streets, and all of us watching on. In another quarter, a five-hundred-year-old mosque is in pieces, its minaret reduced to a stump, and the new home of a nest of brooding pigeons. Amongst all this – amongst such loss of history and life – of course I was unsure whether to be here at all, whether it was frankly absurd to come and talk about ice cream. But I was reassured by locals I had been in touch with long before. Beyond the rubble, they wanted to show what this place once was.

On my first day, a Maraş food historian – dressed all in black, in mourning for the parents and sibling she has lost – insists I come to visit her temporary office, and cooks me boiled *köfte* on a camping stove. She tells me of the city's rich cuisine: its red pepper flakes, in dark and seductive red; its spiced and buttery cookies; and of course its *dondurma*, the dessert she remembers most, on summer Ramadan nights. She puts me in touch with a couple of Maraş explorers, who take me out to the mountains surrounding the city, to the heart of the region's bond with its ice cream. In a battered old Renault Megane, we drive up, past the lower hills, with their olive trees in silvery green, and up into the peaks above, all limestone and pine. Amongst the mountains – still with their snow, like a light powdering of sugar – they point to the highest around: Berid Dağ, Beirut Mountain, so called because, as the legend goes, you can see the Lebanese capital from its summit. This is an area on the civilizational borderlands, tied not just to the Mediterranean in the west and Anatolia in the north, but the flats of Arabia to the south. As we get out the car, on a small mountain plateau, we see a couple of swallows in the sky above – a pair of black boomerangs in the blue, and a sign, despite the cold, of spring on its way. We walk out into the grass, amongst its purple carpets of grape hyacinths, and the yellow of wild pansies, both of which have just bloomed. But still, here in south Turkey, the winter seems to be clinging on. The orchids have not yet opened. Normally, Maraş teems with them: violet ones; yellow ones; ones with flowers shaped like stars. There are dozens of wild orchids endemic in the mountains here, and without them there'd be no ice cream at all.

*

I am sat down at Mehmet's restaurant, the headquarters of his empire with an old-fashioned feel: wood-panelled walls, carpets woven into the tables, leather-backed seats, and soft orange lights. He is a man in demand, and initially I am kept waiting, while he circles around the place slowly, a little sharklike, checking everything is up to standard, occasionally dressing down his employees, and hitting them with tea towels. Then he sits down with a burst of energy, and a lemon tea, and we start. 'Do you know where you are?' he says by way of introduction, 'The birthplace of ice cream . . . You're next to Mehmet Kanbur, from Kahramanmaraş.' I nod along, and he continues, 'Who am I? I come from a family of four generations of ice-cream makers.' He seems a man pleased to be interviewed. At times, conversation disappears into old Maraş poems and obscure sayings. He has a habit too of sharing folksy, motivational quotes before asking me, '*Ne dedim*', 'What did I say?', and waiting for me to repeat – to test my Turkish perhaps, or to check I was listening. 'To look is one thing, to watch is another, *ne dedim?*'; 'Life is not something to write, it's something to live, *ne dedim?*' Slowly, he begins to share enough.

The neighbourhood, he tells me, knew his family as *sütçüler*, milk-sellers. They lived in a small house in central Maraş: Mehmet, his parents, his two brothers, his sister, and three hundred goats in their backyard. It was the 1950s, and a very different city, with little industry, no electricity or gas, and often barely even enough cash to go round. As Mehmet recalls, they used to exchange their milk and yoghurt for a clutch of eggs or a loaf of bread. In the summer though they put their milk to better use. Between April and October – marked by Children's Day at one end, and Republic Day the other – they made ice cream, all under the guidance of their father, who had learnt from his father, and his father before that. 'We were born into ice cream,' Mehmet tells me, 'we opened our eyes to it.'

It was not an easy business. In a place without power, without fridges or freezers, Mehmet and his brothers would first have to go and collect ice. 'Summer, winter, there was always snow,' he says. Indeed overlooking Maraş is Ahır Mountain, like a giant wall at its north face, with barely a jag or ripple, going straight up from brown to green to white, and then into the clean blue of the sky. They would head out early in the morning, Mehmet explains, and scrape away at the cold. For ice cream, they would bundle the snow up and cover it, before heading back down the slopes. But you could make an older recipe too – *karsambaç* – an Ottoman dish of crushed ice flavoured with fruit, molasses, and nuts. 'You never take the first layer of snow,' he warns me, 'it's poisonous.' You need to dig deeper for the older snow beneath. Though over sixty years on, I can still picture Mehmet there now. He has an earthy voice and dark skin, and the air of someone who spent their youth outside, beneath the southern Turkish sun. It was a childhood that spoke to an old Turkish tradition. As one food historian wrote, the Ottoman state had gathered and stored ice for centuries, always ready to cool the Sultan's sherbets. Some wealthy citizens even had their own snow pits, and would distribute ice to poorer neighbourhoods in summer as charity, gratefully received in handkerchiefs and bowls.[1]

Once Mehmet and his brothers had the snow to cool, of course they would need the milk, coaxed from one of their three hundred goats. Though they milked their goats at home, they knew that the ones who grazed on the mountains made it better – rich on a diet of hyacinths, crocuses, and thyme. Then finally came the orchids, and the forty different types that grew up on the Maraş slopes – though only the best, Mehmet insists, from the orchids higher up, are good enough for *dondurma*. Once the plant is ripped out from the earth, you can see its two tubers underneath: one, brown and wrinkled, that developed the plant this year; and the other, white and swollen, ready to do the same the next. The first is thrown away. The second is boiled, dried, and pounded into a powder called *sahlep*. 'You become an expert in it,' Mehmet says, breathing in deeply with his eyes closed, as if there were *sahlep* right there under his nose, 'you can smell it when it's good.' Used for a drink in itself – and long said to cure all sorts – *sahlep* is crucial for how ice cream here is made. Namely, in the words of one writer, because when it's mixed with liquids, it has 'the consistency of drying concrete.'[2]

The process, as ever, has its own mystique. As another ice-cream master in the city once explained, first, over a wood fire, you heat the milk in a copper cauldron, stirring sugar in with a wooden spoon. Then, when it is 'hot enough to burn your finger', you throw in the powdered *sahlep*, which dissolves and 'acts like yarn', threading it all together, as the mix becomes denser and denser by the minute. As it cools, the *dondurmacı* keeps whisking away, to avoid a sugary, milky sludge. A little colder still, it's then transferred into a cylindrical copper bucket, itself placed in a mulberry wood barrel filled with snow. And here the real work begins, as the master beats at it with a cast-iron stick, pounding it around, stretching it out, like a baker kneading dough. Finally, it's left to cool a little more.[3] The result is an ice cream unlike any other: elastic, heavy in your hand, sometimes hard enough to hack with a saw, and able to go days without melting. It is particularly white too, for goat's milk is rich in vitamin A. 'Even more than breast milk', according to one Turkish trade magazine.[4]

If the method of *maraş* ice cream is a little mysterious, its history is too. As the improbable legend goes, it was invented inadvertently by a *sahlep* salesman, used to frequenting Ottoman palaces and mansions around town centuries ago. At the end of one winter day's work – and for a reason never explained – he buried his leftovers with sugar and milk in the ground. The next morning, he came back to unearth a thickened and frozen new dessert, which has been sold on the streets here ever since. Another less romantic account claims it was brought to Maraş just over a hundred years ago, by a trader running from the law in Aleppo over the border, bringing with him a Syrian technique for ice cream.[5] Mehmet, though, is insistent it has an even deeper past. Pointing to the ancient Roman ruins around the city, he tells me that the Romans must have learnt ice cream from Maraş locals thousands of years ago, before bringing it back to Italy, and exporting their *gelato* out from there. When I laugh, thinking he is joking, he asks, both rhetorically and seriously, 'Well did we ever go to Rome?'

Regardless of its origins, it was, as Mehmet I sense is keen to portray, tough and heavy labour. 'You do it manually, by hand with an iron bar. You hit it and hit it and hit it,' he says, 'and your arms grow.' Indeed, he is short, but underneath his shirt, I see his biceps are still large. It was manly work too – the Arabic word for orchids, he tells me, means fox testicles, and they are a famous aphrodisiac. He shows me a picture of him working the ice cream perhaps half a century ago. He was young then, but was already losing his hair – a sign, I remember reading once, of men with too much testosterone to bear.

The family would then do their best to sell what they had made. They hawked on the streets, but they had a little stall too – a small thing of four tables opened by his grandfather – where Mehmet learned not only to make ice cream, but *börek* and *baklava* as well. He was a young man rarely content to sit still, who left middle school to start working full time. One summer, he travelled to İzmir, to peddle ice cream to holidaymakers on the Aegean coast. It was there, he tells me, where he learnt not just to make food but how to sell it. Working an ice-cream cart next to two other young hawkers – one selling pickles, and one almonds on ice – he was taught the importance of market patter. It seems a lesson that he never let go – even now as we speak, every now and again he blurts into a different voice, a different persona. And as his father opened a larger, grander patisserie downtown, both he and Mehmet agreed what he should do next: he would head off to military service, and then return to lead the family business on to even bigger things.

*

One of the restaurant's many suited waiters sets a plate in front of me, and on it, not so much a scoop as a boulder of ice cream: large, bright white, and tough. I force my knife through it, and still it resists a little, as I feel the handle push against the skin of my palm. And then that familiar taste – of childhood holidays out west – and the texture of an ice cream that simply refuses to melt, that unless you chew will sit on your teeth and make them ache with cold.

Maraş saw its first professional patisserie in the 1950s, opened by two brothers said to export their ice cream to other cities in large Thermos bottles.[6] Over the next decade, as electricity spread across the city, bringing fridges and freezers with it, all of a sudden ice-cream masters could cool their ice cream much easier, and store it for longer. The arduous trips to the mountains were no more. Slowly, *dondurma* in the city started to grow – a change, no doubt, that offended the purists. Cow's milk, bleached white, was being used instead of goat's, some complained; *sahlep* was being adulterated with mastic gum and starch, said others.[7] Yet still, the demand increased. And so it was that Mehmet's father Yaşar opened their larger Yaşar Pastanesi in 1964. It would be that patisserie where Mehmet would soon take over, his two younger brothers at his side, but not before learning a few other things first.

In his early twenties, after his military service, Mehmet flew to Rome. He didn't speak Italian, and he had little money, but he was curious: why was this place so famous for its ice cream? Touring around its *gelaterias* for three months, he came, he tells me, to a few different conclusions. The first – and, perhaps, the one he came to Italy with already decided – was that their ice cream was no better. The second though, he would more begrudgingly admit, was that it was more developed, with lots of different flavours, 'like fruit ice cream'. Maraş *dondurma* came only in white, with its natural taste of *sahlep*, sugar, and milk. And the last, and most important, was that they weren't beating out ice cream by hand, they were using new and sparkling machines. 'Allah Allah,' he recalls saying to himself, 'imagine if I used these for ice cream back home.' He returned to Maraş, collecting money and gold from everyone he knew – relatives, neighbours, local housewives, and traders –before heading back to Italy once more. He bought a small ice-cream machine that would allow him to start producing in small batches. 'Without technology,' he tells me, 'we could never have sold outside here.'

Slowly, business was beginning to take off. They started delivering ice cream, first to a military unit stationed nearby, then to the city of Adana down the coast, and then further afield still. They began to transport *dondurma* in refrigerated trucks; they bought more machines, and across the 1970s, they expanded even more. I ask Mehmet exactly when he took over the firm, and when he too wanted to turn it into something bigger, but he is vague again, disappearing into aphorisms and clichés. But clearly, he was a young man who wanted to leave his imprint on the world. In 1980, Yaşar Pastanesi moved to the city's most prestigious, most central street. I had been to visit that morning. Outside it, stood a huge plastic ice-cream sculpture, and streetlights branded with the patisserie's name. Though peering inside the window, as everywhere in this city, it was a different scene: a mess of rubbish and shattered glass.

*

1980, of course, was a pivotal time not just for Mehmet and his family firm, but for Turkey as a whole. After years of political drift and street-level violence, the September coup had sought to set the country on a different course, free from activists, the unions, and their endless strikes and occupations. In the 1983 elections that followed, it could be free from any political parties the military disapproved of too: only three of the fifteen that applied were permitted to stand. Under the stewardship of Turgut Özal – first as Economics Minister under the military junta, and then as vic-torious Prime Minister – it was to embrace the capitalist moment. These were the early years, after all, of Thatcher and Reagan. The currency was devalued, the borders opened to trade, and the full force of capital unleashed – with the ultimate aim of turning Turkey into an exporting powerhouse, selling its goods to the world. And into a nation of consumers too. 'Turkey has changed so much,' my *babaanne* once told my *baba* on the phone, 'you can buy Perrier here now.' It was a project marked by deep, liberalizing reforms, and with substantial international backing too. In just four years, Turkey received a record five structural adjustment loans to smooth its way.[8]

It was a new era for Maraş as well. 'There was nothing here,' Mehmet says to me, 'just red pepper and rice mills', and a few cotton factories. But then Özal came, and 'lifted the curtain', con-tinues Mehmet, 'and asked us, "Do you see the world?"' As one local recalled, gradually the city was changing: new factories were popping up; and their owners, visibly rich, would head to new restaurants and hotels. For a growing business like Mehmet's, the 1980s was an exciting time. By that point, of course, his was still a high street patisserie. But one reform to come would change the course of his family-run firm for good.

It took a few years for Turkey's reforming government to risk pri-vatising its assets. For one, since 1980, when they had been allowed to set their own prices, many of the state-owned enterprises had come to run a profit anyway. But there were deeper reasons too for the hesitancy – some of them had links deep into the early republic, and the hallowed era of Atatürk himself. To sell them off completely – even, God forbid, to foreign firms – was perhaps a repudiation of the past too far. Still, for a programme committed to shrinking the state, it seemed inevitable: most state enterprises were still big loss-makers, bigger employers, and performing roles

the market knew best. A special body was set up to see the privatizations through, responsible directly to the Prime Minister and
his cabinet, and run by a group of technocrats educated in the
US.[9] And so, in the second half of the eighties, they began: cement,
fruit juice, meat and fish, cigarettes, wool, textiles, tourism, and
olive oil.[10] Sector by sector, the state was releasing its grip. *Satalım
kurturalım*, as the saying went, 'Let's sell it and save it.'

The Süt Endüstrisi Kurumu, the Milk Industry Institution, or SEK
for short, had been set up a couple of decades before, in Turkey's
era of five-year development plans. It had been founded by the
Ministry for Agriculture to develop the dairy industry, build milk-
processing facilities around the country, and provide stable prices
for the farmers who supplied them. As SEK would proudly state, it
was responsible in 1968 for the country's first pasteurized milk, in '72
for its mass-produced yoghurt, and later for its first vacuum-packed
white cheese. It also ran at a constant loss, and with its particular
inefficiencies too – years later stories emerged of warehouses full of
spoilt milk. And so it was that in the late eighties a SEK milk factory
in Maraş came up for sale. For an ambitious Mehmet, it was too
good a chance to turn down. After a few opening rounds of negotiation, he tells me, he met with Özal himself, and they talked things
through. The government wanted a guarantee that the patisserie
would sell at least two hundred litres of milk a day, be it in ice cream
or another form; Mehmet said he was aiming for two tonnes. 'Özal
said if you don't do it, I'll take it back.' I ask him how he felt meeting
face to face. 'How are you supposed to feel talking to the country's
prime minister? Like a king or a sultan,' he answers, 'But I had a certain courage. I didn't retreat.' I wonder too if it helped that these two
men, both short and a little round, were also both from deep inside
Anatolia themselves. Whatever the reason, in 1989 Maraş SEK was
sold to Yaşar Paştanesi for the equivalent of seven hundred thousand
dollars, to be paid in instalments from future earnings.[11]

It would still need a little work: the factory, Mehmet explained, had the capacity only to make yoghurt. They would need to bring in their own machines – an oven for pastries, an ice-cream maker for *dondurma*. There would be other changes too. I ask what happened to the employees already there. 'I bought my own men to work there,' he says, 'I told the old ones, "Back to the government for you." ' It was an experience replicated all over. The privatizations across Turkey saw tens of thousands of people lose their jobs; and many of those who worked in the new private firms were paid substantially less. When I ask Mehmet how important the factory was in the history of his business, he refers again to a local Maraş proverb. *Tenceresi olmayan yemeği olmaz.* 'He who doesn't have a pot, won't have any food, *ne dedim?*' He pauses, waiting for me to repeat it, before adding, 'It changed everything.'

*

The next day, we drive half an hour from the city into the Maraş countryside for a tour of Mehmet's model farm. At the entrance he takes me to a vegetable patch, pulls out an orchid, and shows me its tubers underneath. As we walk on, four or five employees trail us with sacks of food, and every now and again he reaches inside, to feed the animals around us by hand: making two enormous dogs jump up for *sucuk* sausage; throwing *börek* to his ostriches; and then more to dozens of gobbling turkeys, and one extravagant peacock amongst them. The whole place feels like the plaything for an Anatolian boy done good – a man of simple tastes who has become a millionaire. As one of his employees told me, Mehmet is traditional through and through: he works with paper, doesn't do emails, and works nineteen hours a day. Yet his business has seen phenomenal success.

Just a few years after the patisserie bought its first factory from the state, Mehmet launched something else entirely: a new brand to sell all over Turkey. It was called Mado – a contraction of Maraş Dondurması, Maraş Ice Cream. And it was not just a new name but a new model too – a franchise of ice-cream patisseries, all contracted to buy their products from Mehmet's factories. The first opened in 1992 in a high-brow district in İstanbul, opposite a Baskin Robbins.[12] 'How did you feel when you were opening that shop?' I ask. 'Like I conquered İstanbul,' he answers, before putting on another one of his voices, 'Sultan Mehmet is coming!' Indeed, he claims he was an early pioneer of the new publicity television offered too, advertising on the private TV channels that opened in the late eighties, as the state retreated from its monopoly on broadcasting as well.

It was a new style of capitalism for Turkey's new age, and the years since have seen it grow and grow. Today, Mado has over three hundred and fifty stores in Turkey. From his grandfather's stall of four tables, and his father's patisserie employing no one but his sons, it now has five thousand direct, contracted workers, and twenty thousand across its franchises.[13] As Mehmet learnt in Rome years ago, they sell not just plain Maraş ice cream, but hundreds of different flavours, from green tea to pepper, and in vegan forms too. The factories that provide them, here in Maraş, can produce over ninety tonnes of ice cream a day. And of course, beside the ice cream, there is *baklava, künefe, kadayif, börek*, and all sorts of savoury meals. They export in refrigerated trucks east to Azerbaijan; in cooled containers down south to the Arabian peninsula; and in planes to Europe too. They have chains in over forty countries.

And here on this site, Mehmet is planning the next step. He takes me to the pride of the farm, to a goat enclosure overlooking a vast green plain below. The secret to their ice cream, he tells me – though there seem to be many secrets – is the quality of their goats, and the milk they produce. Maraş goats, he says, are the best in Turkey, because they are allowed to roam free, and eat the best grass they can sniff out, and Mado buys from thousands of goatherds in the region who tend to them. But Mehmet is hoping to create something even better. We enter the enclosure, long and white, and walk down its middle, as hundreds of goats bleat on either side. He picks one up, and hugs it to his chest, its feet dangling in the air. This, he says, is the Mado Beyaz – the White Mado. They are trying to breed their own goat. Its father is a Halep, an Arabic breed with long hair and drooping ears, famous for how long they can survive without water; its mother is a Saanen, from Switzerland way out west. A little unsure whether this is a marketing stunt, or a real experiment, I ask Mehmet to explain more about it, and why they're doing it. 'Different breeds are different,' he replies, before adding, as the joke forms on his face, 'Isn't your mum English and your dad Turkish?'

*

Few stories surely capture so neatly the changes that the 1980s unleashed in post-coup Turkey, as the country was set on its capitalist path, and generations-old family firms became global business empires. Across the country, across the decade, exports boomed, textile and food factories took off, and the country got richer. Though it was still a place marked by deep poverty in parts, its economy was doubtless changing. Mado perhaps, with its expensive ice cream that you ate with a knife and fork, was a middle-class chain for a country with middle-class aspirations.

It was a decade that shifted the weight of geography in Turkey too. Many of the smaller firms that would prosper were not in the old coastal hubs of İzmir or İstanbul, but in provincial Anatolian towns like Konya, Kayseri, and Gaziantep. Here in Maraş the population increased by a third, as peasants nearby put down their hoes and came to work in the factories, sewing clothes, cutting metalware, and, of course, making ice cream. Today, besides the few owned by Mado, there are more than thirty other ice-cream factories in the city, employing over ten thousand people.[14] And all across Turkey, the business owners thriving in this new economy proved a different kind of capitalist – though Mehmet, banging his fists on the table, insists he is no capitalist at all. They were more pious and conservative, and perhaps more rooted to home too.

Of course, this new wave of capitalism soon brought its own discontents – hot money and financial crises, corruption between government and business, whole regions scarred by environmental neglect. Indeed, the orchid so crucial to *dondurma* is itself at risk, plucked from the mountains at an unsustainable rate. This was an economic growth that could never last.

And if it's a bittersweet story, it seems more bitter in times like this. For much of the Maraş that grew over the last forty years, spreading out across the mountains and down into the plains, has fallen into dust: buildings humbled, their insides turned out, and a city still in mourning. But even amongst it, some energy from those years still pushes on. On my last night here, on a road of rubble, I see a queue amid the cold. At an improvised stall, two young men are shouting out to the dark, advertising their fresh, hot *baklava*, with a scoop of Maraş ice cream. In this new Turkey, there is always something sweet to sell.

10. The Pocket Hercules

1980s, 1990s – Bulgaria

As he had done hundreds of times before, Naum Shalamanov rubs chalk in his hands, inhales his magnesium salts, in through the nose, out through the mouth, and walks onto the platform, where one hundred and forty-eight kilo weights await. As his coach later told me, when the stage is lit up like that you can't really see the audience, but surely the hush, the sense of expectation, comes out from the darkness all the same. He takes his time and bends down, below the height of the advertising hoardings behind him, for Australian supermarkets and office suppliers. Then, as always, as he grips the bar, a puff of his hair, the opening of his mouth, and a grunt of brute strength as he begins to lift. 'Can the little man do it?!' shouts the commentator. 'Up he goes! He's done it!' The two-thousand-strong crowd cheer, as he holds it over his head, his body vibrating underneath it, both steady and quivering. And then the pundit mentions – as everyone knows – how short his arms are, how even when they are fully extended, the bar barely clears his head. He throws it down to a clunk, and punches the air. A world record broken again. And he's only nineteen years old.

The World Weightlifting Championships in Melbourne, 1986, may have been dramatic, but in a sense they were routine too. This was Shalamanov's third World Cup gold. And as a local paper reported – carrying a blurry picture of Naum, a leotard stuffed with muscles – the Bulgarians claimed not just first but second and third.[1] The celebrations that evening though were more unforeseen. The Bulgarian team had organized a meal in a leafy, upmarket Melbourne suburb. They ate, they drank, and they revelled in their success. And Naum, in the words of one Australian weightlifting coach who had come along, was 'as happy as Larry', laughing and joking, and asking about the best discos in Canberra where they were headed next.[2] But when the night was over, and it was time to drive back to the California Motel, the driver noticed something amiss. At the wheel of his twelve-seater minibus, he ran a head count, and Naum wasn't there.[3]

The Bulgarians reported him missing the next morning. 'He is very dear to the public,' said the vice-consul, 'there will be a big reaction from people when they hear the news.'[4] And over the next days – amid claims and counter-claims – the rest of the Bulgarian weightlifting team were taken to a secret location for their own safety. They held a press conference, displaying Naum's possessions to the world: the World Cup trophy with his name engraved at the bottom; two fluffy toy kangaroos; all his clothes, packed in two bags; some car stereo speakers, VHS tapes, cassettes.[5] The Consu-late-General of Bulgaria announced their conclusion: this had been a 'politically motivated kidnapping'.[6]

*

As I navigate the chaos of Esenler, İstanbul's biggest bus station, and step onto the coach, I notice an immediate change: there is not a Turk on board. Instead, it is a bus of blonde hair, blue eyes, and the sounds of another language entirely. And as we head out, another change again: we are going not east, across the Bosphorus and into Anatolia, as almost all the journeys I've ever taken from here go, but west, deeper into European Turkey and beyond.

We move through Thrace, as this part of the world is known, all flat and green, and as we stop and stop, slowly the bus accumulates cargo beyond the passengers: huge sacks of rice, tomato sauce, washing detergent. We are heading to the border, and things are more expensive over there. It takes hours to arrive – to Kapıkule, the border crossing – and then hours more to pass through. We are after all entering not just another country, but Europe proper. The land is unchanged, but the flags lining the road are different on the other side: the white crescent and star on red replaced by a tricolor of white, green, and red, amid the flags of the European Union as well: the circle of gold stars on a background of deep blue. And shortly after the border, the first sign of another freedom perhaps: a supermarket full of slot machines.

We push deeper into Thrace, as the sun ducks under the clouds, starting its descent until it sets somewhere west over Greece. For these are lands in between, split between Turkey, Bulgaria, and Greece. The Maritsa River running just to our south – the Meriç, in Turkish – forms the last of the border between Greece and Bulgaria behind us, before it swings down south to separate Greece and Turkey too. After half an hour inside Bulgaria, we cross it ourselves:

flat, broad, and speckled in the evening light. Along its bank, a boy drives a donkey-drawn cart. We arrive at the first city inland, Haskovo – Хасково – a reminder that I've entered a country with a different script as well. I change, heading down into southern Bulgaria, towards the Rhodope Mountains that form another part of its border with Greece. For now though, it's still flat, and in the distance I see disused factories, their windows smashed in, and stone houses with ramshackle terracotta roofs. Finally, in the dark, I arrive. Momchilgrad, as it's officially known, or Mastanlı, as all the locals call it.

On a fresh and sharp morning, I see it better: this small town of modest old houses and big socialist-era blocks. From the square, the mountains are visible in the distance – like the land has been gently upturned on the horizon. I walk in their direction, towards a six-floor apartment building on the southern outskirts of town. At its entrance, a sign in Cyrillic – put up in its socialist past – asks its residents to be good neighbours and educated citizens, by keeping their shared spaces clean.

I'm here to see someone who lives on the second floor – not to interview, but to meet at least. Hatice is eighty years old and tired. Adjusting the scarf over her head, she welcomes me into her three-room flat, all decorated in white flower wallpaper, and we sit in her 'salon'. Each time she speaks, she sighs deeply and looks down. She is old, she insists to me, and she feels it: her face is wrinkled, and her eyes are sunk deep into her head. She has few teeth, and speaks a Bulgarian Turkish that I only get used to after a little while. Yet still, we have our small talk. After a few minutes, she stands up – to the height of the light switches on the wall – and returns from the kitchen, offering me strawberry-flavoured chocolates. I notice, as she holds out the tray, she has the same trait as her son: her upper and lower arms are the same length. I take one, and we speak a little more, before I head out. And there he is as I leave: by the front door, a picture of a young Naim, smiling at the camera, looking down the corridor of the apartment where his mother lives alone.

i) Naim Suleimanov

I meet Hilmi in his office, a small place where he runs his physiotherapy business across his hometown. Still, his old job – the one he retired from not long ago – he seems unable to quite let go. He has bright blue eyes and a dark blue tracksuit, and an avuncular habit of saying 'Sami' to me halfway through answers, like a teacher making sure he has his students' attention. For decades, Hilmi was a weightlifting coach. And it was Mastanlı where he was first sent to work, over fifty years ago.

He was in his early twenties at the time, and he suited Mastanlı well. He was from a Bulgarian-Turkish family further north; and Momchilgrad was the largest Turkish-speaking town Bulgaria had. Indeed, for centuries it had not been Bulgarian at all, but on the western frontiers of the Ottoman Empire. It was only in 1913, after the humiliating losses in the Balkan Wars, that the Ottomans had to give the region up, to join the Bulgarian kingdom.

By the time Hilmi arrived in Mastanlı in the seventies of course that kingdom had long gone, and the People's Republic of Bulgaria had come in its stead. But there was not much sign of the communist future down in the country's south-east. As one journalist wrote, it was a place of cobblestone streets, of donkeys carrying firewood, and men in traditional wide pantaloons.[7] Though there is little grown here now – the topsoil is thin, like the fuzz of a kiwi – it was back then tobacco country, and the work in the fields was arduous and year-round.

Hilmi had come as a representative of that People's Republic, as one of the thousands of coaches it employed across the country, for socialist Bulgaria held sport in high esteem. And so, even in a small town like Mastanlı, there was a complex to enjoy. Himli started out in a small hall, running weightlifting sessions for kids before and after class. He would go on the lookout for talent too, checking out students at the local schools. He would look, he tells me, 'for those with short arms, short legs, who are a little bit closer to ground.' I ask why it's an advantage, and his explanation couldn't be simpler: you don't need to raise the bar as high.

So it was that one day in the mid-seventies, he came across a boy in third grade. 'It was something just given by nature,' he remembers. For the nine-year-old Naim Suleimanov wasn't just built right, he seemed to understand how to lift better than anyone Hilmi had ever seen.

*

His friends called him Kalemondo, because – like the comic strip character who inspired the name – Naim was short and brave.[8] Even before he started lifting with Hilmi, he was said to have entertained himself by picking up heavy branches and stones.[9] 'I started in 1977,' he once later told a journalist, 'because I wanted to be a powerful man.'[10]

After he first saw Naim at school it was months, Hilmi tells me, before he could get him to train. His parents were unsure – they had never come across weightlifting before. His father was a miner and bus driver; and his mother looked after the home, a little tobacco-farming here, caring for the children there. Hatice, in particular, worried what impact it would have on his nine-year-old body, whether it would stop him growing when he was already so small for his age. So again and again Hilmi visited their family home in Mastanlı's outskirts, a little stone thing with a three-acre garden of tomatoes, melons, and peppers. Slowly, he had them convinced.

Naim found it difficult at first. Not only was it tiring, it was – as

one Olympic weightlifter would admit to me – a boring, monoton-
ous sport. But after one or two months, he started to enjoy it. I
ask Hilmi what kind of training they did, and he springs out of
his chair to an empty space in the room, and gives me a demonstration with an invisible bar. There are two lifts, he explains, the
'snatch' and the 'clean and jerk', the *koparma* and the *silkme*. The
snatch is a one-step move, squatting down, lifting the weight clean
over your head, and then rising up with it. The clean and jerk has
even heavier weights, which require two stages to lift, once up to
the neck and shoulders, and then again over the head, holding the
bar there, arms outstretched, and praying for the horn, or the ref-
eree's call, that deems a successful lift. His lesson over, Hilmi sits
back down again, slightly breathless, and explains that for a child
as young as Naim they did not so much lift heavy weights as work
on technique, and the mastery of all the little movements the sport
requires. 'You just needed to show him once', he says, 'most kids
would need a dozen times.' At nine years old, he was already able
to lift twenty-five kilos, and impressing national coaches at local
youth tournaments.[11] I visit the sports complex in the centre of
Mastanlı where they used to train. In its lobby, for display, is one of
the steel bars he lifted when he was young, now black and rusty. I
see a picture of him around this age: the skin of a child, the biceps
of a sailor.

After two years of training with Hilmi, Naim was ready to progress. All across Bulgaria hundreds of twelve-year-old boys were
selected for the country's specialist sports schools, to be trained by
scores of elite weightlifting coaches. The entrance exam was stren-
uous: sprints, sit-ups, long-distance runs, push-ups, and jumps.
The republic wanted only the best, and those that could cope with
the demands of the schools where they'd live for the next six years.
The programme was relentless, with little but training, class, meals,
and scheduled naps, five times a week. In turn they'd be given all

the weightlifting gear they'd ever need, the tracksuits, the belts, the shoes, and train in gyms with the most modern equipment on offer.[12]

Even in the hardened world of communist weightlifting, it was a controversial project, to start boys training so hard, lifting so young. It had begun around a decade before, the brainchild of the famous head coach of the Bulgarian national team, Ivan Abidjiev, an exacting man with – as one journalist would write – 'a creased, wan face and haunting eyes.' His aim, ultimately, was to produce lifters that would propel Bulgaria past all the other socialist republics, past the USSR itself, and to the summit of the sport. And by the time Naim passed his exam, to enter the sports school in nearby Kircali, Abidjiev's plan seemed to be bearing fruit. Little Bulgaria was a lifting powerhouse.[13]

*

Muharrem is taller than I hoped. He is merely shorter than average and, he tells me, the tallest of his diminutive family. He has a husky voice, deepened by decades of cigarettes – everyone smoked in the tobacco regions where he grew up – and hazel eyes a little lighter than his older brother's. He was born two years after Naim, and remembers his *abi* 'like a role model', who helped teach him to read and write. When Naim went away to the academy in Kircali – just fifteen or so kilometres north – Muharrem was ten, and tells me how keenly he awaited his returns: both because his older brother was coming home, and because his mum would make Naim's favourite meal to mark it, *yaprak sarma*, grape leaves stuffed with rice.

Naim lived like that for a few years, training in Kircali, suffering bouts of homesickness, and returning home every weekend. But it soon became clear to his coaches at the academy – as it did to Hilmi before them – that he was someone with a preternatural gift. At just fourteen, he was transferred further north again, nearly two hundred and fifty kilometres away in Sofia, to train with the Bulgarian national team. He had been earmarked for the World Junior Championships even further away: in São Paolo, Brazil, where he would not only leave Bulgaria for the first time, but compete with lifters up to five years his senior. When the results went out around the world, in the words of one sports journalist, they were thought to be a misprint.[14] Fourteen-year-old Naim had won the juniors lifting 110 kilos in the snatch, and 140 in the clean and jerk. He had nearly broken the men's world record in the process. In his office Hilmi had shown me almost fifty-year-old newspaper clippings he had kept ever since: ripped and soft in my hands, and written in a script I can't read. Yet he pointed out to me the most meaningful parts: Naim, his first coach Hilmi, and the words São Paolo.

It was after this success that Muharrem, his younger brothers, and his mum and dad moved out of the old stone house, and into the flat where I had met Hatice a few days before. It was a gift from the People's Republic, thrilled by the achievements of the family's oldest son. Muharrem was not there for long. Given Naim's talents, the coaches in Sofia wondered if his younger brother might make a good lifter too. So Muharrem joined the junior team in Sofia. 'I didn't love it at first,' he tells me – your fingers callus, your hands ache, your biceps strain at the work. And both of them – Naim in the national team, Muharrem in the juniors – missed their family hundreds of kilometres away. I ask what training was like, and he lets out a long and husky, 'Oof.'

'It was very, very intense,' he explains. For three days a week, there were three, two-hour lifting sessions, morning, noon and night. On Tuesdays and Thursdays, there were 'just' two. On Saturdays there was one. And on Sundays they were free. And all under the watchful eye of the head coach, Ivan Abidjiev, or 'The

Butcher' as he was known – rarely satisfied, occasionally violent, and extremely selective with his praise. Still, one Turkish coach who knew Abidjiev would tell me, outside of training he was a different person – fatherly, and fond of Bulgarian Turks too. Naim was young and far from home, and Abidjiev was perhaps the figure he needed. 'He was not a person satisfied easily,' Muharrem says of his older brother, though it could apply to his coach too, 'and he was a fast learner.'

It was a programme that was pushing against the limits of what was deemed possible, particularly for students so young. It was thought, after all, that the maximum the body could take was three lifting sessions a week, to give the muscles time to rest. In Sofia, they were doing three in a day. How could they recover so quickly? The Bulgarians claimed they had pioneered new techniques: with massages, water therapy, saunas, and periodic fasting.[15] Their competitors around the world were sometimes unconvinced, for this was a sport rarely free of steroids and performance-enhancing drugs. In 1976, the year before Naim started his career, some Bulgarian lifters did indeed test positive.[16] But Naim, his team, and his coaches always rejected the accusations. The only things he took, he would later say, were protein and vitamins.[17]

There was a good atmosphere in Sofia, Muharrem tells me, and lifters would go out together in their spare time, to the capital's cinemas and discos. But inside the training hall, it could be intimidating. 'Almost everyone in the room was a world champion,' he reminds me, 'maybe the worst person, out of ten, will be second in the world in his weight category.' As with any sportsmen, they had their odd tics and habits too. When one American reporter visited a Bulgarian training camp, out on the Black Sea coast, they were surprised to hear all the squatting, grunting, and lifting play out to a soundtrack of country and blues: Willie Nelson, Johnny Cash, and Muddy Waters. Naim's favourite, apparently – and the only English he knew – was Kenny Rogers' 'The Gambler'. *You got to know when to hold 'em / know when to fold 'em / know when to walk away and know / when to run.*[18]

*

At sixteen, Naim was already the best weightlifter the world had ever seen. Competing in the featherweight division, he weighed fifty-five kilos and could lift a hundred and seventy. By fifteen he was already a world champion, and had broken his first world record too – in the next three years, he would break four more. And had the entire Soviet bloc not boycotted the 1984 Los Angeles games, he would surely have won his first Olympic gold. His age alone was unprecedented in the sport, for it was normally dominated by men in their late twenties and thirties, with well-seasoned muscles and well-honed techniques. But here this man-child – barely a hair on his face – was beating them all. He was, as one sports journalist would nickname him, a Pocket Hercules.[19]

Of course, in part, it was Naim's size that made him. Now fully grown, he stood at around a hundred and fifty centimetres tall. His upper arms were the same length as his forearms; his legs the same as his torso.[20] In other words, he was just more muscle than most: more bulging biceps, more strapping thighs, and less of the parts of the body that might give way under strain. But it went well beyond his physique too, for perhaps more important was Naim's ability to control it. He would approach the bar, as some would observe, 'as if in meditation'.[21] While his rivals before a lift might beat their chests or pace the stage, his ritual was almost banal: a puff of his fringe as he crouched down, opening his mouth out wide 'in a silent scream' as he began to pull the bar up, and fixing his eyes straight ahead.[22]

His old coach Hilmi visited Naim at the weekend in those years, taking the Sofia Express up north. He could lift almost perfectly by that point, he says. This sport, he is keen to stress, is not body-building – it is about muscles, yes, but technique and flexibility too. And as he showed me one of his many demonstrations, I could see it: how there is a rhythm to a lift, moving the burden from one set of muscles to another, up from the feet, to the calves, through the knees, then a snap past the hips, and suddenly up above the chest and head. Slowed down, there is a smoothness to it, and you see the subtle shift of weight across the body, the energy, the sway between bar and man, almost like a dance.

*

Perhaps stranger even than the drills, the coach nicknamed 'the Butcher', the programme that took twelve-year-olds away from their home, was the fact that the Bulgarian national team won anything at all. This was a rare success in a decaying regime. The People's Republic of Bulgaria was in its fifth decade; Todor Zhivkov, as its General Secretary, was in his fourth. By the mid-eighties, as all over the communist bloc, it was a country in trouble. Its foreign debt was rising; its economy was stalling; its population was both falling and restless. And its leadership was desperate to stave off reform.[23] So it turned instead to a cause that might rally the people behind it: to the Turkish minority in their midst.

After decades of policies that allowed Turks to develop their own culture and language, in a pique of Bulgarian nationalism, the socialist regime now denied they existed at all. 'There are no Turks in Bulgaria', as General Secretary Zhivkov declared. It wrote a new history too, linking all its citizens to a pure Bulgarian state, right back to the Middle Ages. The peoples in the east – down by the Rhodope Mountains, and up north by the Danube – only spoke Turkish and practised Islam, so it went, because their ancestors had been forced to convert. But ethnically they were Bulgarian, deep down in their bones.[24] Whether it was historically true was debatable – over the five hundred years of Ottoman rule here, there had been big migrations and mass conversions, some forced and mostly voluntary[25] – but in a sense it was irrelevant. Most Bulgarian Turks, centuries on, did not *feel* Bulgarian and nothing else.

To begin with, Turkish was banned, in print and on the street. As Muharrem would remember, it was a change that was particularly difficult for his mum, who spoke little Bulgarian. Traditional Turkish clothes and circumcisions were outlawed – they were backward traditions, by the logic of the Bulgarian state inspired now by one part Bulgarian chauvinism, and one part socialist ideas of Progress.[26] Fasting over Ramadan was portrayed as needlessly depriving workers of their strength.[27] Then, in the winter of 1984, they began to change people's names, to 'return' them to their more Slavic roots. The reports out of eastern Bulgaria grew darker: stories of villages surrounded by policemen and their dogs, troops and their tanks, and officials going into homes, sometimes gun in hand, and providing locals with a list of names.[28] Everyone in Mastanlı remembers the protests, and how the police put them down. As Muharrem tells me, he was sixteen at the time, and back in his hometown to visit. Though he didn't see the protests themselves, he saw their conclusion – out on the volleyball court, in the sports complex where Naim used to train, lay dozens of 'people on the floor, blood everywhere', surrounded by soldiers in red berets. Another local, who was thirteen at the time, says he thinks of that scene 'every time I see the colour red.' For three and a half months there was violence all over the region: protests, arrests, and perhaps as many as a thousand killed. And as tensions increased, the state even opened an old detention camp on an island way up north, to send dissenters and activists who resisted too much.[29]

ii) Naum Shalamanov

In Sofia, Naim was in a sense shielded from all this. The national team was an open, accepting place, and the head coach Abidjiev even spoke Turkish himself. But of course, he still had his family back in Mastanlı. On one visit home Naim was surprised to be told by a policeman that there was an evening curfew, and even more when he saw bullet holes, pocked amongst the cement walls of apartment blocks, and shattered windows.[30]

As Muharrem tells me, because of Naim's fame, the Suleymanovs were the last in Mastanlı to change their name. But even they could not resist. When he came back from a training camp in Australia – preparing for the World Championships in a year's time – the Bulgarian authorities took Naim's passport and handed him a new one soon after. 'Naum Shalamanov', it read. 'It was as if they gave me a number,' he said later.[31] The rest of the family would follow suit. Muharrem went with his father to the municipality, where they were given a list of names. He chose Mavri, after a football player in a local team. His mother Hatice became Anna, and his father Suleyman, Stilian.

It was done more with a sense of resignation than anger, Muharrem tells me. But perhaps for his older brother, a prouder man, and one whose name was known all over, it meant a little more. As one of Naim's coaches would later claim, he went into his room that night, and found him in tears.[32] Though the world would hear it a little differently, filtered through the propaganda of the Bulgarian state. As he was quoted in an article in an East German paper, then amplified across the world by the Associated Press, 'our family has now taken the old Bulgarian name of our ancestors.'[33]

It was around this time that Naim Suleymanov decided to escape.

*

He had, in fact, already been contacted by Turkish-Bulgarian defectors. They lived in Australia, and had heard of how things were deteriorating back home. During Naim's training in Melbourne, just before his name was changed, they were in touch, to share their plans for him through fleeting conversations in his hotel. He said no, but trusted them nonetheless. And if it had tempted him at all before, now Naim – officially Naum – was convinced he had to go. He knew too that there would be another chance, for the World Championships would be held there in less than a year. So the nineteen-year-old Naim spent the next few months secretly preparing to upend his life. As Muharrem says, he didn't even tell his family – it was too risky for them to know. In December, just before he was due to fly back to Australia, he spent two days with them all at home, unsure whether he'd ever see them again.

The defectors contacted Naim in his hotel in Melbourne. As the story goes, one of them, who had escaped Bulgaria underneath a train twenty years before, had a seventeen-year-old daughter who spoke perfect English with an Australian twang. If she approached Naim in the lobby his minders would have no reason to think she was anything but a teenage girl on an autograph hunt. So it was, near the end of the tournament, that she explained to him the plan: when they all gathered at the restaurant on the last night, around nine o'clock, when everyone had relaxed after a few drinks, he would 'go to the toilet', whose door was located by the exit, slip out of the restaurant instead, and look for a car parked to his right, where he'd find two Bulgarian-Turks ready to take him away, first to another car, then to a safe house, and finally out of Australia altogether.[34]

On 7 December 1986, then, that record-breaking performance – the commentator screaming, 'Up he goes! He's done it!', and the cheers of a two-thousand-strong crowd – happened when Naim knew all this. He arrived at the dinner dressed in a suit and tie.

He didn't eat much, and drank mostly fruit juice, as he counted down the hours till nine. Just before it struck, he went once to the toilet, just to see if anyone would follow. Of course no one did. And so, twelve minutes later, he got up from his table again and headed out of the restaurant without looking back. Perhaps, as he left everything behind, he had never needed to control his body as much as this, calmly walking to freedom, and out into the warm summer night.[35]

*

As I leave Mastanlı, back up towards the Turkish border, I read a list of other defectors from the Eastern bloc: that same year, in Tokyo, an opera singer from the Soviet Union escaped during a performance of *Madame Butterfly*; there are figure-skaters, pianists, and spies. In another famous defection in Australia, a few years before Naim, a woman jumped from a boat to swim to Sydney harbour, wearing nothing but a red bikini.

But all around this part of Bulgaria, there were less-known cases too. These borders, between Bulgaria and its neighbours Turkey and Greece, were a green wall of their own: barbed wire ran through the Black Sea woods and down to the Rhodope Mountains; it was guarded by armed guards and their dogs; and locals were forced to spy on outsiders passing through, and denounce those looking to defect. Over four hundred were killed trying to make it to Turkey alone, far more than ever died crossing the Berlin Wall.[36]

And if the world of defections feels another age, it does so particularly here, where the currents of history now move the other way. I return to Turkey, and pass the magnificent Ottoman city of Edirne, all domes and spires. The last time I was here, around the borders between Turkey and the European Union, it was to report on the thousands of refugees – from Afghanistan, Iran, Iraq, and Syria – who had been falsely told that the doors to Europe had been opened, and had flocked from all around Turkey to Edirne to take their chance. And as they waited for the opening that never came, they slept on bus station floors and in fields. A brave few, growing in their frustration and sensing they had been fooled, risked the tear gas, the water cannons, and bullets, and tried to cross the Meriç by themselves. At least one was killed.

It is a transformation that seems to scramble both place and time: Turkey, in the east, is no longer the gateway to the capitalist West; rather, it is the last stop of refugees *from* the east heading west, into the imagined freedoms of Europe.

iii) Naim Süleymanoğlu

Naim landed at Ankara airport on 13 December 1986 in Prime Minister Özal's private jet. As he disembarked, he kissed the tarmac, and then the cheeks of Özal himself. Then, sat immediately in front of a press conference – his first media appearance since going missing six days earlier – he said he defected because of the Bulgarian assimilation campaign that 'someone had to explain to the world'. Naim declared as well that he wanted to win gold for his new nation, at the Olympics in just over eighteen months' time. He had immediately been granted citizenship, and under a new name again: Naim Süleymanoğlu.

As Muharrem says, it was a press conference where Özal, sat next to the weightlifter forty years his junior, would translate 'from Turkish to Turkish', clarifying Naim's Bulgarian-Turkish – its slightly antiquated vocabulary, the odd Bulgarian word thrown in too – to the journalists assembled in front. The Prime Minister 'really adopted him', Muharrem had told me. He was still a teenager, after all, and one who hadn't lived with his own father for seven years. After the press conference, Özal instructed his office to go out and buy Naim some new suits.[37] In Bulgaria meanwhile, his real father, along with his younger brother Muharrem, were being questioned in Sofia on what they had known. They were not treated badly, Muharrem insisted, but the interrogation lasted seven days. And their father Suleyman, a canny man, simply toed the Party line: 'Naum was kidnapped,' he would repeat.

*

The lacquer floor of the *halter salonu*, the weightlifting hall, is dented by years of weights falling on it from a height. There is the light smell of sweat, and the buzz of lights, as the youth team comes out to train: stretching, wrapping belts around their bellies, rubbing chalk between their fingers, and pumping themselves up for their lifts. I am in Ankara, at the home of Turkey's Olympic sports, and a complex that caters not only for lifters but gymnasts, boxers, basketball players, and more.

It was not, perhaps, the ideal place for Naim to launch his bid for Olympic gold. Weightlifting in Turkey was not a storied discipline. While wrestling, a centuries-old Turkish tradition, had earned Turkey almost every gold it had ever won, weightlifting had been started by a few European expats in 1920s İstanbul, and the Turks who took it up thereafter had, at most, won a few medals at the Balkan or Mediterranean Games. There were few active clubs, the facilities were not great, and the best Turkish lifters had long been forced to train abroad.[38] And by the time Naim arrived, though things were slowly improving – this hall was not yet a decade old – it was still a world away from what he had known. For one, all the lifters here were still amateurs. I speak to one retired lifter, who was a teacher in the day, and a member of the national team after class. All his students ever asked him about, he tells me, was Naim.

Slowly after Naim came, the operation professionalized around him. Masseurs, dieticians, and doctors were brought on board, and perhaps a bit of Bulgarian discipline too. Naim was given a one-bed apartment in Ankara, a Ford, and a monthly salary of around $1,000.[39] Yet still, as one of his coaches tells me, he found it difficult to adjust. 'He had come to a new country and a new society,' he explains, 'it was a very different lifestyle.' In Bulgaria, Naim had lived a quiet life, in a society that was a little more reserved. Turks, in contrast, would gather around him on the street, hug him, kiss him – 'we are a warm-hearted, warm-blooded people.' Shy and introverted by nature, Naim wasn't quite sure how to react. 'He had his own inner world,' he remembers, 'he wouldn't open up to anyone.' Maybe as he was approached by strangers, Naim had some deeper fears as well. He travelled everywhere with bodyguards and armed police permanently guarded his home. For he and the Turkish authorities knew what could happen to defectors. Not even ten years before, a Bulgarian dissident writer who had escaped to the UK was killed at a London bus stop with a poison-tipped umbrella, stabbed into his leg.

Perhaps, though, his early difficulties in his new life had the most basic, most intimate explanation of all: he was lonely. He was after all a nineteen-year-old boy who had never lived alone before, far away from everyone he ever knew. He was the subject of huge interest, and occasional drop-ins from the Prime Minister, but as his former coach put it, 'When the evening comes, loneliness collapses in on you.' He could speak to his family on the phone, but even those conversations could be frustrating and stilted. As Muharrem explained it to me, he would call them through the Ankara post office, and it would take half an hour to connect. Once the line was established, they were sure on both ends that the Bulgarian authorities were listening in. To protect each other, they couldn't talk about his defection or their repression, but stuck instead to the mundane. Even today, when Muharrem talks about his brother, he hides certain names and protects certain identities, as if the cold war subterfuge carries on.

But Naim could at least find refuge in the weightlifting hall and its familiar routines. He trained as he always had, and as he started representing Turkey around the world, won as he always had too. As the Seoul Olympics approached, by the rules of international competition, he would need a waiver from Bulgaria to allow him to compete so soon. It was obtained, reportedly, with a payment from Turkey of one million dollars in cash – an episode that speaks to a familiar criticism of those times, of Turkey's capitalist embrace: slush funds, corruption, and money forever off the books. Nevertheless, Naim's exemption was secured.

There were hundreds of Turkish fans in the weightlifting gym at Seoul's Olympic park, 20 September 1988. And back in Turkey, as one newspaper described it, as he took to the stage at around two o'clock local time, the streets were deserted, 'as we watched on TV holding our breath.'[40] Though in truth, it wasn't even close. Naim broke three separate world records, including a one hundred and ninety kilo lift in the clean and jerk. It was more than three times his body weight, about the same weight as a large Shetland pony. The Turks in the audience began to laugh and cry. Naim's goal, he would later say, had been not only to win gold – to reach the pinnacle of the sport he had started in eleven years ago – but to break the records set by Naum Shalamanov. He had also given Turkey its first Olympic gold in twenty years. In Bulgaria, his younger brother Muharrem watched on a black-and-white village TV, its antenna pointed towards the west – the Bulgarian broadcasters were showing another sport; Naim's parents would follow it on Turkish radio. None of them could openly celebrate of course, for by now it was established that the family's eldest son was a traitor to the People's Republic. In the press conference afterwards, Naim asked the Bulgarian authorities to allow them safe passage to see him. That night, when everyone else was asleep, this shy twenty-one-year-old took his bike, and rode around the Olympic village alone for hours.[41]

When he flew back to Ankara, a million people lined the streets from the airport to the city's main square as he was paraded on an open-top bus. Özal, on greeting him, kissed his cheeks eight times, before he was garlanded in flowers, draped over his neck so thick and numerous they look like a petalled fur coat. A Turkish bank promised him three hundred and forty-two one-kilo gold coins, in honour of the total weight he had lifted; he received nine more apartments and a Mercedes in gifts from the government, newspaper campaigns, and proud and wealthy Turks.[42] And as one former team-mate told me, his fame became something else entirely: policemen waved him through at checkpoints; restaurants would refuse to charge him for meals; for a month after Seoul, 'the TV news was "Naim came here, went there, ate this dinner". As Özal put it – in the business terms of the new age – when he justified the payment he had authorized to Bulgaria to allow Naim to compete, it was more than worth it, because he 'had advertised the Turks to the world.'

*

For weeks after the Olympics, Naim toured around the world, talking about the persecution of Bulgarian Turks. He travelled to West Germany, France, and the US, where he met Nancy Reagan in the White House, before speaking at the United Nations in New York. Eventually the pressure told. As Muharrem had told me, he and his parents had convinced themselves they would never see Naim again. It was easier to live that way. But only a month after Seoul, they were all taken to the Kapıkule border crossing and handed over to the Turkish authorities on the other side. There they took a helicopter to İstanbul's airport, and then their two-year separation came to an end. 'It was a very different feeling,

I can't explain.' And so they lived together once more, in one of Naim's many Ankara flats.

That, though, was just the beginning. By 1989, Bulgaria was in turmoil – shaken both by the reforms of its socialist neighbours across the Eastern Bloc and by protestors at home demanding the same. Seeking a pressure valve to open, its leadership made an abrupt change. After years of claiming there were no Turks in Bulgaria, they now accepted that there were . . . and that it would be better if they went. As General Secretary Zhivkov told the nation on TV, 'Turks are infidels to the Bulgarian state and should leave.'[43]

The exodus in May 1989 was historic, as three hundred thousand people – around one in two Bulgarian Turks – headed east. Many were forced to go, pressured by local authorities to be on the road the next morning, and many went willingly. They abandoned their houses and jobs, sold their property and furniture. They could only take with them what they could pack in their vehicles. The queue to the border – of cars and trucks, stacked with fridges, beds, family members, and pets – was longer than twenty kilometres.[44] It was a migration – rushed and chaotic as it was – that seemed to affirm a particular, long-held Turkish ideal. For some Turkish nationalists had dreamed for a century of uniting all the Turkic peoples under one banner, from Xinjiang in the east to the Balkans in the west. Here at least was proof of their common ties, made real in a traffic jam to Kapıkule.

Amongst it was Hilmi, Naim's first ever weightlifting coach. As he described it, after being told by the police to leave, he took his wife, son, daughter, and three bags of things into their car, and drove. When they eventually entered Turkey, and went to stay with their family in Bursa, it was 'a loop', he says, 'our ancestors came from the Ottoman Empire six hundred years ago, and now we go back to Anatolia.' After three or four days there, he took a midnight bus to Ankara, walking across the city in the early morning to see his old pupil again. They hugged, and drank tea together. He hadn't changed at all, he tells me, though he lived under pressure like never before. He never lost the fear that the People's Republic – even now as it collapsed – might take its ultimate revenge.

*

Naim went on to have a career like no other. He won gold in Barcelona, and again in Atlanta, becoming the first weightlifter ever to win three consecutive Olympic titles. But whether he was satisfied by it was a little less clear. He suffered ligament damage to his lower spine; he began to smoke and drink more; twice, he retired, only to return, begged back by his fans, and by politicians too, always keen to capitalize on his triumphs. Maybe also he couldn't resist the lure of the sport – and the thrill of the lift – that had defined his whole life. As his brother Muharrem described it to me, 'that dust, that breath, the atmosphere of that hall is different.'

It ended at the Sydney games in 2000, in an atmosphere that showed how far he had come from the cold war. The competition, as one report noted, was constantly interrupted by 'the incessant ringing of mobile phones.'[45] Undertrained and overweight, a thirty-three-year-old Naim tried and failed three lifts, wobbling under the bar 'like a punched boxer.' By that point, the boy from tobacco country smoked fifty cigarettes a day.[46] Then his life in retirement: more drinking, more smoking, brawling, a failed nationalist political career, and all in the public eye. He died, aged fifty, of liver cirrhosis, leaving four daughters from different women, all outside of marriage. In a final indignity, his body was disinterred after his death to prove that he shared with one of them the same DNA.

If it was, in one sense, the typical postscript of a childhood star, perhaps it suggested something else as well. For how well did this reserved boy from Bulgaria ever fit in, once he left his homeland behind? It was a life that at once showed how much Turkey means to the Turks living beyond its borders, but the limit of those bonds too. Of the hundreds of thousands of Bulgarian Turks who travelled to Turkey in that early summer of 1989, over a third of them soon headed back. Materially, life in Turkey wasn't always what they had hoped, but neither was it their real home. As Hilmi – who did end up staying in Turkey – said to me, moving 'wasn't something you wanted . . . I lived under that flag in Bulgaria for nearly thirty-five years. I served there, I grew up there, I studied there.' And of course, it was a Bulgaria that transformed in no time at all: less than six months after the exodus, and one day after the Berlin Wall collapsed, Zhivkov was ousted in a palace coup; Bulgaria would have its first multi-party elections the following summer, and vote to end the anti-Turkish laws at last.

And few would experience this life in between – of loyalties split – more than Naim's parents themselves. His father Suleyman, so long separated from his son, moved back to Mastanlı nonetheless, where he lived until his death. His mother Hatice now spends her winters in Turkey and her summers in Bulgaria. She has lost her husband and her eldest son, and her children and grandchildren are scattered across Turkey and Europe beyond. I suspect, in the end, she would have been happier if they had never left their home at all. As she told me with a sigh, of her son, the greatest athlete his sport has ever known – 'Keşke bir halterci olmasaydı.' 'If only he hadn't been a weightlifter.'

But for his adopted nation, there would be no such doubts at all. The celebrations at his Olympic victory had been wild, relived again and again in books and films; his funeral was attended by the great and the good. Of course, every nation has its sporting heroes, but perhaps it betrayed something deeper too. For in those heady days after his first gold, what is notable about the Turkish coverage is not only its descriptions of Naim's lifts, but the pride in how he was being feted elsewhere: mentioned in *Newsweek*, on the front cover of *Time*, invited to the headquarters of Adidas and Coca-Cola. For over sixty years, Turkey had after all had a curious relationship to the modern world and the powers that ran it: at times resentful, at times jealous, at times wanting above all to belong to it. Maybe then their newfound son Naim, in all his success, had proved something about Turks after all, and had eased an insecurity deep within – one betrayed by a question I'm asked wherever I go, half-in, half-out as I am, 'What do they think about us over there?' At least in those fleeting moments when the bar was above his head, Turkey had not just been accepted into the comity of nations, but had risen to its peak.

11. Ahmet Kaya

1990s, 2000s – İstanbul, Paris

THE NIGHT BEFORE, THEY WATCHED A FILM TOGETHER and laughed. They had seen it many times, but still it made them smile, and Gülten remembers wondering if they had become like those migrants abroad who relive bits of Turkish culture over and over again because it feels like home. They went to bed soon afterwards: Gülten read a book about Turkish prisons, Ahmet went straight to sleep. He woke up after a while when the light was still on, and asked why she was reading something like that, when she had lived through it once already. It was interesting, she replied, and banned in Turkey as well. Then he asked her whether she had remembered to take the headphones off Melis, their twelve-year-old next door, who liked to fall asleep listening to her Walkman at an incongruously high volume. She hadn't, so he went into her room, removed the headphones, gave her a quick cuddle, and came back. Then they both slept.

The next morning, Gülten woke up to a noise, to a thud in the corridor – the sound of falling. She rushed out, to find Melis already there, and Ahmet on the floor. 'This could be a heart attack,' she remembers thinking, while also trying not to panic her daughter. Gülten asked Melis to call an ambulance, for her French was pretty good, while she put her mouth to her husband's, and tried to breathe him back.

The paramedics came and did their best, as Gülten and Melis listened from the next room – to the massage of his heart, and the shocks of the defibrillator. 'Deeet – deeet – deeet,' says Gülten, almost in song, recalling the flat sound of the machine over twenty years ago. 'He's not coming back.' Her memory is poor these days, she tells me, but those moments she will never forget.

*

Gülten vapes silently as we talk. We are in her basement office in Cihangir, an İstanbul neighbourhood both bohemian and upmarket, sharply up a hill from the Bosphorus. It is a warm day in the middle of spring, and on the way here, crossing the straits on a ferry, I saw dolphins swimming on the surface – this is the season where they head north, to the cooler waters of the Black Sea. Gülten is in her early sixties, and seems to tread lightly through the world: she speaks gently, and even when she shows me around, walking with a cane, she moves with a certain grace. She works here in her studio, she tells me, part business, part museum to the husband she has lost.

It is a story that starts back in the mid-eighties, in a military prison on the outskirts of İstanbul. Gülten was a student on the radical left, and detained in 1980 like thousands of her comrades. She was sent to Metris, a new and brutal place, where she was heavily beaten. And there, if only for a few months, she was joined by the famous Selda Bağcan – folk singer, activist, and voice of the revolution that never was. Though Selda was ten years Gülten's senior, they quickly became very close. 'We took her in,' she remembers, of the group of young and hardened leftists on their ward. When Gülten's five-year sentence came to an end, they soon met up again. It was, Gülten remembers, a hard step back into normal life. She needed long-term treatment for the beatings she had endured in Metris, and perhaps a job to pay for it – 'I couldn't keep taking pocket money from my father.' Selda offered her a place at her new recording studio.

One day early on, Selda handed Gülten an album of an artist she had recorded, and suggested she listen. So it was that night, putting the cassette in the tape player, and lying down in bed, she heard his voice for the first time:

Aglama bebeğim / ağlama sen de. 'Don't cry my baby / don't you cry too.'

It was an inescapably eighties sound, all synth and drum machine, plus the more distinctive plucked strings of the *bağlama*, the Turkish long-necked lute. It was beautiful, she remembers thinking, but it was also brave. The lyrics were mostly taken from dissident poetry of the left – an album of longing, imprisonment, and exile. 'Who is that boy?' she asked a friend over breakfast the next morning. 'That's Ahmet Kaya.'

*

Up to that point, his life had not seen much success. A teenage school drop-out, he had floated from job to job: waiting in restaurants, peddling on the streets, even working off the books in

Germany for a few months. He was divorced, with a little daughter he rarely saw. And his music career was struggling. With no record label interested, he paid for his album's production himself, selling his beloved camera in the process, and with a little money from his mother too. When it was finally released, because of its political content – and this would happen many times in the repressive atmosphere of 1980s Turkey – the tapes in one city were briefly seized by prosecutors, before a judge deemed the album suitable for release. Regardless, *Ağlama Bebeğim* didn't sell much anyway. As Ahmet put it himself about those times: 'There was no work, we roamed the streets hungry, I was rejected, and I didn't see my baby.'[1]

Indeed, when Gülten met him a little while later at the studio, she wasn't immediately impressed. He had arrived dressed in a suit for a promotional picture – 'not my style at all', she laughs. Still, when he heard her story, he started asking her lots of questions: about her politics, which prison she was in, whether she was tortured. And if it was a little intense, it seemed at least they came from a similar place. Like her, he had spent time in prison – five months for hanging up leftist propaganda. Like her, he had many friends inside now too. And like her, she learnt, he was Kurdish.

*

In no other decade of Turkey's history had the denial of Kurdishness been so intense. This was a time dominated by the military junta, and the generals hanging over Turkish politics even once the civilians had formally taken back power. They were nationalists and statists, and resolved to never again let the country fall apart. Their approach to the Kurdish issue – that age-old question of what to do with the peoples of the south-east – was particularly hard line, and always underpinned by a soldier's threat of force. While the 1960 constitution had permitted only Turkish to be used in print and broadcast, the 1982 constitution went one step further still: 'no language prohibited by law shall be used in the expression and dissemination of thought.' Here then was an article that not only banned Kurdish in speech, but did so – consistent with the new era of denial – without explicitly naming the language either.[2] In the same year, an education minister sent out a reminder to all provincial governors that all folk songs must be sung in Turkish;[3] thousands of books, papers and magazines were burnt; a book published by the military after the 1980 coup claimed 'Kurd' was just the sound made when people living in the mountains stepped onto the snow.[4]

Yet it was a time when Kurdishness asserted itself all the same, and in new and bloody ways. Though Kurdish activism had never disappeared, since the rebellions of the twenties and thirties it had been a quiet few decades. It changed almost out of nowhere on a single day in August 1984, just a year before Ahmet and Gülten met. In a small south-eastern town, thirty militants killed one gendarme and announced their presence through the speakers of the local minaret; nearly four hundred kilometres away, others read out a statement in the town square. They were announcing the arrival of the PKK.[5]

In truth, the Partiya Karkerên Kurdistanê, the Kurdistan Workers' Party, had formed six years earlier, at a meeting in a village teahouse, papers taped over its windows. Most there – of the few dozen graduates, high-school students, university drop-outs and teachers – had been active on Turkey's left for years. And though their new organization was also Marxist-Leninist, it differed in two crucial ways: it sought to establish an independent Kurdistan across Turkey's south-east, and it would achieve it first and foremost through armed struggle. As one scholar wrote, the PKK – and its leader Abdullah Öcalan hiding out in Syria – viewed Kurdish history as one of corruption, shame, and betrayal, one from which only violence could set them free.[6] It was therefore a movement not just against the Turkish state, but the conservative forces that had dominated the region for so long – the *ağas*, sheikhs and tribal leaders. The first few years of the PKK's existence had been spent targeting those local elites. Now they were turning their attention to the Turkish state itself.

In response, the Turkish army moved five divisions down to the south-east, increased the number of gendarmes, and built more military outposts across the mountains. It began to enlist civilian Kurds in its efforts too. Within a year, there were over ten thousand 'village guards', locals armed and equipped to fight the growing threat in their home towns for seventy dollars a month.[7] Meanwhile, the slow erosion of Kurdish identity carried on: by 1986, thousands of Kurdish villages had been renamed. The conflict that would shape the region for the next decades was beginning, though of course its effects would be felt everywhere: the villager who ran away to join the PKK; the young Black Sea boy conscripted to serve in the south-east; and the Kurds like Gülten and Ahmet who lived way out west, and watched.

*

That after all was another experience they shared: not just that they were Kurdish, but that they were here in İstanbul. Gülten had moved from Elazığ as a student, while Ahmet had come even younger. He was from a poor family of seven in Malatya, who had migrated west when he was fifteen. It was then, looking at the Bosphorus, that he saw the sea for the first time. And while he had come to love the city, his early life in İstanbul hadn't been easy. He realized on the first day, he said later, that he spoke and dressed differently, and he would find it hard to fit in.[8] He would not be alone. As many Kurds living in western Turkey would say, discrimination was all too common: children asked by their classmates if they had a tail; or drivers stopped by the police because their licence plate betrayed a car registered in the south-east.

Gülten and Ahmet understood each other's lives before that too. Both Malatya and Elazığ were in the south-east, but they were not cities like Diyarbakır, Hakkari, or Batman: long opposed to the state and unashamedly Kurdish. They were instead more divided and fraught. Malatya had been on the border of the old Ottoman province of Kurdistan, and – as one activist once put it a little condescendingly – was full of Kurds who thought they were Turks.[9] It was conservative and, in Ahmet's time, a mixed population of Kurds and Turks, Sunnis and Alevis, leftists and rightists. A few years after Ahmet's family left for İstanbul, Malatya – like so much of Turkey in the late seventies – witnessed its own sectarian violence. Ahmet's childhood, in that context, seems at times to stand apart: his father was Kurdish, his mother Turkish, and though they were Sunnis, he spent hours learning music with the Alevis of his city, for the *bağlama* had a special place in Alevi culture. Its melody, as one singer had it, 'allows human spirits to rest.'[10] Still, the tension across Malatya was felt even within his family – his grandparents had fallen out with his parents over their marriage. Elazığ, where Gülten grew up, was similarly strained. Her family were Alevis in a predominantly Sunni and Turkish neighbourhood, and she remembers that her parents wouldn't speak Kurdish out on the street.

Both on the left and proud of their Kurdishness, they knew then the experience of feeling out of place, first in their home towns, and secondly in the city where they had moved. Beyond the broader outlines of their lives, of course, they shared something more human. They laughed at the same things. They liked the same poems. She went to his concerts and saw how the audience warmed to his music. But perhaps what she found most affecting about Ahmet was how convinced he was, despite his troubles, that this was what he was meant to do. 'He always believed in himself,' she remembers.

He had been playing all his life. As the story goes, his father, a factory worker, had given him a *bağlama* when he was six, and Ahmet practised behind their house, with impromptu concerts to the family chickens. At just nine, he had his first proper gig, for his father's fellow workers for May Day, before beginning to travel the region as a teenager – to Elazığ and Diyarbakır – playing at weddings and circumcision ceremonies.[11] He had his own self-taught style – at times plucking the strings in the traditional mode, at times hitting them roughly, or even all together like chords. By the time he met Gülten, he could play not only the *bağlama* but the oud, the violin, the piano, and the guitar.

They toured around with Selda, growing closer all the time. He was twenty-eight, she was twenty-five. She was beautiful and book-ish, he had almond eyes and a deep baritone voice. They fell in love. Working on his second album, they spent all night together talking about their pasts, and discussing their favourite poets. Indeed even now, when Gülten speaks, she refers to writers and thinkers – not in a showy way, just that it's clear it's how she understands the world. The album was not a big hit on its release, but slowly for Ahmet, things were starting to move.

Starting straight away on another, Gülten pushed him to be more daring still. There was a poem she had read in prison and found deeply moving. She thought it could be the title song on the next tape. It was called 'Şafak Türküsü', 'Dawn Song', and had been written by a leftist poet on death row. They tracked it down together, and Ahmet set to work – for he had a gift for seeing melodies in the written word. At times, Gülten remembers, the music in him seemed almost overwhelming. 'There are a million songs in my head!' he would complain, occasionally as an excuse for not listening. Some nights together, she would see his toes twitching to a rhythm as he slept.

'Şafak Türküsü', when he recorded it, sounded different from his previous songs. The drums are stripped back, the music a little slower. For the first forty seconds, it is just a flute and a *bağlama* weaving between each other, and then Ahmet starts to sing:

Beni burada arama / Don't look for me here
Arama anne / Don't look, Mum
Kapıda adımı sorma / Don't ask for my name at the door
Şaçlarına yıldız düşmüş / The stars have fallen on your hair
Koparma anne ağlama / Don't break, Mum, don't cry

It is a heartfelt plea, almost an apology, from a son to his mother, on the morning of his execution. And the way he sings it – his voice softer, more intimate – you feel less like listeners of a song, more like intruders in their final moments. He repeats the lines *şaçlarına yıldız düşmüş*, his baritone playing with the words, hovering over them at times with a slight vibrato. At other points, he reads out verses of the poem at a time. It goes on in total for nine minutes. And it seems like the moment a young artist has found his voice.

'"Şafak Türküsü" was the cry of millions when it met with the sound of Ahmet Kaya,' as one writer put it to me.[12] Though the album had the usual problems at first – a prosecutor seeking to ban it for its content, cassettes being confiscated at the record company headquarters[13] – it was eventually allowed to be sold, and did so in numbers that Ahmet had never seen before. At the heart of it, it seemed to recognize that Turkey was a nation of lost boys and grieving mothers. As Gülten explained, Turks on the left and right had been rounded up in their hundreds of thousands since the coup. Though few of them would be sentenced to death, the longing, the separation, and the resignation of 'Şafak Türküsü' resonated all the same. 'It was often mothers defending the rights of children at the prison gates, against the generals,' Gülten says. She adds another reason for the song's power: the words meant a lot to Ahmet himself. Not only had he spent time in prison, he was very close to his mother. He had lost his father in his early twenties, and it was her who had supported his career up to that point. 'In our culture,' Gülten continues, 'the matriarch of a family is like the roof of the house.'

*

Before I spoke to Osman, I had watched him in black-and-white funk videos from decades ago. In the 1970s, he had released an album setting old Ottoman classics to a disco beat, and played it with his orchestra live on state TV. He was a composer at the time, grooving along at the front of the stage in shades, an open suit, and an extravagant goatee. Nearly fifty years on, the goatee is still there, though all is now more white than black. He's still making music. As a producer, he has made over eight hundred albums since he started. 'Classical, Turkish classical, instrumental, disco music, protest music, Turkish jazz . . . in almost every genre across the seventies, eighties and nineties,' he tells me, 'more or less there is no Turkish artist I haven't worked with.'

Soon after the release of 'Şafak Türküsü', Osman met Ahmet for the first time in his studio. He had never heard of Ahmet before, and he came 'dressed in such a shabby outfit, it was ridiculous.' But the moment he heard him sing, he was convinced. 'The tone of his voice, it was really impressive.' It was a full bass-baritone, he remembers, but it had its own softness, 'it goes straight to someone's heart.' He could hear somewhere in it some part of his upbringing as well. As Osman and many others would tell me, though Ahmet didn't speak Kurdish, he sang 'with a Kurdish throat', wavering it up and down the notes. They began to discuss Ahmet's next work. Indeed, from that point on, Osman produced every one of the fifteen albums Ahmet released in his life.

It was a fertile time in Turkish music. For by Osman's description, when he started in the 1970s, things had become a little stale.

There was a derivative Turkish pop – 'based entirely on Western culture' – which often just lifted melodies wholesale from the US and Europe and translated the lyrics. There was 'Turkish folk', but oddly, as Osman puts it, 'Turkish music wasn't listened to by anyone in Turkey.' It was a genre almost entirely confected by the state. Musicologists had travelled the country to collect 'pure' Turkish music, then to be performed on the radio by large choirs and orchestras, sounding almost nothing like what Turks knew as local music.[14] There had been a lively dissident rock movement, but it had been largely driven underground by the coup.

By the mid-eighties though, it was a changing scene. Decades of migration to İstanbul were beginning to have an effect. There was a new urban audience, and new types of producers amongst them. As Osman sums it up a little bluntly, 'People sold their fields and cows, came to the city, and started making different kinds of records.' They brought with them a genre known as *arabesk*, full of silky violins, large string orchestras, *bağlama*s, and most importantly, the plaintive cries of a solo singer. Lyrically, it was a music of laments, heartbreak, and abandonment to fate. 'If your love was poison,' went one of its pioneering records, 'I would still drink it.' Even the structure of the music was disposed to the sad – its modes were built not around Western scales but Arabic *makams*. As one academic wrote, the most used *makam* in Turkish *arabesk* has a 'friendly and gloomy character', ever popular with Turks.[15]

It was a genre long in the making. While in the 1930s and 1940s Turkish state radio was trying to promote its reconstructed folk, listeners instead were tuning into Egyptian and Lebanese stations abroad, and were captured by what they heard.[16] Over time, local musicians responded, and created an *arabesk* that was ever more Turkish, with their own lyrics, their own instruments, and even their own regional variations too. Though it was banned on Turkish radio, it was the music of Anatolia all the same. Of course, after decades of migration, İstanbul by the 1980s was more Anatolian than ever. So while *arabesk* may have been initially met with a degree of snobbery by the city's oldest residents – it was the music of the *dolmuş* and the *gecekondu* – by now it had more or less eclipsed all else. As Osman told me, he had been classically trained, and had to learn the *makams* and melodies of *arabesk* as he went. Indeed, by the middle of the decade, it had become so pervasive, and was selling so many records, it was hard to categorize as a single genre any more.

Ahmet, who had grown up playing the *bağlama* in provincial Malatya, of course knew *arabesk* well. But he was steeped in older traditions too: in Anatolian folk, and the Kurdish epics he heard from his father. During his military service, he played in the army band, and learned about the violin and cello, and various Western motifs. At home, as Gülten tells me, he listened not only to local stuff but classical music as well. In other moods, he would go for Pink Floyd or Iron Maiden instead. Then, of course, was perhaps the genre that drew his heart most: the long and storied line of Turkish protest music. His music then was often difficult to define: the melancholic sound and instruments of *arabesk* perhaps, but with none of the fatalism of its lyrics.

It was a composite style well suited to a composite age: his first single with Osman, a rousing, almost anthemic rendition of a poem by another socialist poet, topped the local charts; the bestseller from abroad – the lists were split – was 'La Isla Bonita' by Madonna.[17] This, Gülten reminds me, was just his official success. He was listened to on bootlegged tapes all over.

*

Over the next few years, Ahmet's career finally took off. Though of course – as a protest singer in 1980s Turkey – no rise could ever be completely smooth: he was banned on the radio, and his albums

were subject as always to legal threats, prosecutions, and confisca-
tions. But still, through word of mouth, and particularly on the left,
his reputation grew. Osman recorded with him in his own complex
in İstanbul – 'a factory', he remembers, with its three studios and a
mastering suite. And if it was one of the most advanced production
houses in Turkey, it didn't seem to faze Ahmet. 'He would turn it
into a restaurant', Osman says, bringing in *köfte* and meat stews
he had made at home, or sleeping there through the day, only to
record his songs at night. With a bear-like presence, shabby black
hair, and thick beard, he was perhaps a little more down-to-earth
than the stars Osman normally worked with. 'He loved life', he says,
'he was very positive.' Slowly, the production on his records grew
bigger, the strings more sweeping, and they were sold by larger
record companies.

By the early nineties, his fame had reached new heights, as the
state relinquished its monopoly on TV and radio and private channels began playing Ahmet to those who had never heard of him.
Just a few years after he was, in his words, 'wandering the streets
hungry', he could now buy a motorbike, a BMW, and a summer
house on the Aegean coast, though Gülten objects a little to the
insinuation. They moved into their first place shortly after they got
married, she tells me, and it was a converted 'office of a friend's
uncle', with no curtains on the windows, and barely any furniture
in the rooms. Most of the money, she explains, went to labels and
middlemen. When I ask about the summer home, she answers that
it was really very small, 'but the left-wing magazines were saying
we were hugely rich, composing songs sipping whisky by a seaside
villa', she continues, laughing at herself, 'and I tried to disprove
them like an idiot.'

It was always, Gülten tells me, a slightly ragged, family affair.
When Ahmet would do concerts, Gülten would cook meals for
the band, helped out by her older brother Yusuf too. Indeed, Yusuf

was a poet himself, and Ahmet set many of his words to music in those years. It was a creative trio behind much of Ahmet's work, bound not just in song but by blood. A couple of years after they fell in love, Ahmet and Gülten had their daughter Melis. There is a picture of him with unruly bed head, curls all around, serenading her in her cot with his *bağlama*. She looks around six months old, and is staring straight back at him, sporting, like her father, a mop of wild dark hair.

It was around this time that Ahmet's live performances – up till then, small gigs here and there – were transformed into something much grander, with stages, open arenas, and atmospheres he had never seen. As one artist who once sang alongside him told me, Ahmet suited live performances: he was warm and extroverted, 'the type to call everyone *canım* and *çiğerim*', little Turkish terms of endearment that literally mean 'my life' and 'my liver'. At his first mass concert in the summer of 1990, at least a hundred and fifty thousand fans filled İstanbul's Gülhane Park with an energy that was almost uncontained.[18] As the papers reported the next day, members of the audience yelled and surged; the police, at times fighting them back, fired into the air. As Gülten remembers, at the end of it, Ahmet was drenched in sweat. And in the next few days, as always, another prosecutor opened a case against him. During his performance, a spectator had jumped up on stage, and wrapped a yellow, red, and green scarf around Ahmet's neck. They were the colours of the Kurdistan flag.

*

The last few years – the very same when Ahmet's career had lifted off – had seen the skirmishes in the south-east transform into an all-out civil war. Most of the region was under some kind of martial law, and the number of soldiers and gendarmes was increasing all the while. Their raids on villages suspected of aiding or housing militants became feared all over – marked by arbitrary arrests, beatings, and all sorts of petty humiliations. As one journalist at the time wrote, he saw children in one village who had learned to put their hands on their heads whenever they saw the police.[19] Besides the security forces, over a hundred thousand village guards were recruited too. It was a military response as heavy-handed as it was brutal, and symbolized for many by the prison to which many Kurdish activists, journalists, and militants were sent: Diyarbakır No. 5. It was a place of systematic torture – of electric shocks, sexual assault, and *falaka* foot whippings[20] – where inmates were dressed in uniform, and made to sing the Turkish national anthem.

The PKK meanwhile saw an almost inexorable rise in its recruits, taking in thousands of young men from across the south-east – still, as ever, the poorest region in Turkey. As one historian writes, their relentless guerrilla war, and their refusal to wilt, had earned many locals' trust and respect.[21] But they were not immune from exacting some brutality of their own. They would kill not just village guards but their families. In one hilltop village somewhere near Mardin, after a shootout with local guards, thirty militants descended on the settlement and killed eight men, six women, and sixteen children. In the inhuman logic of a civil war, it was a village indelibly tainted by its collaboration with the state.

Still by the late eighties, most of the rest of the country was not so aware of what was happening in the south-east. Or more accurately perhaps, they seemed unwilling to hear. When a Social Democrat deputy talked of 'the Kurdish problem' in the assembly in 1988, members from the main party drowned him out by banging on their desks, yelling, and spitting in his direction. But it was becoming more difficult to ignore. For one, the PKK had a growing following amongst Kurds in western Turkey. But perhaps even more significantly, it seemed to have become a cause taken up not just by militants, but by people right across the south-east. After a funeral for one rebel, there were mass protests in Nusaybin and then Cizre. As one Turkish newspaper put it, there was 'the air of revolution.'[22]

Tentatively, politicians were beginning to recognize this was not a problem to be solved through denial and force. Turgut Özal – a more radical voice now as President rather than Prime Minister – repealed the Kurdish language ban in February 1991, though it was still in place for broadcast, print, and education. And if it was in some ways just an acceptance of reality – it had proved impossible, of course, to ban a language 'for the dissemination of thought' – it was a major breakthrough all the same. Still, there was only so far Turkish politics was willing to go. On the same very day, the assembly passed a new anti-terror law, with wording so wide it threatened to prosecute anyone involved in the promotion of Kurdish culture – to charge, in the words of its article 8, individuals engaging in 'oral and written propaganda that aims to destroy the national unity and the indivisibility of the Turkish republic.' As Gülten tells me, Ahmet always felt Kurdish to his core. So as the conflict in the south-east grew more intense, there was a notable change in his music too. While all around him, *arabesk* singers were embracing the fame and money of the early nineties scene – their lyrics growing more banal, their *makams* that bit poppier – Ahmet's art was going somewhere else entirely. If only obliquely and occasionally, his lyrics were beginning to address the situation down south. 'I fell in love with the peaks', he sang in one song; another spoke of three bandits in the mountains. His melodies were growing a little more eastern too – more violin strings, more *darbuka* drums.

Things soon got much darker. In the spring of 1993, Özal – who had recently not only acknowledged 'the Kurdish Issue' for the first time, but managed to orchestrate a ceasefire too – died suddenly of a heart attack. The respite had been cruelly short; the violence returned less restrained than ever. In May, near the eastern city of Bingöl, PKK militants intercepted a bus carrying thirty-five unarmed Turkish soldiers, and killed all but two of them. In October, after a PKK attack on Lice killed one gendarme, soldiers closed off the roads to the town of ten thousand and started firing on the houses. Over thirty people were killed.[23] Around the mountains of the Turkish and Iraqi border – where PKK militants were based – villages were bombed from above ever more indiscriminately. Yet it was the Turkish army's decision to empty the Kurdish countryside that had the longest lasting effect. They had realized that militants depended on local villages for food to eat, places to stay, and information to accrue. So beginning in the eighties, and intensifying in the early nineties, they developed a new strategy: draft or destroy, as some described it.[24] They turned up at villages early in the morning; locals were given the choice either to join the village guards, or leave within twenty-four hours. The scenes, at times, seemed medieval: houses and fields set on fire, lines of villagers escaping on foot, leading donkeys laden with their possessions.[25] A thousand villages were evacuated in 1994 alone.[26]

'Living in İstanbul didn't help us', Gülten tells me, for they were both still deeply attached to the south-east. They would visit their wider families around Elazığ, Adiyaman, and Dersim, and see for themselves what was going on. 'Villages in Kurdistan are being emptied, people are being massacred', Ahmet wrote in a newspaper column, 'the demand of the Kurdish people to live humanely is being suppressed by the Turkish republic with blood and slaughter.' If no doubt instinctively he sympathized with the wider Kurdish cause, calling it a 'just war' too, he called for a peaceful solution all the same. 'I am sad for the young who die in a soldier's uniform, and for the death of the guerrilla on the mountain', he continued, 'let the parties sit at the table and solve the problem.'[27]

'We saw a black cloud over ourselves', Gülten says, as the war came ever closer to their home. It was already a little tense for

İstanbul Kurds – the PKK had bombed a train station in the city, killing five military students, and outraging the wider population – but for Ahmet and Gülten there were more personal terrors to face. This was the age of the unsolved murder, of death squads targeting politicians, activists, and journalists. Hundreds were killed every year. It was a murky underground world drawing in conservative Kurdish tribesmen, mafia bosses, and far-right nationalists. But somewhere behind it was the state's involvement too. Famously, victims were often kidnapped first in 'white Toros' cars, the Renault model preferred by the counter-terror agency. As Gülten tells me, some of their friends and acquaintances had already been killed. Ahmet, who had made a very good friend high up in the police force, was told that they had seen his name on a death list too.

*

The most popular album that Ahmet ever made starts with fifty seconds of drums and violin. And then the words he wrote himself, and that familiar voice: '*Martılar ağlardı, çöplüklerde / Biz seninle gülüşürdük.*' 'The seagulls used to cry in the rubbish dumps / We used to laugh.' It's admittedly a slightly enigmatic opening, but soon it becomes clear. This is a deeply personal love song, set against the backdrop of war:

Şehirlere bombalar yağardı her gece, / The bombs used to drop on the city every night,

Biz durmadan sevişirdik / And we'd make love without stopping

Acımasız olma şimdi bu kadar, / Now don't be cruel,

Dün gibi, dün gibi çekip gitme / Don't go away like yesterday, like yesterday

Bırak da sarılayım ayaklarına, / Let me hug you, let me wrap around your feet

Kum gibi, kum gibi ezip geçme. / Don't crush me like sand, like sand.

'Kum gibi' is perhaps the masterpiece of Ahmet's career – his best-known song, and the distillation of his sound: the arabesk rhythms, the gravelly voice, the words that addressed something beyond. Yet it showed also, as Gülten tells me, that Ahmet was an artist who at heart sang not so much about politics but about the human relationships caught up in it: sons and mothers, friends and lovers. Here was a singer – whose Turkish, Kurdish parents had risked the wrath of their families to marry thirty years before – who was moved by love and what it could transcend.

It was the first song of the album *Şarkılarım Dağlara*, 'My Songs to the Mountains' – fifty minutes of music that spoke to the civil war in a way that Ahmet had never done previously. 'Murder Hour', 'Freedom Call', 'Death Quatrain', as the song list goes. Gülten wrote the lyrics to one of its other hits, a song with an almost bruised-sounding clarinet and an electro-*bağlama*, and ending with Ahmet, far from the microphone, shouting in rage. Of course, she tells me, he was angry at what was happening, at 'the injustice done to the Kurdish people'. 'If the outside world was butterflies and blooming flowers,' she continues, 'maybe we'd write just romantic songs.' The album went on to sell nearly three million copies, bought not just by Kurds or those on the left but by people all over Turkey. When I ask her if she was surprised at all by its success, she shrugs. 'Not really,' she explains, because the feelings it expressed were being felt on all sides. Whether Turkish conscripts or PKK militants, 'children were dying in the mountains all the same.' Indeed, some recruits to the PKK by the mid-nineties were as young as fourteen. Osman his producer has a further explanation for *Şarkılarım Dağlara*'s popularity. The last song on it is just a classic arabesk tune about a heartbroken man, waiting for his love. Upbeat and very danceable, apparently after recording Ahmet didn't want it on the album at all, but was overruled. 'That song appealed to everyone in Turkey,' says Osman, and helped him be heard in circles that, perhaps, wouldn't normally be drawn to an album dedicated solely to the country's civil war.

Now a household name, Ahmet soon became a star not only on the radio but on television too. In 1995, a private TV channel contracted him to his own weekly show, *Ahmet Abi'nin Vapuru*, 'Big Brother Ahmet's Boat' – an eclectic thing of music performances, guest interviews, and political discussion. As he said in his first episode – suited up, but still a casual presence on screen – he wanted to help the country 'learn to live lovingly together.' Of course, he was wealthier than ever too. He had bought a Mercedes and a jeep, as well as some more extravagant purchases: a motorbike, cameras, and an Atari video console. He had – as many attest – a boyish side, and an endless wonder of gadgets. 'He never knew the concept of money,' Gülten says – even now a little despairingly – and would give it out to friends, or would be so disorganized he would run out of cash on tour. Even the fancy cars, she tells me, had a slightly charming, childlike explanation: he was afraid of flying, and so would drive to his concerts even in Europe.

Still, he was criticized often. As Ahmet's biographer told me, Kurds thought he had forgotten himself, drinking wine and driving a Mercedes; those on the broader left despaired of his lavishness. He would make more painful decisions for them in time. Though his TV show only aired for a dozen or so episodes, one was filmed at the resort of a notorious nationalist mobster in Elazığ out east. As the biographer said, it was a decision typical of a man who often moved between the various groups split across Turkish society, and perhaps even enjoyed provoking them, mocking them as he went. As he found while researching his life, 'one of his friends was a right-wing chief of police, another was a Turkish restaurant owner, another a Kurdish folk singer.' They all hated each other, he says, 'the only thing they had in common was Ahmet Kaya.'[28]

It was not just his music then that was hard to categorize. Though

Kaya described himself as a leftist, democrat, and revolutionary, at times he seems like a kind of rough Anatolian liberal, who valued freedom above all. When a young Recep Tayyip Erdoğan – then Mayor of İstanbul – was sentenced to prison for reciting a poem, Ahmet defended his right to free speech. He supported the right too of female students to go to university in headscarves. In the atmosphere of mid-nineties Turkey – where the military had just forced Turkey's first Islamist government to step down – both were stances to court risk. He seemed to be walking a fine line: going to the same balls and restaurants as the old elites, but not quite accepted by them all the same.

Ahmet still of course had his causes. In 1995, he met the 'Cumartesi Anneleri', the Saturday Mothers who gathered in İstanbul every week at noon and held vigils for their children, missing somewhere in the south-east. He released an album in their name the same year. The conflict itself had reached a new, more nihilistic phase. As the Turkish military strategy to empty out the villages stretched PKK supply lines, causing heavy losses and retreats, the group turned to new tactics of its own: women, who had joined the PKK in their thousands over the last couple of years, staged a few suicide attacks. Meanwhile, the number of internal refugees grew ever higher. And as they migrated, in a sense Ahmet's life in İstanbul became more emblematic again, as Kurdish geography shifted from the mountains to cities, from the south-east to out west, and beyond to Europe too. By the end of the decade, up to two million Kurds were displaced.[29]

For his part, Ahmet in those years was drawn increasingly to the Kurdish language itself, and in particular to an old Kurdish love song called 'Karwan'. Of course, he couldn't speak Kurdish, but he had grown up with its music nonetheless. As Gülten tells me, they had both listened to Radio Yerevan on little battery radios as a child – a station from across the Soviet border that had beamed in an hour of Kurdish radio into Turkey once a week. 'He was sad he didn't know it,' she says, and would always be a little regretful at his silences when they visited distant family in villages across the south-east. In a way, it was a typical experience for Kurds all over Turkey: proud of a language they didn't speak, at times embarrassed that they couldn't understand, and resentful too of a Turkish state that had repressed it for so long.

It is something I have noted in my own time in Turkey at least. Often I am scolded by Turks for not speaking better Turkish – 'shame!' – as if it is a moral failing. But travelling around the south-east, the reaction has a different tone: not reproachful but understanding – for many of them are less than fluent in a language dear to them as well – and a recognition that languages, who can talk them and how well, are social, political things too.

*

As the nineties neared their end in Turkey, the country was a febrile place. After the government had finally, successfully convinced its Syrian counterpart to stop hosting the PKK's leader Öcalan in 1998, he embarked on a long and at times public tour of possible countries for his next safe haven – Greece, Russia, Italy, Tajikistan, Belarus, and finally Kenya. It outraged mainstream Turkish opinion, aghast that they would not simply hand over a man deemed worldwide to be the head of a terrorist organization. It was an international story that would have inevitable consequences for Kurds at home. In November, just a few days after Italy decided it could not extradite someone to a country where they faced the death penalty, Turkish authorities raided the offices of the country's biggest Kurdish party, arresting three thousand.[30] In January 1999, a prosecutor sought to close it down entirely at the Constitutional Court, alleging that it had too close a tie with the PKK. To stoke the flames a little further, there were local elections coming up as well, with the party predicted to scoop up votes and mayoralties all across the south-east.

It was in this context then that in early February, Ahmet went to the Princess Hotel in İstanbul, dressed in a dark silk suit. He was attending a glitzy award ceremony hosted by the magazine journalists' association, and Gülten accompanied him. Midway through the night he won 'Best Artist of the Year', and went up to accept his prize. He dedicated it, he said, to the Saturday Mothers still holding their vigils. And then he utters the sentences that would change his life for ever. 'On my upcoming tape, because I have Kurdish roots, I'm doing a Kurdish song,' he says, a smile on his face, 'and I'm going to do a video in Kurdish. I know there are brave people who will broadcast it. And if they don't, I know they will be called to account by the Turkish people as well.'

He finishes, and the camera pans to some stony faces amongst the crowd. And unbeknownst to Ahmet, as he begins to sing his latest hit, he seems to have tapped into some deep history: the same history that had been changing village names for nearly eight decades, that took Kurdish children into regional boarding schools to 'educate them properly', that, two years after Ahmet was born, arrested a Kurdish poet for publishing a Kurdish poem in a newspaper, that even now, where Kurds were being tortured a thousand kilometres away, had written across the entrance of Diyarbakır Prison *Türkçe konuş, çok konuş*, 'speak Turkish, speak it a lot'.[31] He finishes, and a kind of spontaneous rage ripples across the room. As he sits down, as Gülten once put it, 'all of these chic men and women turned to monsters'.[32] They throw knives and forks, shout, 'There is no such thing as a Kurd', and call him a pimp. Out of nowhere, a group of singers go on stage and start singing an old independence anthem, led by a young starlet in a shimmering scarlet shirt and leather trousers. The audience clap and pound their fists in the air, turned both to the front and directly to Ahmet and a smoking Gülten too. Faced with this – this collective strength of cowards – they escape with security, looking slightly bewildered, and are spirited away in an old yellow taxi.

The reaction doesn't stop there. Over the next few days, Ahmet's posters are ripped off walls and his CDs publicly crushed in stores. Much more seriously, they receive death threats in their letter box and on the phone. Neither of them dare leave the house, and they notice as well that few of their friends are calling to check in either. Melis, eleven years old, asks her parents what 'traitor' means after watching the news.[33] Then a newspaper publishes a picture of Ahmet, supposedly from a concert he gave in Berlin in 1993. Behind him is a map of putative Kurdistan, and pictures of Öcalan; it carries quotes from him at the gig too, in support of the PKK.

As if to complete the nationalist frenzy, that very week Öcalan is captured in Kenya by Turkish agents, handcuffed, blindfolded, and flown back to Turkey. He is tried in May that year, and sentenced to death in June. One more to the conflict's death toll, then – by that point, it had killed six thousand Turkish soldiers and gendarmes, twenty thousand PKK militants, and five thousand civilians.[34]

*

Ahmet was charged twice over for aiding and abetting an illegal terrorist organization: once for his speech at the awards ceremony, and once for his alleged remarks in Berlin. He would be tried at a type of court – dating back to the 1980 coup – set up specifically to deal with cases of national security. By the time the hearings began in April he was already on the decline: embittered, struggling with his health, and putting on weight. His lawyers had at least managed to have a travel ban lifted – for he had a tour of Europe ahead. So faced with the prospect of years in prison, he left Turkey for good. On a warm June night, he recorded 'Karwan' – the Kurdish love song that had started all of this – and slipped out of the country at

4 a.m. the next day. He didn't – it must be said – help his own cause while he was away. At one gig in Germany, faced with thousands of migrant Kurds chanting for Öcalan, he changed the lyrics of one of his songs – a mischievous look on his face – to express his support as well. More charges would come, and more furious headlines too.

As he settled briefly in Paris, Gülten moved between there and İstanbul, where her daughter was at school and her husband was on trial. Their defence was simple enough: that he had never given a concert at the alleged time, that the quotes were fake and the pictures doctored. After first publishing them, they noted, the paper had not even handed over the originals to the court. He was first asked by the judge, before he left, why he wanted to sing in Kurdish if he didn't speak it; he replied that plenty of singers in Turkey sang songs in English without knowing what they were saying either.

'Every day Ahmet said, "I want to go back", Gülten tells me, 'that he would get on a boat and row in the dark waters towards Turkey.' He missed sleeping in the same bed, but Gülten told him it was too dangerous, and they would have to trust in justice and the law. 'In one moment,' she says, recalling the time she was sitting on a bench in an İstanbul court, trying to read the body language of the judges before her, 'those concepts were destroyed. They immediately collapsed in my head.' Ahmet was acquitted for the awards speech, but given three years and nine months in absentia for the supposed concert in Berlin.

At times speaking to Gülten, she flitters to the present tense, as if it is all happening again now. She still, she tells me, can't believe the verdict. Minutes later, she went out of the courtroom, and called her husband to share the news.

*

He was living in a small apartment in Paris. He tried to learn French and Kurdish, worked through his legal appeals, but more than anything, eagerly awaited the visits of his wife and daughter. 'He never liked loneliness,' Gülten tells me, 'he was always asking when I would come . . . If I came twice a month it wasn't enough.' He was someone, she continued, 'who loved being at home, to be home and be protected.' It wasn't just his family he missed, but Turkey too – even on three-month tours, she says, he would tend to come back home every few weeks, for he was never so comfortable abroad. He would walk by the Seine and pretend it was the Bosphorus, and scour supermarkets and petrol stations for something that tasted like the soups he knew. Every night, Gülten tells me, they would watch Turkish news together, and talk on the phone as if they were side by side. While he started with the hope he would soon return, it gradually dawned on Ahmet that this was the shape of his life. He became depressed, put on even more weight, and suffered with stomach ulcers. 'The disease of exile,' Gülten says. His heart began to trouble him too. And though he was unable to write music, his ability with words at least was not lost. As he wrote one day:

'Instead of being in the middle of Paris right now, I would be in my house in İstanbul, by my barbecue with its crooked leg. Instead of drinking wines whose names I do not know, I would like to drink a glass of *rakı* whose smell and taste I have never forgotten, or to go down to the Bosphorus and eat *köfte* and bread, and afterwards drink a glass of beer. And then go home, as always, joking with the cops on the streets . . . You think you sent me out of my country and you wonder if I'll ever come back. But I'm already there, and I have no intention of going anywhere else.'[35]

And then that night in November, when Gülten and Ahmet laughed at a film they'd seen many times before, and the next morning she woke up to a thud in the corridor. He was forty-three years old. 'He was a cactus with thorns, used to the tough and sandy soils of Turkey,' she says, 'but they plucked him from his earth and planted him in the soft soil of Europe. He faded and withered. He was an artist that fed from here.'

*

When Ahmet died in November 2000, the landscape that had defined much of his adult life was changing. After Öcalan's capture the year before, the PKK was sapped by defections and surrender – its fighting force of around fifty thousand dwindled to around six.[36] And as their leader's death sentence was commuted to life imprisonment, he called on all his militants to withdraw from Turkey entirely. A kind of peace – fragile and temporary – was restored. Meanwhile, as Turkey began talks to join the EU, it passed a series of dramatic reforms. In October 2001, a constitutional amendment package eased language laws further; the following March, radio and TVs were allowed to broadcast in Kurdish; the next June, Kurds found it much easier to give their children Kurdish names. Martial law – which had been applied in various provinces as far back as 1980 – was finally lifted completely. So it was that in 2003, just a few years after Ahmet's announcement to that awards ceremony in İstanbul, İbrahim Tatlıses – the old Kurdish king of arabesk – sang a Kurdish song live on TV. Amidst all the changes, there was a flourishing of Kurdish literature, cultural festivals, and music across the south-east. But without a political settlement, it was all built on shaky ground. In 2004, the PKK called off their ceasefire. And beyond a few years' brief respite, they have been fighting ever since.

As Ahmet's biographer told me, all those criticisms of Ahmet, from the left and from his fellow Kurds, faded away after his death. He became an iconic martyr instead – one I've heard in music bars not just in Van, Diyarbakır, and Mardin, but in İstanbul and beyond. In part, perhaps, it is because some part of his music – and its human spirit – speaks to a hope that Turks and Kurds have all over. Those years saw huge numbers of Kurdish migrants move to cities across Turkey, to Adana, Mersin, Antalya, as well of course to İstanbul and Ankara too. And while they have felt discriminated against when trying to rent a flat or find a job, they did not tend to see racist violence either. After fifteen years of bitter civil war, Turkey stretched and strained, but it did not rip.

But his story of course speaks to pain too, not only of the point-less destruction of those years – the lives lost and lands razed – but of the sense of exile left amongst those who survived. That exodus from the south-east was not like those of Turkey's past, where migrants could leave their village house intact, return every now and again, and keep the flame alive. Instead, many of the Kurds of the nineties were more or less severed from their homes. The villages were changed for good, or lost completely. Instead they were stuck in new cities they didn't know, surrounded by a lan-guage they didn't understand. Even death brought its own kind of space between. The PKK for years kept no records of its casualties, so many did not know whether, or how, or where, their sons and daughters had died.

That afternoon after we talk, Gülten goes home to pack her things once more. She is off to Paris again, where she spends half her time, and where Melis will be waiting for her as well. Zoom out a little, and you see hers as a life of exile upon exile, of Turkish history folding back in on itself. Though she grew up in Elazığ, it is not where she first lived. Her parents were originally from Dersim, where her family had to leave like all others. But even in the first town where they went – after some Sunni and Alevi clashes – they did not feel safe, and decided to leave once more. The journey on is her first memory. She was five years old, and they had packed all their things into a truck. Somewhere along the way down south to Elazığ, her ginger cat Minnoş jumped off and fled.

12. The Prison Nation

2000s to present – Silivri Penitentiaries Campus

SEVENTY KILOMETRES WEST OF İSTANBUL, SILIVRI IS A getaway town, of fish restaurants along the marina, day boats waiting in the harbour, and hawkers working the promenade with balloons in the form of SpongeBob SquarePants. It had, I'm told, a more prestigious past: an important, ancient Greek port on the Marmara. But that was long ago, and it is a sleepy place now. Even the sea – a bluey grey haze – can barely muster a ripple. I take a *dolmuş* out of town. The earth looks like it is made of different stuff here in Thrace – rolled flat and green – and there are wildflowers by the side of the road. We pass artichoke fields. It's the season, and they are sold in jars in the market, stripped and squashed, next to bunches of Silivri's famous lavender. We roll on down the motorway, past shopping malls, wind turbines, and big expanses of grass, keeping the sea to our left. At the sign for Marmara Ceza İnfaz Kurumları Kampüsü, we hang right and turn inland. There are only a few of us on the minibus – the others are all laden with plastic bags. They are, I guess, staff who have gone shopping in the town centre, before coming back to their homes.

I am a little nervous as we step off. I am, in fact, unsure as to whether I'm allowed to be here at all. Certainly I can go no further. The road ahead, and the fields to my right, are closed off with fences and barbed wire. To my left, the entrance lies behind a giant manned barricade. Behind it, I see the two spires of a mosque rising up above, and rows and rows of apartment blocks, all in salmon pink. I know what lies beyond them, spreading out south-west towards the sea. I have seen it in pictures: nine separate prisons lying low to the ground, walled off even from each other, each containing their own separate wards, each containing their own separate cells. Worlds within worlds within worlds.

*

For as long as there has been a Turkey, there have been Turkish prison stories – tales of imprisoned writers writing epics, or of activists and politicians bravely suffering their fate. Şule Yüksel Şenler went to prison; Yusuf Sönmez went to prison; Ahmet and Gülten Kaya went to prison. Famously, before he became Prime Minister, Recep Tayyip Erdoğan spent four months inside too. But Silivri is on a different scale.

Its origins go back to those early years of Erdoğan's time in power, when Turkey seemed at last a country again on solid ground. The 1990s had seen a bewildering array of coalitions and parties, economic crises that had left millions unemployed, three-digit inflation, and of course the conflict in the south-east. Under the AKP majority government from 2002, things soon felt different:

Kurdish rights were in some part acknowledged, the economy was growing, and politics was stable. And all under the leadership of a man who may have been a devout Muslim with an Islamist past, but who seemed also a modernizing force.

Away from the public's attention, their reform programme extended to Turkey's prisons, to make them, as a law passed in 2004 put it, dedicated to prisoners' 'improvement'. In truth, they were in part carrying on changes that had preceded them, to move Turkey's prisoners from institutions with rooms of forty or fifty to more manageable ones with cells of one to three. It had already been a bloody transition: marked by hunger strikes, death fasts, and violent transferrals of thousands of prisoners to the new jails.[1] But the AKP, once in power, resolved to press ahead.

Construction of a new generation of prisons began in 2005. For the flagship prison of the new era a site was chosen just west of Silivri, part of which had been – as the story goes – a mulberry orchard. And covering one million square metres, it was to replace not just one prison but two. Bayrampaşa was İstanbul's primary prison, but it was – in the words of one national newspaper – 'neglected and inadequate'.[2] Opened in the mid-sixties for a capacity of around one thousand two hundred, it now housed over four thousand. According to one report, there were bunk beds lined up in the corridors, only enough hot water for one shower a week, and a shortage of toilets.[3] Its population would be transferred wholesale. Silivri would also take over from the small county jail in the town's centre. By chance, I spoke to someone who grew up next to it as a child, and used to make food at home to bring to those inside. It was a small stone thing under ash trees, he told me, with a capacity of around sixty. And the only crimes they had committed, he went on, almost nostalgically, were drunken fights and traffic accidents.

For the huge prison being built on the outskirts was not at all popular in the town itself. As one local put it to me, 'Silivri' had meant summer houses, beautiful sand, and plentiful fish. It was known for its buffalo and their yoghurt. 'We want the region to be associated with tourism,' said the Mayor at the time, begging at least for the prison's name to be changed.[4] Many were afraid that the town – whose population was only around sixty thousand itself – would be changed beyond recognition. As one local baker told a newspaper the year Silivri opened, she was afraid to go out after 9 p.m.[5] But there was no stopping Silivri being built, and by the spring of 2008 it was ready to start taking prisoners. It was separated into nine units – eight closed prisons and one open – each administered independently by separate directors and staff. Inside, for most of the prison, the large room system of old was replaced by smaller units of twenty-one prisoners, split across cells of three. The cells had access to TV and radio, and a panic button to call the officers. Beyond them, each unit had common areas and courtyards. Across the wider complex, there was a hospital, a library, classrooms and workshops, an indoor sports centre, and two open-air pitches.[6] The sports facilities, as one BBC reporter put it, 'would be the envy of any local school.'[7]

And that was just for the inmates. For the staff who worked there, there were five hundred separate flats, a mosque, a market, a restaurant, and for their wider families – if needed – a primary school and nursery. As one prisoner later wrote, from his cell, every Monday and Friday he could hear the flag ceremonies of the officers' children at school.[8] There were kitchens of course, and a bakery that could produce thirty thousand loaves a day. For high-security cases, there were two courtrooms within the prison walls.

Across the Turkish press at its opening there were repeated, gleeful mentions of Silivri's technology: retina scans at exits and entrances, 2,592 cameras, and an X-ray check to prevent contraband. It was an institution, in the words of one prison manager, 'that many countries in Europe should take as an example'. Indeed, many early prisoners from Bayrampaşa were quoted saying how much happier they were now: it was cleaner, more modern, and open prisoners could work in the canteen. Some however were slightly less sure how to react. For there were a few other facts about Silivri that were hard to ignore: for one, it was called officially 'The Silivri Penitentiaries Campus', a name that suggested a type, a scale of prison they had not seen before; it had cost $80 million to build; and its stated total capacity was eleven thousand men. *Avrupa'nın en büyük cezaevi maalesef bizde*, as one headline put it, 'Europe's Biggest Prison is Ours, Unfortunately'.[9]

*

Silivri had not even been completed by the time it saw its first mass trial. As the Director General of Prisons told the press in the summer of 2009, prisons Nos 1 and 2 were still being prepared. But Silivri would be ready regardless. Its courtrooms had proved too small for what was required, so instead, they had converted a gym hall into a court instead, with a capacity in total for 753: lawyers, journalists, and a section of 180 down the middle for the defendants.[10]

The accused were quite the cast. Over the last few years, state prosecutors had claimed to have unearthed a series of plots, from bombings to coups that aimed to overthrow the Erdoğan government as soon as it came to power. Hundreds were arrested – generals and police chiefs, journalists and lawyers – an alleged nationalist, republican conspiracy desperate to remove Turkey's Islamists from office. They were housed in Silivri Prison Nos 4 and 5 as they awaited trial. Indeed, the newspapers enthusiastically reported which commander or police officer was where, who they were bunking up with, and how they would go to the prison's special computer room to prepare their defence. They added that the whole campus was being guarded by six hundred gendarmes.[11]

When the hearings began, it seemed Silivri was hosting a historic moment. For many observers, it seemed undeniable that the secular republican establishment *had* been determined to remove the government – by now twice elected – from power. The military, for example, had famously issued a memorandum threateningly warning about 'the unchangeable characteristics of Turkey'; a chief prosecutor had come close to closing the party down at the constitutional court. Let alone the deeper history, of hats and headscarves, and coups threatened and real. Besides, as one activist described it to me, many on trial were 'the usual suspects', ultra-nationalist 'dark forces'. Perhaps this was the moment, after all, when Turkey was reconciling in some way to its past. At least belatedly, some locals were happy. As one restaurant owner told a journalist, he had seen a thirty per cent increase in business since the trials started. 'The longer the case lasts, the better.'[12]

Silivri, meanwhile, was filling up with less well-known prisoners too. Amidst a slight moral panic about urban crime – thefts, drug offences, and muggings – in 2005 the assembly passed laws mandating longer times in prison before conditional release, and longer sentences in total for certain crimes. The following year, an amendment to Turkey's broad terror laws made them even broader. At the same time, the police were both expanded and empowered. The result was that all over Turkey, without any notable increase in actual crime, the prison population started to soar.[13]

In 2012 and 2013, the conspiracy cases came to their conclusion – most of the hundreds who were tried were found guilty. And though one international news organization was still able to write that the AKP had been 'the only force able to take on the deep state and survive', many Turks themselves were having their doubts.[14] For the Silivri trials in the years in between had been deeply flawed. The first indictment – 2,500 pages – was full of spelling mistakes and paranoia. Subsequent evidence included doctored documents and inaccurate dates. Key witnesses for the defence were ignored entirely. The prosecution in turn relied on anonymous informants and tapped phone recordings. As twenty-three separate cases were all merged together, defence lawyers claimed the total indictment was an impossible four million pages long. When even the most important defendants were called to the stand, they were given only two hours.[15]

Within a few years, all of those found guilty were released. There was no evidence, as a higher court concluded, that any of the plots ever existed at all.[16] But in a sense it didn't matter. By that point, the military – so long the force that had hung over Turkish democracy – had been tamed once and for all. Looking back, I had been naive as the rest of them, as those who had cheered on a few years before as Turkey 'faced up to its past'. As if history could just right itself, that there was some natural balance to be restored. Perhaps there is a more unsettling truth: that history is unmoored, and a country can always turn to a new, darker place; that there is no innate sense of justice amongst its victims once they're in power themselves.

*

It started with a sit-in. It was May 2013, and a group of environmentalists had heard about plans to cut down trees in İstanbul's Gezi Park, inside the city's historic Taksim Square, to make way for a shopping centre. It was a new digital age of politics: of protesters wearing *V for Vendetta* masks, of organizing on Facebook and Twitter, and, inevitably, of sharing videos of police brutality throughout the virtual world. When security came to break up their demonstration – with days of dawn raids, tear gas, and water cannon – it seemed to touch a nerve all over. All of a sudden, thousands were coming to set up camps in Gezi Park. Of course, they chanted and protested and clashed with the police but – as so many would later say – there was a festive atmosphere too, as people sang, painted, and even gardened together in this rare patch of İstanbul green. Soon, the demonstrations were spreading throughout the country: to İzmir on the Aegean coast, to Ankara in central Anatolia, to Diyarbakır in the south-east. In all, there were protests in over seventy cities in Turkey, with three million people taking part.[17] Amongst them, of course, was the old opposition one might suspect: the traditional secular, republican Turks. But the protests went far beyond them: there were Kurds and liberals, headscarved students and the socialist left. Taksim Solidarity – the umbrella group loosely organizing some of the protests at Gezi Park – included scores of member organizations ranging from radical worker parties to the İstanbul Dentist Association.[18] What united them above all was a fear not about another shopping mall in İstanbul but how powerless they felt about the plan to push it through, and what it said about the direction in which Turkey was heading. Erdoğan, by that point, had won three general elections and two constitutional referendums, and had increased his share of the vote to nearly half the electorate. More and more, he seemed almost hostile to the other half who did not vote for him – to the politicians who represented them, to the lifestyles they led, and the rights and spaces they held dear.

His hard-line approach to the Gezi protests surprised even his allies in government. He 'dismissed them as looters' at first, and after two weeks, it was decided to shut them down for good.[19] With tear gas and rubber bullets, water cannon and bulldozers, hundreds of riot police made their way to Taksim Square and brought the demonstrations to a violent end. All in all over Turkey, eight people were killed, more than eight thousand wounded, and five thousand arrested.[20] As one rights organization put it, Taksim Square was closed off afterwards, 'like a crime scene.'[21] But beyond the immediate response – a government's desire to reassert its control, to reclaim its space – there was something deeper happening too.

For increasingly in conservative circles, and seemingly in Erdoğan's own head, there was a narrative growing that cast the Gezi protests as something else entirely.

The year saw Turkey wear in other ways too. The economy, growing for so much of the AKP's first decade, began to stutter and fail – a dip that it has not recovered from even now. The Syrian civil war on its border entered a new and bloodier stage. And increasingly, the Turkish government was pulling itself apart. An Islamist sect that had been the AKP's allies for so long – that had, indeed, infiltrated the state once they entered power, and provided so many of the prosecutors and police chiefs who had humbled the military just a few years before – was now targeting Erdoğan and his cadre. As the two groups turned on each other, the judicial system became a battleground once more: there were indictments and counter-indictments, arrests and counter-arrests. Slowly, however, Erdoğan and his AKP allies won out, and purged the state of hundreds of judges, thousands of police officers.[22] Silivri, as ever, welcomed many of them, its numbers growing all the time. Turkey's prison population trebled from the previous decade.[23]

The mood was souring, and Turkey's state was fraying, but there was still some semblance of institutional strength, of power diffusely held. When, for example, a journalist published pictures exposing Turkey's role in the violence in Syria, he was sent to Silivri, where 'the soil ended and a heap of concrete began.'[24] Yet, despite the fury he had provoked, of Erdoğan and of the country's intelligence services too, after three months the Constitutional Court ordered his release, in February 2016.* It would be hard to imagine just five months later.

The attempted coup of 15 July was a trauma the nation over.

---

* The ruling concerned his pre-trial detention only. Can Dündar, the journalist in question, was later convicted of espionage and fled to Germany.

Carried out by that very Islamist sect that been ousted from power – and a faction loyal to it within the Turkish armed forces – it saw tanks on the streets, fighter jets over major cities, and the national assembly bombed. In total, two hundred and fifty people were killed, and President Erdoğan was reportedly nearly one of them: on holiday on the Aegean coast, he escaped an attempt on his life. Yet by the morning of Saturday, 16 July, as Erdoğan returned to İstanbul to address crowds and journalists at the airport, two things had become clear: that the coup had failed, and that Turkey was about to become a different place all the same.

Under a state of emergency, within a month, over twenty thousand people were imprisoned over alleged links to the coup. As the months and years went on, eventually one hundred and fifty thousand were detained. Another one hundred thousand civil servants were dismissed, including more than three thousand judges. Two hundred media outlets were shut down.[25] If it seemed a squeeze not just on those connected to the coup but on anyone who had opposed Erdoğan in the past, it was about to be ratified in law. Still under a state of emergency, and the shock of post-coup Turkey, a constitutional reform package in 2017 was put to a referendum that would create an all-powerful presidency, a rubber-stamp assembly and a judiciary subservient to them both. It was narrowly and controversially passed.

*

I meet Hande in the courtyard of an old state brewery. It's a converted space now, for galleries and cafes, full of artists and students. Behind us, a giant orange monkey sculpture hangs off the building at the entrance. We are in Bomonti, an upmarket neighbourhood in İstanbul, full these weeks of the pink splashes of Judas trees, and the hanging purples of wisteria. There is another seasonal decoration too. On the walls and the sides of buildings, I see graffiti stamped in black, of the figure of a man and words written below: *Ben Kemal Geliyorum*. He is the opposition candidate, Kemal Kılıçdaroğlu. 'I, Kemal, am coming'. The presidential elections are just weeks away. All over the city hang campaign posters of Erdoğan too, pictured humbly holding his hand to his heart. '*Doğru zaman, doğru adam*', goes the slogan. 'The right time, The right man', as if he hadn't been in power for the last twenty years. Hande, though, is hopeful for change. 'I'm wary of saying this', she tells me of her husband and the others, 'but they'll be out quite soon'.

They met in 2017. Her voice warms a little at the memory. She was in her late twenties, and organizing a week-long programme for Turkish Roma and civil society groups that represent them. Hakan was the project's advisor – a renowned academic whose book on global civics had been translated into five languages. He had founded a politics school, at one of İstanbul's most prestigious universities, a few years ago. Every year, it took in students from all over Turkey for a week, and got them to talk. There were lectures and workshops on human rights, the rule of law and democracy. He was more than fifteen years her senior, and with the scars of an older life: a divorce and a cancer scare not long past. But as they worked together over the week, 'there was a spark', Hande tells me. He listened a lot, she says. They were soon together, spending time in İstanbul, and in his summer house. It was a one-storey stone cottage with a garden, in Çanakkale to the south-west, near where the Marmara spreads wide into the Aegean Sea. 'It was his happiest place'.

The journeys there, though, were a little fraught. Driving south-west from İstanbul, heading down the E84, they would pass Silivri Prison to their left, where one of Hakan's old colleagues was detained. His name was Osman Kavala, a businessman and philanthropist who had spent decades funding various causes on Turkey's civil society scene: art exhibitions and civic initiatives, many aimed at promoting the rights of Turkey's smaller ethnic and religious groups. In 2001, he had helped to establish the Open Society Foundation in Turkey, part of the global civil society network founded by George Soros. Hakan had been the institute's founding director. When Osman was first detained at an airport in October 2017, he initially assumed it was a mistake, but things soon became even more serious still. He was placed in pre-trial detention after two weeks, and accused of trying to violently overthrow the government: once during the attempted coup the previous year, and once again at the Gezi Park protests in 2013. 'Every time we passed,' Hande tells me, of their drives by Silivri, 'we would go silent. And every time I would say from inside me to Hakan, "God, please don't make me a visitor of that place."'

For Hande, it began at dawn, as it does for so many. It was 6 a.m. on a November day in 2018, and Hakan was waking her up, telling her that there were ten policemen in their house. They were searching through everything: their possessions, their books, 'every bit of paper'. It's a trauma, she says, a form of assault. And one with its own gender politics as well. As she recounts with a particular sense of disgust, 'some *men* touching every belonging you have.' For days, she tells me, she didn't want to clean or touch anything she owned. They stayed for an hour, and then took Hakan into police custody.

They found out that day that there were more than a dozen others being questioned too. Though at first they had no idea what they were accused of, after Hakan was questioned for nine hours – made to listen again and again to tapped phone conversations from 2013 – they had worked out enough: the Gezi protests, and their putative links to Osman Kavala. After thirty-six hours in detention, Hakan was released, but he was a free man no more.

The indictment came in February. It was a sprawling thing of six hundred and fifty pages, full – in the *style du jour* – of factual inaccuracies and wild conspiracies. But at its core was a simple reframing: that what happened at Gezi Park was not a spontaneous protest, but a planned coup – one funded from abroad by George Soros, effected by his representative in Turkey, Osman Kavala, and organized through the Open Society Foundation. As it states at one point, 'no element of the actions was accidental, and that it was a very clear and definite operation with foreign support to bring the Republic of Turkey's state to its knees.'

The other suspects, it claims, were all parts of the same conspiracy. The evidence – such as it is – comprises hundreds of pages: receipts of plane tickets abroad, transcripts from tapped phone conversations, and tedious details of meetings. None link to any acts of violence, let alone the charges alleged, of trying to overthrow the government. As even one senior AKP figure would admit of the indictment, 'not even a child would write this.'[26]

Of the six hundred and fifty pages of the indictment, almost painfully, Hakan's section lasts just four. Even those, Hande tells me, are full of inaccuracies. Though prosecutors would insist he worked for the Open Society Foundation, he had left his job as director as far back as 2009. Though he continued on the board afterwards, even that he left before Gezi kicked off. Besides, of course, the Open Society did not plan a coup in Turkey in 2013. The rest of the evidence against Hakan mostly entails phone transcripts *after* the protests had been put down. As Hande says, not even exasperated, Hakan only went to Gezi Park twice. An academic – and not really one for demonstrations – he wanted to observe what was going on, and see how it might fit in to his career-long thinking on civics.

Of course, in this Turkey, it did not really matter. For the prosecutor knew too what was important was the political winds. Gezi, said Erdoğan months before the indictment was released, had been financed 'by that Hungarian Jew Soros.' Indeed, perhaps in all the indictment's length, the only part of it that really counted came as early as page three. Under a list of victims and aggrieved parties of Gezi, there are dozens and dozens of names. The very first one, there in the right-hand column, is 'Recep Tayyip Erdoğan'.

The first hearing was held in Silivri in June 2019. As one human rights activist described it, sitting in a new courtroom with space for two hundred and fifty defendants, she got chills down her spine – this was a place 'designed for mass trials'.[27] For Hande and Hakan, who had spent months working on his defence, it was perhaps a more poignant time than for most. Just one month after the trial began, Hande discovered that she was pregnant. When I ask if she worried how they'd cope, she looks almost bemused. Before they started trying, she tells me, they didn't even talk about the case. 'We didn't want to stop our lives.' A few months later, they got married. Still, she admits, she worried about her stress, and what effect it would have on her growing baby. Silivri – the prison, not just the courtroom – was heaving into view.

*

As one prison lawyer told me, Silivri's decline started on the very night of the attempted coup – many guards, he claimed, simply abandoned their posts, left the prisoners inside, only to come and unlock them again at some point the next day.* And in the months ahead, thousands would be rounded up and sent to Turkey's jails.

The prison population, around fifty thousand in 2005, had risen by now to two hundred and ninety thousand.[28] At the reported cost of over a billion dollars, dozens of new prisons – new campuses – were built.[29] Of course, much of the growth was from the longer sentences for petty crimes, but it was the vast increase in political

---

* The author put this claim – and many other allegations about Silivri Prison – to the Turkish Directorate of Communications, but received no response.

prisoners too. In 2005, there were two hundred and seventy-three people convicted of terror offences[30]; by 2019, there were over forty thousand, either convicted or merely charged, but all in prison nonetheless.[31] There were thousands more prosecuted for 'insulting the president', as the space for free speech dwindled ever more.[32] As many citizens would find, even prosecutors opening cases against them was a threat enough in itself, hanging over people's lives for years, ready to proceed whenever they 'transgressed' again. First under the state of emergency, and then under the executive presidency, the judiciary, as one academic wrote, had become 'a target and a weapon': subject to waves of purges and interventions; characterized by show trials and absurd indictments.[33] Silivri had grown with the rest of them. As a rights commission had reported in August 2019, this prison built for eleven thousand now had a population of twenty-two thousand.[34] Let alone the largest prison in Europe as a paper once despaired, according to the *Guinness Book of Records* that year, Silivri was now the largest prison in the world. Of course, its size – its notoriety – had not gone unnoticed. A phrase – half joke, half warning – had begun to pop up online and in conversation, whenever someone said something controversial. *Silivri soğuk.* 'It's cold in Silivri.' As I talked to former inmates all over İstanbul, they could only agree. It's all iron and concrete, one told me, and the winter cold penetrates deep into its cells; with the humidity of the sea air, it smells of mildew and mould.

Of course, it had always been an inhuman place, with a certain cruelty written into its rules. As the writer Ahmet Altan described – during his own imprisonment after the coup – occasionally in the spring, passing birds would drop flowers for their nests into his small and sunless courtyard. Once he took one and put it in a plastic bottle to decorate his cell. The next day, the officers took the flower away.[35] But the overcrowding was now bringing sufferings of its own. I speak to one ex-prisoner of Silivri, there on terror offences, who tells me that in his unit – built for twenty-one inmates – there were forty-nine. Even with some added bunks, there were not enough to go round. They had shifts on the beds, with people sleeping on the floors and in the corridors too. They shared just two toilets between them. At times, the crowding seems almost comically absurd. How do you fit forty-nine inmates in a courtyard of thirty steps by thirty steps, he asks. Another, convicted of drug possession, says during their weekly exercise sessions – on Silivri's much vaunted outdoor pitches – there were forty people playing football at a time.

Lawyers began to receive more and more complaints. Some were merely the symptoms of a system overstretched. Books and letters were delivered late. Meals became smaller and smaller. It was harder to receive medical care. But even these routine failures could have devastating effects. One inmate who suffered from cataracts wrote to a human rights group, saying that the lack of access to treatment had lost him his right eye.[36] I meet one former prisoner, a cancer patient, who did not receive his high-dose painkillers for four and a half months. He was, he tells me, simply unable to leave his bed. Then there were the wrongs that were more deliberately inflicted. They tended to start before Silivri itself. As many rights groups and prisoners attested, beatings were frequent when in police custody, at the first entrance to prison, and during court transfers as well. One prisoner told me he had spent a week or so in an underground police station – the lights on the whole time – as guards told him they would 'fuck his mother'; once he came into Silivri and refused a strip search, he was beaten by officers with batons.

Though Silivri has always been marked by allegations of abuse, the coup was perhaps a turning point again. In the days afterwards, all over TV, suspected plotters were paraded on screen with broken noses and bloodied scalps. It seemed a message from the top, a prison lawyer told me, that torture and mistreatment were now OK. It was not, he said, as systematic as it had been in the 1980s, but it was certainly tolerated. Indeed for some prisoners the very randomness – the uncertainty each day over what would happen to your own body – was a punishment in itself. As one explained to me, some guards were nice, and seemed to hate what was happening; others, 'I think they wanted to kill us.' There were allegations of sexual assault with truncheons, of repeated and unnecessary cavity searches, intense, humiliating room searches, and prolonged periods of isolation. As one resident of Silivri No. 9 – its highest security unit – complained to a rights group, he had been living in isolation twenty-four seven, twelve months a year. 'It was like being kept alive in a grave.'[37] Of course, though they are rare, there have been unexplained deaths in Silivri as well.[38]

Many make special mention of a particular place in Silivri, to the *süngerli oda*, the sponge room. Designed with padded walls to hold prisoners at risk of self-harm, it had become instead synonymous with violence – a place on units free of cameras, where officers take inmates specifically to beat. As one prisoner told me, he had been left in a sponge room once as punishment, handcuffed and rough-handled. And across the wall, someone had written *Allah Yok, Muhammed tatilde*. 'There is no God. Muhammed is on holiday.'

*

It is early afternoon, up on the cliffs. We're in Silivri town, overlooking the sea and the orange sparrowhawks diving down in front of us. Ali – which is not his real name – is about to embark on a twelve-hour night shift. He is an officer in the prison, middle aged but looking older, losing his hair and overweight. Behind his sunglasses, he is tired too.

He seems a kind man, and relatively loose-tongued – not

enamoured by his job, but not embarrassed by it either. He fell into it years ago, and now, even if he wanted to, it is too late to change paths. Besides, he tells me, his kids like it here, going to the beach and swimming in the sea. There is nothing like that in the central Anatolian town where they're from. Their accommodation in the prison complex is heavily subsidized too. Still, they're not immune from the problems of Turks all over: his civil servant wages, he says, cannot keep up with inflation.

It is of course difficult work. Once, he explains, he found a prisoner who had killed himself, and failed to revive him with his own hands and mouth. And though that was one rare and painful episode, the daily grind of Silivri – the counts, the lock-ups, the confrontations – has worn him down. I am reminded of what a prison sociologist wrote of Silivri: that not only are the prisoners far away from their home towns, but the staff are too. They live on the premises, socialize with other guards, and slowly the prison subsumes their whole identity.[39] 'You start to become what is around you,' Ali tells me more than once.

We share a soda together, and he picks a bunch of lavender by our knees, and holds it under his nose, breathing it in. I ask him more what it's like in there, and in truth he depicts a place like any prison I have ever known:* full of alcoholics, drug addicts, and the homeless; corrupt around the edges, 'as the officers don't earn very much, and the gang leaders inside do'; and marred by violence – he has a friend, he says, with a scar from a knife slashed right across his face. Still, I find his answers slightly unsatisfying, given all I know of the place where he works. Do you ever have any doubts, I ask him, do you ever think people are there when they shouldn't

* My first job was based in a prison in London, for which I travelled to over thirty others across the UK.

be? 'There was a father imprisoned after he caused a traffic acci-
dent,' he tells me, and he wondered if his punishment hadn't been
excessive.

The start of his shift is nearing. He takes another handful of
lavender – to give to his children when he returns home – and we
depart.

*

There had been six hearings in total – starting in the summer,
stretching past the autumn, and now into the winter too – but the
Gezi Park trials were nearing their end. It was 18 February 2020,
and the day of the verdict had come. Hande, by that point, was
seven months pregnant. So while Hakan and the others were in the
courtrooms of Silivri, she was waiting for the news with her family
back home. She was afraid, she told me, how her body might react
if the decision went the wrong way.

She found out in a text, she says, 'they were all acquitted.' It
seemed against all odds. They hugged and cried, and got straight
in the car, to drive the seventy kilometres west from İstanbul. The
defendants – newly freed men and women – and their families
had gathered at one of Silivri's many fish restaurants along the
pier. They laughed and ate, then headed back towards the prison
itself, to greet Osman Kavala too – he, unlike the others, had been
inside since the moment of his arrest. Yet as they waited in a car
park nearby, 'waiting and waiting,' as Hande remembers, someone
saw the news on a TV. Another arrest warrant had been issued
for Osman, on new charges relating to the attempted coup. Hande
says she saw Osman's wife as she received the news, and will never
forget 'the complete destruction on her face.' It would be a heartbreak shared. As the story goes, somewhere in that complex, the
authorities had even put Osman in the car to drive him to the gate,
only to then tell him he wouldn't be released.

As they drove home, they all knew too what it meant thereafter. That – not just for Osman but his eight co-defendants – it couldn't be over. Sure enough, all the acquittals were appealed; the judge who issued the verdict was subject to disciplinary hearings; and the very next day, President Erdoğan was on TV, signalling – to any future judge who had somehow missed it – what he felt about the case. 'They attempted to acquit,' he said a little darkly, 'with a manoeuvre yesterday.'

*

The pandemic came a month later. For those in Silivri, for the first time in years, it did at least provide some room to breathe. All over Turkey, given its swollen prison population, a hundred thousand inmates were given early parole, though it excluded many: those on pre-trial detention, those convicted of serious violent and sexual crimes, and the tens of thousands inside on terror offences. And though Silivri's numbers fell a little, for those still there – including of course every one of its political prisoners – conditions did not much improve. As one told me, as all the world adjusted to its new normal, the usual delays of Silivri grew even longer: newspapers came later, bread arrived stale, phone conversations with family were curtailed, with fewer staff around to manage them.

For Hande and Hakan, it was a happier time. In late April, their son was born. They called him Ege – 'Aegean' – after the region they both loved, with its dark pine forests and sparkling seas, the place where they had spent so many days together in Hakan's summer home. Hakan, Hande tells me, had spent most of his life never wanting to be a dad, but now – in his fifties and with his first-born son – he found himself transformed. 'He says it's the most magical thing that can happen to someone.' She's glad, she tells me, that Ege was born in the pandemic – it meant he could spend much more time with Hakan.

So they watched Ege grow, and prepared for the next steps. When Ege was nine months old, his father's acquittal was officially overturned; when he was just past one, his trial restarted. Over the several hearings to come, it seemed a show trial that could barely even muster the energy for the act: no witnesses were called to the stand, no defendants were cross-examined. There was instead a simple formula – the prosecutor made his case, and the defendants responded.

Hakan and Hande had spent weeks altogether drafting his statements, patiently pointing out the basic mistakes, and protesting his innocence once more. When they were read out, as Hande and many others would say, the response of the judges was particularly galling. They would never look at the defendants; often, they would play with their phones instead. Meanwhile, they would try and be the best parents they could. Hakan, Hande once said, would take Ege to the park, and make him laugh by falling over each time Ege came towards him on the baby swings.

And so they came to the verdict once again, a few days after Ege's second birthday. It was not in Silivri, but in a massive courthouse in İstanbul – supposedly also the biggest in Europe – a multi-storey 'Justice Palace' of three hundred and twelve separate courts. This time Hande was there, along with around two hundred others: defendants and their lawyers, activists, ambassadors, and journalists. After the final proceedings, the judges retired for about forty-five minutes – as one lawyer told me, about five minutes for each of the accused – and came back, ready to announce it. As Hande remembers, in those few seconds when the judgement is revealed only on the lawyers' computers, 'everyone's faces froze.' She sensed something coming, and then the judge said it: life imprisonment without parole for Osman Kavala; eighteen years for everyone else. They had been found guilty under Article 312 of the Penal Code, of attempting to overthrow the government. Hande hugged Hakan, and kept asking how this could happen. People cried and shouted at the judges. The guilty verdict may not have been a surprise, but the sentences handed out were a shock. Hakan, before being taken away, handed Hande his keys and wallet, and told her they'd be OK.

Amnesty International called it a 'travesty of justice'. The US State Department said it was 'deeply troubled'.[40] In Turkey, beyond the activists following the trial, the response was more muted. On the major news outlets – now almost exclusively owned or close to the government – there was no focus on the case at all. Instead, they reported on the long-awaited removal of mask regulations, and the granting of toll-free travel for drivers on the upcoming Eid.

*

That, then, is where they are when I meet Hande in an old state brewery in an upmarket part of İstanbul. Hande and Ege are living in their home, Hakan is in a prison of twenty-two thousand people an hour's drive to our west. It has nearly been a year.

She received a lot of advice, she tells me, for her first visit: when she should set off from the city, which bus to take once inside the campus, not to wear a bra because it would set off the metal detectors. It was the first Friday after the judgement, just a few days later, and she was waiting in the closed visits room. Then she saw him behind the glass. 'The first thing we did – and this I'll never forget – we just looked at each other and laughed. We laughed and said, "What the fuck?"'

Hakan was in Silivri No. 9, its highest security prison. While the other prisons in the campus may have filled up over the years, in No. 9 each unit has strictly only one to three inmates. These are often the highest-profile political prisoners, and all efforts are made to keep them away from others. Hakan's unit was typical: a small shared duplex with a bedroom on the top floor, and then a bathroom and common area, next to a courtyard, below. He was sharing it with two others, Can and Tayfun. They were also defendants in the Gezi trial, and though the state viewed them as co-conspirators in the same plot to overthrow the constitutional order, Hakan had never met them before the hearings began.

As Hakan would tell Hande from the start, the conditions were OK: physically, the place was not so bad; he got the books he wanted, he had access to his legal team, and the staff treated them well. And so, as the weeks went by, he fell into the rhythms of his new life. From the plastic seat and table in his 'kitchen', he started to write a bi-weekly column for an independent news organization. They focused mostly on civics – quoting Aristotle and Kant, discussing deliberative democracy and freedom – and always stressed the restorative power of conversation, the same lesson he had been teaching to students all over Turkey for nearly ten years. He had meetings more or less every day, with lawyers and MPs, professions that had always been granted easier access inside.*

He settled into his new domestic life. As Hande tells me, the three of them are quite different characters: Hakan is mellow and relaxed; Can, a human rights lawyer, is high-energy; Tayfun, an urban planner, is serious and melancholic. They have their petty squabbles over house rules, but they have learnt to iron them out. Once a week, they are let out onto Silivri's outdoor football pitch, and joined by their fellow plotter, Osman Kavala, living alone. Then for an hour, these four middle-aged men play together like school kids again. 'They are very, very competitive,' Hande says laughing, and Hakan spends long stretches of their conversations describing

* I wrote a letter to Hakan's address in Silivri Prison to ask him questions directly, a letter which, to my knowledge, he never received.

particular moments of their weekly two-on-two games. If it was sweet, it was a little unexpected – Hakan had never shown any interest in football before. Underneath it of course was a more painful truth: that there is little else of note happening in his life.

The visits are every Friday. Some are open, some are behind glass, but they are all bittersweet. As Hande explains, she is sure there are lots of hardships he is suffering and doesn't want to show, as there are for her as well. 'That one hour is all performance,' she says. Beyond those conversations – so unnatural, even between husband and wife – there are all the normal obstacles of prison rules as well. It is the randomness, Hande explains, that is 'so frustrating.' One week, she is told she can no longer give him red clothes; another, their weekly phone conversations are cut without warning from twenty minutes to ten. Still, she tells me, it's an arbitrariness that can go both ways. The day after we talk is Ege's third birthday, and Hakan's open visit that week has been unexpectedly, and without explanation, moved forward to meet it. 'Maybe there is an angel in administration,' she says, after all.

Of course, for all three of them, it is Hakan's separation from Ege that hurts most of all. Hande does her best to turn the visits into something fun: making games on the bus to Prison No. 9, or telling him that he was being searched by the guards because they love sugar, and wanted to see if he had any. She says, at least, the officers are nice to him, that they hand him chocolates and little sweets. Still, the trips are not easy. He gets bored or tired or hungry, and Hande feels both the need to entertain her son, and reassure Hakan – so excited to see him – not to take personally any toddler moods Ege might have. On the open visits, they can at least touch each other, play, talk, and eat cashew nuts, Ege's favourite. Hande shows me a picture from one visit: Hakan with a salt and pepper beard, and in his arms, smiling for the camera, a fair-haired boy with an orange juice moustache. The closed sessions, behind glass, are much harder. For one, when Hakan entered Silivri, Ege was only just learning to speak, and had no idea how to use a phone. He managed to make him laugh all the same, renewing the game they used to play in the park – this time Hakan would fall back not when Ege reached him on the swings, but every time he hit the glass between them. As the year has gone on, Ege has begun to understand more and more. *'Bu hafta oda mı?'* he asks Hande before their visits – 'Is it the [open] room this week?' Still, some things he still cannot grasp, or maybe cannot accept. As he says sometimes at the end of visits, looking behind him, *'Baba gel,'* 'Daddy come.'

I ask Hande how on earth she can explain all this – the injustice, the randomness, a life completely out of your control – to a three-year-old. 'There has been a mistake,' she tells Ege, 'and Daddy has to stay somewhere else until it gets sorted out.'

*

It is a system like no other I have come across, Turkish politics in 2023: a President in almost total control, a subservient assembly, a cowed judiciary, a media brought thoroughly into line. Yet still, there are elections. They are not, perhaps, 'free and fair' as the terminology goes, but they are free *enough*, fair *enough*, and close enough to offer the opposition hope.

Speaking to Hande, it is impossible to ignore the campaign backdrop, and what the results might mean for them all. When she talks about hearings and appeals, I notice, she speaks in a certain tone: flat and distant, as if she is talking about a life that isn't her own. But when I ask her about the election, I can see the hope spread across her face, almost a muscle in itself, lighting up her eyes, turning up the corners of her mouth. She is suppressing a smile just at the very idea of what the future might hold. We are four weeks out, and all the polling points to an opposition win. After all, there is three-digit inflation and the currency is collapsing; Erdoğan – normally so present – seems fading and tired; and just two months ago his government was unable to respond to the moment as thousands of buildings collapsed that February morning. But spring, the opposition promises, will come again.

'It's something I think about every single day,' Hande says. Indeed, she has started therapy only now, to cope with the drama of the campaigns. The first time, she says, after months of numbness, she cried all the way there, and then for the entire forty-five-minute session. 'It's existential,' she tells me. Though she knows, ultimately, Hakan's and the others' fates will be decided in the courts, it feels unimaginable that the Gezi Park defendants will spend much longer in prison if the opposition comes to power. It is not only that they promise to reform the whole political system once more, and vastly reduce the power of the presidency; it is that this whole trial has been political, and seemingly personal to Erdoğan, from the start. If he goes, why would the show carry on?

A month later, as I move through İstanbul late on a Sunday evening, the streets are completely empty, and my taxi driver is watching the preliminary results roll in. Could this really be it? My aunt opens the front door to let me in to her flat, sparking with nerves. 'Rakı?' she asks me, as I enter. In the living room, my uncle and his dad are already shouting at each other. More numbers come in, and we argue over what they might mean. Hours pass, they are going the wrong way. Baffled and embittered, we slink off to bed, and he – the President in power for the last twenty years – is on TV, singing on a balcony, victorious again.

This, surely, is the singular quality of Turkey in 2023, its centenary year. Not the repression, but the hope that it might end, raised only to be crushed. And the knowledge, somewhere over another part of this city, that your son's father won't be coming home.

13. Epilogue

I HAD WANTED THIS TO BE A REDEMPTIVE STORY, A history of a young country that, in its hundredth year, somehow found a new peace with itself. I had wanted to finish with scenes of packed squares and streets: a would-be dictator voted out; a people unbowed; dancing, singing, drinking, long into a warm spring night. I had wanted to write too on the deeper promise of what it meant, and about the opposition call for *helalleşme* – for healing, forgiveness, and making good on historic wrongs: to Greeks expelled, to Kurds tortured, to Islamists repressed, and on, and on. Here at last – I would have written – seems a nation ready to reconcile with its past. But Turkey, May 2023, as a historian once said of another place and time, was the turning point that didn't turn.

Amongst the broader sweep of things, there would be a more personal redemption as well: that my *baba* had left Turkey, and I had come back. In truth, as much as I had a plan, it was not to move forever. I have after all, in London, a small and growing family of my own. But I wanted at least to know Turkey better, and the person who left it over forty years ago, that eighteen-year-old I've seen in photos, in skinny flares and black curls. Re-reading this book, I'm struck by how many of the stories – hat protests in the north, Alevi rebellions in the east, communist utopias on the Black Sea – are also about sons and fathers, fathers and sons.

As it was, we almost learned Turkey together. In the last few years, my *baba*, after decades of estrangement, found an appetite to rediscover his country once more. Alongside my mum – his forever companion, who loved even the 1970s Turkey she first saw – he travelled to places he never would have before: to Balıkçılar, our ancestral village; to Mardin, the ancient mountain town; to Gaziantep, the spiritual home of Turkish food. For him, what once seemed backward – power cuts, dirt roads, 'dry' towns – had become romantic. As part of their tours, they visited Sinop, a small and historic city on the coast. It was there, in its prison, that a dissident socialist poet wrote the words *Aldırma Gönül*, the song my *baba* plays on the piano every day. It has since been turned into a museum. Entering his cell, and reading those same words on the plaque on the wall, my *baba* broke down and wept.

Of my own embrace of our Turkishness, he once said it was an 'unexpected blessing'. In part, it was for me an awe at the place itself: the sunsets in İstanbul, with their ribbons of orange, purple and blue; the ripple of mountains going out east; the clear waters of the Aegean, the first sea I had ever known. In part it was the people too, right down to how they said my name: the depth of it, leaning into the first syllable, *Saaami*. Even beyond that, I liked who I was in Turkish, and in Turkey: warmer, more tactile, at ease.

Despite the insistence of Turks all over – '*Baban Türk sen Türksün*', 'Your father's Turkish, so you are Turkish' – I knew I was not exactly one of them, and never would be. For my real answer to the question *nerelisin?* – where are you from? – is not Rize but Londra. Perhaps I had remained a little 'betwixt and between', but I learnt to love that space for what it was.

Of course, my work was in some sense to deliberately pierce that film my *baba* had placed between us and Turkey, the one that muffled its noise, dulled its sting. Without it, both him and I were a little rawer, more exposed. And in the year it took me to write this book in particular, it could hardly have caused more hurt.

When the earthquake struck on that February morning, we were lucky in one sense – our immediate family and friends were safe – but we were at the same time surrounded by loss, by people we knew with loved ones buried under their homes. I first went to Maraş six weeks later, when the ground had not yet stilled, hoping to write stories of what was left. Yet I found myself treading lightly not just on the rubble strewn over the city, but on people's pain too. Faced with children reeling off the names of friends lost, or pensioners staring at their homes as they were picked apart, I found myself unable to work, to ask the usual journalist questions of 'What happened?', 'How do you feel?' Instead, I offered condolences, a few whispered *geçmiş olsuns*, I held some hands, and the moment I flew back to İstanbul, I – a thirty-two-year-old man with a son of my own – called my mum and cried.

It wasn't just the pain I was more open to either. There was an uglier side to it all, when people weren't just victims but perpetrators themselves: the many daily injustices of modern Turkey, the dawn raids, the show trials, the state-led cruelty. Following the Gezi trial, and the verdict handed down to Hakan and the seven others, I was filled not only with anger, but with shame.

*

No father and son story did I find more affecting than Hakan and Ege – a boy so sensitive, Hande told me, that he hugs the sad characters in his children's books. Thinking about him, I could not help but see my own son, just a little younger, and ache for Ege and Hakan both.

As it turned out, the endless country was even more endless than I had thought. Months after I finished the book, Hakan's sentence, and those of two of his co-defendants, were overturned. It was so unexpected, and his release so sudden, that he called Hande from his taxi driver's mobile phone to deliver the news, telling her he was on his way home. But this was no happy ending, or even an ending at all. At the time of writing, Hakan faces lesser charges in the new year, and potentially hearings that could drag on for months again. In the meantime, as Hande wrote to me, the three of them will be busy 'putting their lives back together.'

Besides, as they explained in their one public statement since, their minds are on the other five still inside, still facing eighteen-year sentences or worse. They include Hakan's two cellmates, as well as Osman Kavala – the final player in their weekly football two-on-twos. One family, of another of the released, explained to me that they feel mostly 'survivor's guilt.'

All of it – the lives of those inside and out – spoke to something more, to perhaps the cruellest part of the Turkey I had seen over the last few years: the brute fact of unaccountable power, and how callously, how capriciously it decides the fates of others.

*

And that historic redemption, then? For now, it is yet to come and hard to foresee. But even in Silivri, there is a spirit that will surely have its time: the courage of prisoners who stand up to officers for the rights of their sick cellmates; the solidarity of others, who throw recipes in bottles from courtyard to courtyard, detailing how to make toasties in between radiator slats; a refusal to give in to hatred or despair. As Hakan insisted once in an open letter to Ege, written on the plastic table in his cell, 'we're lucky, son, to be born and raised here.'

I think too of my own *baba*, and the song we now sing together, its words written in another prison cell decades ago: *Gönül aldırma / Görecek günler var daha*. 'Don't mind my heart / there are still more days to see.'

Acknowledgements

To have a book to write and a one-year-old to raise is to always feel you are failing at something. So my first thanks will always be to those who were there when I wasn't. To Michi, above all, but also to the whole cast of people who fill Tommaso's life, not least his beloved *nonna!* and *baanne!*

They have all been irreplaceable in the year or so it took to write and research this book, but its own story has been longer than that. So my thanks also to my agent Doug Young, who was the first stranger to ever think it was possible – even interesting – and to the team at Picador who commissioned it. Mary Mount, my editor since, has been a reassuring presence – mostly in that I always felt she understood what I wanted to do. In terms of my other, actual work, I am indebted to Phil Maynard and Nicole Jackson at the *Guardian*, who supported my request for a lengthy sabbatical. I will never know – and never ask – what hurdles they had to jump through to achieve it.

A work like this, covering different topics in different places, is only possible with the help of a great many people. Among them, before even any research is possible, are the patient Turks who have spoken Turkish with me over the years, particularly Gül and Muhammed. Zehra Aslan is always my guide in Rize and its history. Scholars like Cemal Taş and Ahmet Kerim Gültekin were indispensable in understanding the sad past of Dersim; Hüseyin Kasim showed me the place's beauty too. Of course, I am particularly grateful to Hasan Erdoğan, who shared with me his time and his story. 'Write, write', he told me, and I hope I haven't let him down.

Demet Tezcan was a friendly authority on the life of Şule Yüksel Şenler, while Ayşenur Alev-Yılmaz and her brother Fatih were kind enough to share their memories with me of their famous aunt. Many journalists and researchers helped me try and uncover the mysteries of Koçero, among them Ahmet Özcan, Hüseyin Bakır, Recep Kavuş and Ali Mehmet Izmir. The chapter on the bridge featured no interviews and no tracking anyone down, but it was inspired by an unforgettable picnic breakfast with my friend Dilara. Kerem Morgül and Hade Türkmen both wrote brilliantly – as students! – on the history of Fatsa, and were generous in helping me on the ground. I am grateful too to Yusuf Sönmez's two sons, Naci and Yusuf. The communications team at Mado organized my interview with Mehmet Kanbur under impossible circumstances. My thanks, and condolences, to all those in Maraş, including Hatice, Mürüvvet Alparslan Nazlı and Ertuğrul Aslan.

Muharrem Süleymanoğlu was invaluable not just in learning about the life of his brother Naim, but about Mastanlı, the Bulgarian town where they grew up. Sevim, his hometown friend, was hospitable when I arrived. If writing about Ahmet Kaya was a daunting experience, his wife Gülten did much to put me at ease – warm, welcoming, and willing to talk about all they went through. His biographer, Ferzende Kaya (no relation), helped me understand not only the arc of his life, but why his work meant so much to so many. Finally, Hande Yalnızoğlu Altınay gave me time during an ordeal I could barely imagine. My profound thanks to her and the former Silivri prisoners I spoke to. I wish them all the best.

On all these subjects and more, I have spent many evenings talking with my *hala* – laughing, arguing, and sharing chocolate ice creams. She has become not only my forever-host in Turkey but my closest friend. I'm so glad also to have passed so many hours with my *babaanne*, whose life I have seen anew.

To loop back onto family matters, then, there are characters who loom large over the pages you have just read, even if they are rarely named. Thanks to my *baba*, who taught me how to tell stories, and to my mum, who taught me how to read them. And how to listen to people too. I owe them both more than I could ever describe.

But even they could have nothing on Michi, and the amount she has done, at every step, to make this book real. She encouraged me to write the proposal, and then to send it out to agents. She despaired at my inability to 'negotiate' with publishers, and celebrated with me once the deal was signed. She sat down with me to work out how we could carve the time out for research, and then looked after our son while I was away. She put up with my moods on bad writing days and was, of course, the book's first reader too. Where I have failed as a parent over the last two years, she has succeeded. He is beautiful and happy, loving and loved, and it is only down to her. She has done all that, while also flying at a job far more important than my own. *Grazie amore*, what more can I say?

Bibliography

GENERAL READING

Feroz Ahmad, *Turkey: The Quest for Identity*, Oneworld, 2003

Nicholas L. Danforth, *The Remaking of Republican Turkey: memory and modernity since the fall of the Ottoman Empire*, Cambridge University Press, 2021

Metin Heper and Sabri Sayarı, eds, *The Routledge Handbook of Modern Turkey*, Routledge, 2012

Kemal Karpat, ed., *Ottoman Past and Today's Turkey*, Brill, 2000

Alexandros Lamprou, *Nation-Building in Modern Turkey: the 'People's Houses', the State and the Citizen*, I. B. Tauris, 2015

Andrew Mango, *Atatürk*, John Murray, 2004

Aziz Nesin, *Turkish Stories from Four Decades*, selected and translated by Louis Mitler, Three Continents Press, 1991

Umut Özkırımlı and Spyros A. Sofos, *Tormented by History*, Hurst, 2008

Esra Özyürek, *Nostalgia for the Modern*, Duke University Press, 2006

Christine May Philliou, *Turkey: A Past Against History*, University of California Press, 2021

Ellen Churchill Semple, 'The Regional Geography of Turkey: A Review of Banse's Work', *Geographical Review* 11:3, 1921

Umut Uzer, *An Intellectual History of Turkish Nationalism, Between Turkish Ethnicity and Islamic Identity*, University of Utah Press, 2016

Erik Zürcher, *Turkey: A Modern History*, I. B. Tauris, rev. edn 2002

CHAPTER TWO: ON THE CUSP OF THE REPUBLIC

Arif Atılgan, Yeldeğirmeni Öyküsü, 12/09/2022 – http://mimdap. org/2017/12/yeldedhirmeni-oykusu-arif-atylgan/ – accessed 12/09/2022

Gökhan Akçura, Paris Mahallesi, 19/06/21 – https://manifold.press/paris-mahallesi – accessed 12/09/22

Yiğit Akın, *When the War Came Home: the Ottomans' Great War and the Devastation of an Empire*, Stanford University Press, 2018

Alexis Alexandris, *The Greek Minority of Istanbul and Greek-Turkish Relations 1918–1974*, Centre for Asia Minor Studies, 2nd edn, 1992

Anon., 'Geographical Elements in the Turkish Situation: A Note on the Political Map', *Geographical Review* Vol. 13, No. 1, 1923

Abe Attrep, '"A State of Wretchedness and Impotence": A British View of Istanbul and Turkey', *International Journal of Middle East Studies* 9:1, 1978

Grigoris Balakian, *Armenian Golgotha: a memoir of the Armenian Genocide*, trans. Peter Balakian with Aris Sevag, Knopf, 2009

Phillip Marshall Brown, 'From Sevres to Lausanne', *American Journal of International Law*, 18:1, 1924

Nur Bilge Criss, *Istanbul under Allied Occupation 1918–1923*, Brill, 1999

Lerna Ekmekçioğlu, *Recovering Armenia: The Limits of Belonging in post-Genocide Turkey*, Stanford University Press, 2016

Meltem Ersoy and Esra Özyürek, eds, *Contemporary Turkey at a Glance II: Turkey Transformed? Power, History, Culture*, Springer, 2017

Herbert A. L. Fisher, 'Mr Lloyd George's Foreign Policy, 1918–1922', *Foreign Affairs* 1:3, 1923

Ryan Gingeras, *The Fall of the Sultanate: the Great War and the End of the Ottoman Empire, 1908–1922*, Oxford University Press, 2016

Adnan Giz, *Bir Zamanlar Kadıköy, 1900–1950*, İBB Yayınları, 1988

Erdağ M. Göknar, 'Turkish-Islamic Feminism Confronts National Patriarchy', *Journal of Middle East Women's Studies* 9:2, Spring 2013

Nâzim Hikmet, *Memleketimden İnsan Manzaraları*, YKY, 2002 (Originally 1966)

— , *Human Landscapes from my Country: an epic novel in verse*, trans. Randy Blasing and Mutlu Konak, Persea Books, 2002

Clarence Richard Johnson, *Constantinople To-day, or, The Pathfinder Survey of Constantinople; a study in oriental social life*, Macmillan (New York), 1922

Kadıköy Life, January / February, 85, 2019; March / April, 86, 2019; May / June, 87, 2019

Charles King, *Midnight at the Pera Palace: the Birth of Modern Istanbul*, W. W. Norton, 2015

Albert Howe Lybyer, 'Turkey Under the Armistice', *The Journal of International Relations* 12:4, 1922

Daniel-Joseph MacArthur-Seal, 'Intoxication and Imperialism, Nightlife in Occupied Istanbul, 1918–23', Comparative Studies of South Asia, Africa and the Middle East 37:2, 2017

— , *Britain's Levantine Empire, 1914–1923*, Oxford University Press, 2021

Elif Mahir Metinsoy, *Ottoman Women during World War I: Everyday Experiences, Politics and Conflict*, Cambridge University Press, 2017

Karl E. Meyer, 'Ghosts along the Bosphorus', *World Policy Journal* 24:3, 2007

A. E. Montgomery, 'The Making of the Treaty of Sèvres of 10 August 1920', *Historical Journal* 15:4, 1972

Katie Nadworny, 'Good Vibrations', *Cornucopia* Issue 56, 2017

Çiğdem Oğuz, *Moral Crisis in the Ottoman Empire: Society, Politics and Gender During WWI*, I. B. Tauris, 2021

Robert Olson, 'The Second Time Around: British Policy toward the Kurds (1921–22)', *Die Welt des Islams* New Series, Bd. 27, Nr. 91, 1987

Irfan Orga, *Portrait of a Turkish Family*, new edn, Eland, 2002

Pınar Şenışık, 'The Allied Occupation of İstanbul and the construction of Turkish national identity in the early twentieth century', *Journal of Nationalism and Ethnicity*, Nationalities Papers, 46:3, 2018

Ronald Grigor Suny, *"They Can Live in the Desert but Nowhere Else": a History of the Armenian Genocide*, Princeton University Press, 2015

CHAPTER THREE: THE LEGACIES OF HATS

Songül Alşan, '1923–1950 Yılları Arasında Rize'de Nüfus Yapısı', Atatürk Universitesi Türkiyat Araştırmaları Enstitüsü Dergisi (66), 2019

Zehra Aslan, 'Rize'de, Birinci Dünya Savaşi Yıllarinda Rus Donanmasinin Faaliyetleri Ve Göçmenlerin Durumu (1915–1917)', *Karadeniz İncelemeleri Dergisi* 9:17, 2014

Omer Bartov and Eric D. Weitz, *Shatterzone of Empires: Coexistence and Violence in the German, Habsburg, Russian, and Ottoman Borderlands*, Indiana University Press, 2013

Ildikó Bellér-Hann and Chris Hann, *Turkish region: state, market & social identities on the east Black Sea coast*, James Currey, 2001

Gavin D. Brockett, *Islamic Reaction to the Turkish Revolution*, Master's Thesis 1990, University of Victoria

— , 'Collective Action and the Turkish Revolution: Towards a Framework for the Social History of the Atatürk Era, 1923–38', *Middle Eastern Studies* 34:4, 1998

Gazi Doğan, *The Establishment of Kemalist Autocracy and Its Reform Policies in Turkey*, PhD Thesis, Kansas State University, 2016

Yasemin Doğaner, 'The Law on Headdress and Regulations on Dressing in the Turkish Modernization', *Bilig* 51, 2009

Pablo Dominguez Andersen and Simon Wendt, eds, *Masculinities and the Nation in the Modern World: Between Hegemony and Marginalization*, Palgrave Macmillan (New York), 2015

Kaya Genç, 'Turkey's Glorious Hat Revolution', *Los Angeles Review of Books*, November 11th 2013 – https://lareviewofbooks.org/article/turkeys-glorious-hat-revolution/ – accessed 10/10/21

Ryan Gingeras, *Eternal Dawn: Turkey in the Age of Atatürk*, Oxford University Press, 2019

Mona Hassan, *Longing for the Lost Caliphate: a Transregional History*, Princeton University Press, 2016

Recep Koyuncu, *Ankara İstiklâl Mahkemesinin Rize Duruşmaları*, Heyamola Yayınları, 2023

Michael E. Meeker, 'The Black Sea Turks: Some Aspects of Their Ethnic and Cultural Background', *International Journal of Middle East Studies* Vol. 2, No. 4, 1971

— , *A Nation of Empire: the Ottoman Legacy of Turkish Modernity*, University of California Press, 2002

Murat Metinsoy, 'Everyday Resistance and Selective Adaptation to the Hat Reform in Early Republican Turkey', *International Journal of Turcologia* 16:8, 2013

Camilla T. Nereid, 'Kemalism on the Catwalk: The Turkish Hat Law of 1925', *Journal of Social History* 44:4, 2011

Zeki Sarıgil, 'Ethnic Groups at "Critical Junctures": The Laz vs. Kurds', *Middle Eastern Studies* 48:2, 2012

Jeremy Seal, *A Fez of the Heart*, Picador, 1995

Nesim Şeker, 'Forced Population Movements in the Ottoman Empire and the Early Turkish Republic: An Attempt at Reassessment through Demographic Engineering', *European Journal of Turkish Studies* 16, 2013

Owen Tweedy, 'Turkey in step with twentieth century civilization', *Current History (1916–1940)* 29:2, 1928

Uğur Ümit Üngör, *Young Turk Social Engineering: Mass Violence and the Nation State in Eastern Turkey, 1913–1950*, University of Amsterdam, 2009

Hale Yılmaz, *Becoming Turkish: Nationalist Reforms and Cultural Negotiations in Early Republican Turkey, 1923–1945*, Syracuse University Press (New York), 2013

CHAPTER FOUR: '38

George J. Andreopoulos, ed., *Genocide: Conceptual and Historical Dimensions*, University of Pennsylvania Press, 1997

Nick Ashdown, 'Turkey's Alevis and the myths of the mountain goats', *Middle East Eye* 07/12/20 – https://www.middleeasteye.net/discover/turkey-dersim-tunceli-zaza-alevi-goat-myth – accessed 26/01/2024

Ezgi Başaran, *Frontline Turkey: the Conflict at the Heart of the Middle East*, I. B. Tauris, 2017

Michael Benanav, 'Finding Paradise in Turkey's Munzur Valley', *New York Times*, June 26 2015 – https://www.nytimes.com/2015/06/28/travel/finding-paradise-in-turkeys-munzur-valley.html – accessed 12/02/2023

Soner Çağaptay, 'Reconfiguring the Turkish Nation in the 1930s', *Nationalism and Ethnic Politics* 8:2, 2002

Berfin Çiçek, 'Telling the Memories of a Massacre: Testimonies from Dersim's 38', History, Culture, and Heritage, AHM Conference 2022: 'Witnessing, Memory, and Crisis', Volume 1, June 2022

Cuma Çiçek, *The Kurds of Turkey: National, Religious and Economic Identities*, I. B. Tauris, 2016

Dilşa Deniz, 'Re-assessing the Genocide of Kurdish Alevis in Dersim, 1937–38', *Genocide Studies and Prevention: An International Journal* 14:2, 2020

Oya G. Ersever, 'Women's Rights and Education in the Republic of Turkey', *Peace Research* 30:4, 1998

Özgür Fındık, *Kara Vagon: Dersim Katliami*, Belgesi [Documentary], 2011

Erdal Gezik and Ahmet Kerim Gültekin, eds, *Kurdish Alevis and the Case of Dersim: Historical and Contemporary Insights*, Lexington Books, 2019

Özlem Göner, 'Histories of 1938 in Turkey: Memory, Consciousness, and Identity of Outsiderness', *International Review of Qualitative Research* 9:2, 2016

— , *Turkish National Identity and its outsiders: memories of state violence in Dersim*, Routledge, 2017

Ahmet Kerim Gültekin, 'Dersim as a Sacred Land', Chapter 16 in Stephen E. Hunt, ed., *Ecological Solidarity and the Kurdish Freedom Movement: Thought, Practice, Challenges, and Opportunities*, Lexington Books, 2021

Randy Blasing and Mutlu Konak, *Poems of Nazim Hikmet*, Persea, 2003

Çiçek Ilengiz, 'Erecting a Statue in the Land of the Fallen: Gendered Dynamics of the Making of Tunceli and Commemorating Seyyid Rıza in Dersim', *European Review of Feminism*, Heft 2, 2019

Mehmed S. Kaya, *The Zaza Kurds of Turkey: a Middle Eastern minority in a globalised society*, I. B. Tauris, 2011

Zeynep Kezer, 'Spatializing Difference: The Making of an Internal Border in Early Republican Elazığ, Turkey', *Journal of the Society of Architectural Historians* 73:4, 2014

Hans-Lukas Kieser, 'Dersim Massacre, 1937–1938', *Mass Violence & Résistance* [online], 27 July 2011

L. Molyneux-Seel, 'A Journey in Dersim', *The Geographical Journal* 44:1, 1914

Leyla Neyzi, 'Gülümser's Story: Life History Narratives, Memory and Belonging in Turkey', *New Perspectives in Turkey* 20, Spring 1999

Robert Olson, 'The Kurdish Rebellions of Sheikh Said, Mt Ararat, and Dersim: Their Impact on the Development of the Turkish Air Force and on Kurdish and Turkish Nationalism', *International Journal for the Study of Modern Islam*, March 2000

Gözde Orhan, 'Remembering a Massacre: how did the rise of oral history as a methodology improve Dersim studies?', *Wrocławski Rocznik Historii Mówionej*, June 2020

David Shankland, *The Alevis in Turkey: the Emergence of a Secular Islamic Tradition*, RoutledgeCurzon, 2003

Şule Toktaş, 'Nationalism, Modernization and the Military in Turkey: Women Officers in the Turkish Armed Forces', *Oriente Moderno* 23, 2004

Annika Törne, 'Dedes in Dersim: Narratives of Violence and Persecution', *Iran and the Caucasus* 16, 2012

— , ' "On the grounds where they will walk in a hundred years' time" – Struggling with the heritage of violent past in post-genocidal Tunceli', *European Journal of Turkish Studies* 20, 2015

Erol Ülker, 'Assimilation, Security and Geographical Nationalization in Interwar Turkey: The Settlement Law of 1934', *European Journal of Turkish Studies* 7, 2008

Nicole Watts, 'Relocating Dersim: Turkish State-building and Kurdish Resistance, 1931–1938', *New Perspectives on Turkey* 23, Fall 2000

CHAPTER FIVE: A TURKISH TINA TURNER

Amélie Barras, 'The Struggle of Devout Turkish Women for Full Citizenship', *Middle East Report* 32, 2012

Ebrar Beşinci, *Şule Yüksel Şenler*, Master's Thesis, TC Marmara Universitesi, 2017

Ebrar Beşinci Şimşek and Ali Coşkun, 'Tarihsel Süreç İçinde İslamci Kadin Kimliğinin İnşasi Ve Şule Yüksel Şenler'in Rolü', *Toplum Bilimleri Dergisi* 11:21, 2017

Ali Çarkoğlu and Ersin Kalaycıoğlu, *The Rising Tide of Conservatism in Turkey*, Palgrave Macmillan, 2009

Emel Çokoğullar and Bakko Bozaslan, '1967–1980 Arası Dönemde Cemiyetin Kurtarılması Misyonu ile Tanımlanmaya Başlanan "İslamcı Kadın" Kimliği', SBF Dergisi 69:4, Ankara Universitesi, 2014

Rüstem Ertuğ Altınay, 'Şule Yüksel Şenler: An Early Style Icon of Urban Islamic Fashion in Turkey', Chapter 5 in Emma Tarlo and Anneliese Moors, eds, *Islamic Fashion and Anti-fashion: New Perspectives from Europe and North America*, Bloomsbury Academic, 2013

Sema Genel and Kerem Karaosmanoğlu, 'A New Islamic Individualism in Turkey: Headscarved Women in the City', *Turkish Studies* 7:3, 2006

Cemal Karakas, 'Turkey: Islam and Laicism Between the Interests of State, Politics, and Society', Peace Research Institute Frankfurt, January 2007

Nilüfer Göle, *The Forbidden Modern: civilization and veiling*, University of Michigan Press, 1996

Nazan Maksudyan et al., *Women and the City, Women in the City: a gendered perspective on Ottoman urban history*, Berghahn, 2014

Şerif Mardin, *Religion and Social Change in Modern Turkey: The Case of Bediüzzaman Said Nursi*, State University of New York Press, 1989

Mehmed Mazlum Çelik, 'Zulümle mücadeleyi cinsiyet değil, şahsiyet meselesine dönüştüren yazar: Şule Yüksel Şenler',

Independent Türkçe, 28 August 2020 – https://www.indyturk. com/node/234901/k%C3%BClt%C3%BCr/zul%C3%BCmle-m%C3%BCcadeleyi-cinsiyet-de%C4%9Fil-%C5%9Fahsiyet-meselesine-d%C3%B6n%C3%BC%C5%9Ft%C3%BCren-yazar-%C5%9Fule – accessed 12/04/23

M. Sait Özervarli, 'Reconstruction of Islamic Social Thought in the Modern Period: Nursi's Approach to Religious Discourse in a Changing Society', *Asian Journal of Social Science* 38:4, 2010

Ayşe Saktanber and Gül Çorbacıoğlu, 'Veiling and Headscarf-Skepticism in Turkey', *Social Politics: International Studies in Gender, State and Society* 15, 2008

Tuba Sarı, 'Changing Urban Pattern of Eminönü: Reproduction of Urban Space via Current Images and Function', *Athens Journal of Architecture*, January 2018

Şule Yüksel Şenler interview, 02/03/2012 – https://www.timeturk.com/tr/2012/03/02/sonradan-hidayete-erenler-daha-suurlu.html accessed 26/01/2024

Sule Magazine archive – https://katalog.idp.org.tr/dergiler/67/sule

Seher Vakti Magazine archive – https://katalog.idp.org.tr/dergiler/65/seher-vakti

Kim Shively, 'Religious Bodies and the Secular State: The Merve Kavakci Affair', *Journal of Middle East Women's Studies* 1:3, 2005

Demet Tezcan, *Bir Çığır Öyküsü / Şule Yüksel Şenler*, Timaş Yayinlari, İstanbul, 2007

Jan-Markus Vömel, 'Global Intellectual Transfers and the Making of Turkish High Islamism c. 1960–1995', Chapter 9 in Deniz Kuru and Hazal Papuççular, eds, *The Turkish connection: global intellectual histories of the late Ottoman Empire and republican Turkey*, De Gruyter Oldenbourg, 2002

Jenny B. White, 'State Feminism, Modernization, and the Turkish Republican Woman', *NWSA Journal* 15:3, 2003

CHAPTER SIX: THE LAST OF THE BANDITS

Serat Akcan, *Batman'da Petrolün Bulunmasi, Kente Sosyoekonomik Ve Sosyokültürel Etkileri (1940–1970)*, Master's Thesis, Batman University, 2018

Seda Altuğ, 'Culture of Dispossession in the Late Ottoman Empire and

Early Turkish Republic', in Yael Navaro, Zerrin Özlem Biner, Alice von Bieberstein, and Seda Altuğ, eds, *Reverberations: violence across time and space*, University of Pennsylvania Press, 2021, chapter 3

Arif Arslan, *Yüz Yüze Batman*, Berdan Matbaacılık, 2015

Senem Aslan, 'Everyday forms of state power and the Kurds in the early Turkish republic', *International Journal of Middle Eastern Studies 43*, 2011

Karen Barkey, *The Ottoman Route to State Centralisation*, Cornell University Press, 1994

Ryan Gingeras, *Heroin, Organised Crime and the Making of Modern Turkey*, Oxford University Press, 2014

Mehmet Gürses, *Anatomy of a Civil War*, University of Michigan Press, 2018

Şan Ararat Halis, 'Representation of Bandits in Turkish Cinema', *Online Journal of Art and Design*, 4:1, 2016

Mehmet Ali İzmir, *Son Eşkıya Kocero*, Birey, 2004

Fuat Keyman, ed., *Symbiotic Antagonisms: Competing Nationalisms in Turkey*, University of Utah Press, 2011, chapter 10

Ahmet Özcan, 'The Last Kurdish Bandits in Modern Turkey: Analysis of Kurdish "Spontaneous" Individual Uprisings or Banditry Against the Turkish Nation State', *L'homme et la société*, 187, 2013

Francis O'Connor, *Understanding Insurgency: popular support for the PKK in Turkey*, Cambridge University Press, 2021

Zeynep Oğuz, 'Unintended Consequences of Turkey's Quest for Oil', *MERIP*, 296, 2020

Ahmet Özcan, *The Missing Link in the chain of Oppression and Resistance: Last Era of Kurdish Banditry in Modern Turkey, 1950–1980*, PhD thesis, Bogazici University, 2014

Hayriye Özen, 'Latent dynamics of movement formation: The Kurdish case in Turkey (1940s–1960s)', *Current Sociology*, 63:1, 2015

Murat Sunkar and Sadettin Tonbul, 'Batman Şehrinin Kuruluş Ve Gelişmesi', *Coğrafya Dergisi*, 21, İstanbul 2010

Ömer Tekdemir, *Constituting the Political economy of the Kurds*, Routledge, 2021

Uğur Ümit Üngör, 'Rethinking the Violence of Pacification: State Formation and Bandits in Turkey, 1914–1937', *Comparative Studies in Society and History 54*:4, 2012

Paul White, 'Economic Marginalization of Turkey's Kurds: the failed promise of modernization and reform', *Journal of Muslim Minority Affairs*, 18:1, 1998

Veli Yadırgı, *The Political Economy of the Kurds of Turkey*, Cambridge University Press, 2017

Mesut Yeğen, 'Prospective Turks or Pseudo-Citizens', *Middle East Journal*, 63:4, 2009

— , 'Banditry to Loyalty: The Kurdish Question in Turkey', in Ayse Kadioglu and Fuat Keyman, *Symbiotic Antagonisms: Competing Nationalisms in Turkey*, University of Utah Press, 2011, chapter 10

Sinan Yıldırmaz, *Politics and the Peasantry in post-war Turkey*, I. B. Tauris, 2017

CHAPTER SEVEN: INTERLUDE – THE FIRST BRIDGE

Anon., 'Bosporus Bridge, Proc. Brown Parsons and Knox Discussion', *Instn Ciu. Engrs*, Part 1, 1976

Anon., *Dünden Bugüne İstanbul Ansiklopedisi*, Cilt 2, Kültür Bakanlığı ve Tarih Vakfı'nın ortak yayınıdır, İstanbul, 1994

Anon., 'First Intercontinental Bridge', *Science*, 126: 3285, 1957

Esra Akcan, 'The Melancholies of Istanbul', *World Literature Today*, 80:6, 2006

Türkan Akkaya-Kalaycı, Christian Popow, Dietmar Winkler, R. Hülya Bingöl, Türkay Demir and Zeliha Özlü, 'The impact of migration and culture on suicide attempts of children and adolescents living in Istanbul', *International Journal of Psychiatry in Clinical Practice* 19, 2015

Sevim Aktaş, 'The Urbanisation Issue and the Culture of Gecekondus in Turkey', *Oriente Moderno*, 2013, 93:1

Sencer Ayata, 'Migrants and Changing Urban Periphery: Social Relations, Cultural Diversity and the Public Space in Istanbul's New Neighbourhoods', *International Migration* Vol. 46 (3), 2008

Sirel Ayşe, 'An Analysis of the Relationship Between Transport and Urban Structure In Istanbul', *Journal of Urban and Landscape Planning* 6, 2021

Hale Çıracı and Seda Kundak, 'Changing Urban Pattern of Istanbul; From Monocentric to Polycentric Structure', 40th Congress of the European Regional Science Association: 'European Monetary Union and Regional Policy', 29 August to 1 September 2000

Nora Fisher-Onar, Susan C. Pearce, E. Fuat Keyman, eds, *Istanbul, Living with difference in a global city*, Rutgers University Press, 2018

Murat Gül, *Architecture and the Turkish City, An Urban History of Istanbul Since the Ottomans*, I. B. Tauris, 2017

Christopher Houston, *Istanbul: City of the Fearless*, University of California Press, 2020

Çağlar Keyder and Ayşe Öncü, 'Globalisation of a third-world metropolis', *Review* 17:3, 1994

Cengiz Orhonlu, 'Boat Transportation in Istanbul, an historical survey', *Turkish Studies Association Bulletin*, 1989

Emin Özgür Özakın, 'Becoming Gap of the (bosphorus) bridge', *International Studies in Philosophy* 40.1, 2011

Jean-François Perouse, 'Istanbul Since 1923', in Nicolas Monceau, ed., *Istanbul: Histoire, Promenades, Anthologie & Dictionnaire*, Bouquins, 2010

Henry Petroski, 'Bridges of the Mediterranean', *American Scientist* 99:1, 2011

Ö. Burcu Özdemir Sarı, Suna S. Özdemir, Nil Uzun, eds, *Urban and Regional Planning in Turkey*, Springer, 2019

Esra Tekeli, Dinemis Kuşuluoğlu, Melike Ersoy, 'Kentleşme ve Yeşil Alan Değişiminde İstanbul Boğaz Köprülerinin Rolü', *Anadolu Doğa Bilimleri* 6:2, 2015

Ahmet Topçu, *Anlatımlı Resim Galerisi*, Eskişehir University, 2016

Nil Uzun, 'Urban Governance in Istanbul', *Analise Social*, 45:197, 2010

Jenny White, *Islamist Mobilisation in Turkey, A Study in Vernacular Politics*, University of Washington Press, 2002

Murat Cemal Yalçıntan and Adem Erdem Erbas, 'Impacts of Gecekondu on Electoral Geography of Istanbul', *International Labour and Working Class History*, 64 2003

William Zuk, 'Bridge Engineering', *The Military Engineer*, 73:474, 1981

CHAPTER EIGHT: THE END OF THE LEFT

Anon., *Turkey: OECD Economic Survey*, April 1980

Anon., *Unutturulanlar – 1) Fatsa Gerçeği*, Açılım Belgeleme Filmcilik, 2007

Onur Acaroğlu, 'Paris 1871 and Fatsa 1979: revisiting the transition problem', *Globalizations*, 2018

Pertev Aksakal, *Bir Yerel Yönetim Deneyi*, Simge Yayınevi, 1989

Ahmet Becioğlu, *Fikri Sönmez*, Su Yayınevi, 2020

Sumercan Bozkurt, *The Resistance Committees: Devrimci Yol and the Question of Revolutionary Organization in Turkey in the Late 1970s*, Master's Thesis, METU, 2008

Ö. Burcu, Özdemir Sarı, Suna S. Özdemir, Nil Uzun n *Civilisation*, 12:1, 2019

Yeşeren Eliçin, 'Social Capital, Leadership and Democracy: Rethinking Fatsa', *International Journal of Social Sciences and Humanity Studies* 3:2, 2011

Ekin Erdem, '80'lerin Doğuşu: Turk Siyasal Hayatinda 1979–80 AP Azinlik Hukumeti', International Congress on Critical Debates in Social Sciences, Conference Paper, September 2022

Derya Fırat, 'Sites of Memory of the 1980 Military Coup in Turkey', in Maria Theresia Starzmann and John Roby, eds, *Excavating Memory*, University Press of Florida, 2016, chapter 2

Michael Gunter, 'Political Instability in Turkey During the 1970's, *Conflict Quarterly*, 1989

Ali Islam, 'Hazelnut Culture In Turkey', *Akademik Ziraat Dergisi*, 7:2, 2018

Elifcan Karacan, *Remembering the 1980 Turkish Military Coup d'État*, Springer VS, 2016

Kerem Morgül, *A History of the Social Struggles in Fatsa, 1960–80*, Master's Thesis, Bogazici University, 2007

— , 'Fatsa, Sol Popülizm ve Yerel Yönetimler', *Birikim* 239, 2009

Göze Orhon, *The Weight of the Past: Memory and Turkey's 12th September Coup*, Cambridge Scholars Publishing, 2015

Jim Paul, 'The Coup', *MERIP* Reports, No 93, 1981

— , 'Turkey: The Generals Take Over', *MERIP* reports 1981

Hade Türkmen, *Radicalisation of Politics at the Local Level: The Case of Fatsa During the Late 1970s*, Master's Thesis, METU, 2006

Utku Utkulu, 'The Turkish Economy', in Debbie Lovatt, ed., *Turkey since 1970*, Palgrave Macmillan, 2001

Jenny White, *Turkish Kaleidoscope*, Princeton University Press, 2021

Altan Yalpat, 'Turkey's Economy Under the Generals', *MERIP*, March/April 1984

Atilla Yayla, *Terörizm ve Fatsa Örnek Olayı Çerçevesinde Türkiye'de Terör*, PhD Thesis, Ankara University, 1986

— , 'Terrorism in Turkey', *SBF Dergisi: Ankara Universitesi*, 44, 3 (1989)

BIBLIOGRAPHY

Alp Yenen, 'Legitimate Means of Denying: Contentious Politics of
    Martyrdom in the Turkish Civil War (1968–1982)', *Behemoth* 12:9,
    2021
Deniz Yildirim and Evren Haspolat, eds, *Değişen Karadeniz'i Anlamak*,
    Phoenix, Ankara 2016
Ergin Yıldızoğlu, Ronnie Marguilies, 'Trade Unions and Turkey's Working
    Class', *MERIP* 121, 1984
Erdem Yörük, *The Politics of the Welfare State in Turkey*, Michigan Press
    2022

CHAPTER NINE: THE ORCHID ICE CREAM

Izak Atiyas, 'Recent Privatisation Experience of Turkey – A Reappraisal',
    in Ziya Onis and Fikret Senses, eds, *Turkey and The Global Economy*,
    Routledge, 2009, chapter 6
Ayşe Buğra, 'Class, Culture, and State: An Analysis of Interest Represent
    Action by Two Turkish Business Associations', *International Journal
    of Middle East Studies* 30, 1998
Ömer Demir, Mustafa Acar and Metin Toprak, 'Anatolian Tigers of
    Islamic Capital', *Middle Eastern Studies* 40:6, 2004
Gastro Dergisi, Metro Yayınları, 43, Ocak/Subat 2008
Priscilla Mary Işın, *Sherbet and Spice*, I. B. Tauris, 2013
— , *Bountiful Empire*, Reaktion Books, London, 2018
Nadire Karademir, 'Kahramanmaraş Kentinde Tarihsel Konutlar ve
    Turizm', *Erdem* 81, Aralik 2021
Ziya Onis, 'The Evolution of Privatisation in Turkey: the Institutional
    Context of Public-Enterprise Reform', International Journal of Middle
    East Studies 23, 1991
— , 'Turgut Özal and his Economic Legacy: Turkish Neo-Liberalism in
    Critical Perspective', *Middle Eastern Studies*, July 2004
Cenk Özbay, Ziya Umut Türem and Ayşecan Terzioğlu, eds, *The Making
    of Neoliberal Turkey*, Routledge, 2016
Gül Berna Özcan and Hasan Turunç, 'Economic Liberalisation and Class
    dynamics in Turkey', *Insight Turkey* 13:3, 2011
Ekrem Sezik, 'Turkish Orchids and Salep', *Acta Pharmaceutica turcica*, 44,
    2002
Kemal Kaan Tekinşen, Yusuf Biçer, 'Salep Orchids and Salep in
    Kahramanmaras Region', *Turk Bilimsel Derlemeler Dergisi*, 11:2, 2018

Selcuk Uygur, 'The Islamic Work Ethic and the Emergence of Turkish
    SME Owner-Managers', *Journal of Business Ethics* 88:1, 2009

CHAPTER TEN: THE POCKET HERCULES

Victor Bojkov, 'Bulgaria's Turks in the 1980s: a minority endangered',
    Journal of Genocide Research, 6:3, 2004
Frederick de Jong, 'The Muslim Minorities in the Balkans on the Eve of
    the Collapse of Communism', *Islamic Studies* 36:2/3, 1997
Ali Emonov, 'Islam and Muslims in Bulgaria: A Brief History', *Islamic
    Studies* 36:2/3, 1997
Kapka Kassabova, 'Border', *Granta* 2017
Oguzhan Keleş, *Examining the 'Pocket Hercules'*, Electronic Thesis and
    Dissertation Repository, University of Western Ontario, 2021
Craig Neff, "Heroic and Herculean," *Sports Illustrated*, 9 May 1988
— , 'Little Big Man Pound For Pound, Turkey's Naim Suleymanoglu Is The
    Best', *Sports Illustrated*, 14 September 1988
Jean-François Polo, 'Istanbul's Olympic Challenge', John Karamichas
    and Graeme Hayes, eds, *Olympic Games, Mega-Events and Civil
    Societies*, Palgrave Macmillan, 2012, chapter 4
Gary Smith, 'The Weight of the World', *Sports Illustrated*, 22 July 1992
Tamer Taşpınar, *Naim: Cep Herkülü*, Türkiye Halter Federasyonu, Ankara,
    2019
Terry Todd, 'Behold Bulgaria's Vest-Pocket Hercules', *Sports Illustrated*, 11
    June 1984
Tufan Türenç, *Naim Süleymanoğlu*, MD Yayıncılık, 2020
Darina Vasileva, 'Bulgarian Turkish Emigration and Return', *International
    Migration Review* 26:22, 1992
Çınar Yazıcı, *Halter: Temel Ağırlık Çalışmaları ve Güç Geliştirme*, Ertem
    Basin, 1999

CHAPTER ELEVEN: AHMET KAYA

Ozan Aksoy, 'The Soundtrack of Social Movements among Kurdish Alevi
    Immigrants from Turkey in Germany', *Journal of Ethnic and Cultural
    Studies* 6:2, August 2019
Ezgi Başaran, *Frontline Turkey*, I. B. Tauris 2017
Eliot Bates, 'Socal Life of Musical Elements', *Ethnomusicology* 56:3, 2012

BIBLIOGRAPHY

BBC Witness 11th November 2016 – https://www.bbc.co.uk/programmes/po4f319d

Hamit Bozarslan, Cengiz Güneş, and Veli Yadırgı, eds, *The Cambridge History of the Kurds*, Cambridge University Press, 2021

Ayşe Betül Çelik , "'I miss my village!": Forced Kurdish migrants in Istanbul and their representation in associations', *New Perspectives on Turkey*, no. 32, 2005

William Gourlay, *The Kurds in Erdogan's Turkey: Balancing Identity, Resistance and Citizenship*, Edinburgh University Press 2020

Mustafa Gurbuz, Jan Willelm Duyvendak, James Jasper, *Rival Kurdish Movements in Turkey, Exogenous Shocks on the Eve of the Millennium*, Amsterdam University Press 2016

Mehmet Gürses, *Anatomy of a Civil War: Sociopolitical Impact of the Kurdish Conflict in Turkey*, University of Michigan Press, 2018

Joost Jongerden, 'Villages of No Return', *Middle East Report* 235, 2005

Songül Karahasanoğlu, Gabriel Skoog, 'Synthesising Identity: Gestures of Filiation and Affiliation in Turkish Popular Music', *Asian Music* 40:2, 2009

Ilkay Kara, 'Açık Yaranın Sesi, Bir Politik Anlatı Olarak Ahmet Kaya Şarkıları', *İletişim*, 2019

Gülten Kaya and Emrah Aydoğdu, *Ahmet Kaya*, Gam Yayınları 2005

Aysun Kıran, *Re-presenting the Conflict: Multilingualism, Intertextuality, and non-translation in new Turkish cinema*, PhD thesis, UCL, 2019

Kevin McKiernan, 'Turkey's War on the Kurds', *Bulletin of the Atomic Scientists*, March 1999

Aliza Marcus, *Blood and Belief: The PKK and the Kurdish Fight for Independence*, New York University Press, 2007

Irene Markoff, 'The Ideology of Musical Practice and the Professional Turkish folk Musician: Tempering the Creative Impulse', *Asian Music* 22:1, 1990

Iren Özgür, 'Arabesk Music in Turkey in the 1990s and Changes in National Demography, Politics and Identity', *Turkish Studies* 7:2, 2006

David Romano, 'Modern Communications Technology in Ethnic Nationalist Hands: The Case of the Kurds', *Canadian Journal of Political Science*, 35:1, 2002

Reuben Silverman, 'Ahmet Kaya: Witness to the Age', 16 May 2015, https://reubensilverman.wordpress.com/2015/05/16/ahmet-kaya-witness-to-the-age/

Ibrahim Sirkeci, 'Exploring the Kurdish population in the Turkish context', *Genus* LVI, 1, 2000

Martin Stokes, 'Music, Fate and State', *Middle East Report*, 1989

— , 'The Media and Reform: The Saz and elektrozaz in Urban Turkish Folk Music', *British Journal of Ethnomusicology*, 1, 1992

— , 'Voices and Places: History, Repetition and the Musical Imagination', *The Journal of the Royal Anthropological Institute*, 3:4, 1997

— , 'Turkish Urban Popular Music', *Middle East Studies Association Bulletin*, Vol. 33, No. 1 (Summer 1999)

Welat Zeydanlıoğlu, 'Turkey's Kurdish Language Policy', *International Journal of the Sociology of Language*, 217, 2012

CHAPTER TWELVE: THE PRISON NATION

Ahmet Altan, 'I Will Never See The World Again', *Granta*, 2019

Noah Blaser, Foreign Policy, 8 August 2021 – https://foreignpolicy.com/2021/08/08/turkey-prison-complex-erdogan/

J. Bohannon, 'Grim Day for Turkish Science as Six Academics get long prison terms', *Science* 341, August 2013

Soner Çağaptay, *The New Sultan*, I. B. Tauris, 2017

Council of Europe 2021 penal statistics - https://www.coe.int/en/web/portal/-/council-of-europe-s-annual-penal-statistics-covid-19-pandemic-helped-reduce-europe-s-prison-population

Jim Crow and Sam Turner, 'Silivri and the Thracian hinterland of Istanbul: an historic landscape', *Anatolian Studies* 59, 2009

Yasin Doğan, *1970'li Yıllardan Günümüze Türkiye'de Hapishane Tipleri ve Kaza/İlçe Tipi Hapishanelerden Kampüs Tipi Hapishanelere Geçi*, Turkey's Center for Prison Studies 2015

Can Dündar, *We Are Arrested*, Biteback, 2016

Mustafa Eren, 'Osmanlı'dan Günümüze Türkiye Hapishanelerinin Üç Dönemi', *Toplum ve Kanun*, 8, 2013

Maureen Freely, 'The Prison Imaginary in Turkish Literature', *World Literature Today* 83:6, 2009

Zeynep Gönen, *The Politics of Crime in Turkey, Neoliberalism, Police and the Urban Poor*, I. B. Tauris, 2017

Serra Hakyemez, 'Margins of the Archive: Torture, Heroism and the Ordinary in Prison No. 5, Turkey', *Anthropology Quarterly* 90:1, 2017

Marmara Bölgesi Hapishaneleri, Hak İhlalleri Raporu, İnsan Hakları
    Derneği , Istanbul Şubesi, Ekim – Kasım – Aralık 2022
International Commission of Jurists, *The Gezi Park Case, A Trial
    Monitoring Report*, 2020
Gürcan Koçan and Ahmet Öncü, 'From the Morality of Living to the
    Morality of Dying: Hunger Strikes in Turkish Prisons', *Citizenship
    Studies* 10:3, 2006
Middle East Eye, 30 August 2019 - https://www.middleeasteye.net/
    big-story/ergenekon-trials-turkey-gulen
İrfan Neziroğlu, 'A Comparison of Law and Practice within the Turkish
    Prison System with Relevant International Prison Standards, with
    Special Reference to F-Type High Security Prisons', *Turkish Studies*
    7:3, 2006
OMCT, Briefing Note in *The Situation of Prisons and Prisoners in Turkey*,
    2022
Margaret Owen, 'First hand account oF the Fifth hearing oF the Kurdish
    Lawyers' trial held in the Silivri Prison courtroom, outside istanbul,
    on 20 June 2013', *New Journal of European Criminal Law* 4:3, 2013
Prisons of Turkey Report, 'Civil Society in the Penal System Association
    for European Prison Observatory', 2019
Reuters, 'How Turkey's courts turned on Erdogan's foes', 4 May 2020 –
    https://www.reuters.com/investigates/special-report/turkey-judges/
Dani Rodrik, 'Ergenekon and Sledgehammer: Building or Undermining
    the Rule of Law', *Turkish Policy Quarterly* 10:1, 2010
Kent Schull, *Prisons in the Late Ottoman Empire*, Edinburgh University
    Press, 2014
Herman Schwartz, Omer Karasapan and Joe Stork, 'Prison Conditions in
    Turkey', *Middle East Report*, 160, 1989
Murat Sevinç, 'Hunger Strikes in Turkey', *Human Rights Quarterly* 30:3,
    2008
Ali Sipahi, *The Labor-Based Prisons in Turkey, 1933–1953*, Master's Thesis,
    Bogazici University, 2006
Merve Tahiroğlu, 'How Turkey's Leaders Dismantled the Rule of Law', *The
    Fletcher Forum of World Affairs* 44:1, 2020
Özgün E. Toprak, 'The Authoritarian surveillant assemblage:
    Authoritarian state surveillance in Turkey', *Security Dialogue* 50:5,
    2019
Turkey Chapter. Human Rights Watch World Report 2019

Türkiye Büyük Millet Meclisi, İnsan Haklarını İnceleme Komisyonu, Silivri Ceza İnfaz Kurumları İnceleme Raporu, 2019

İhsan Yılmaz, Greg Barton, James Barry, 'The Decline and Resurgence of Turkish Islamism: The Story of Tayyip Erdoğan's AKP', *Journal of Citizenship and Globalisation Studies*, 2017; 1(1)

Deniz Yonucu, *Police, Provocation and Politics, Counterinsurgency in Istanbul*, Cornell University Press, 2022

Notes

1   Adnan Giz, *Bir Zamanlar Kadıköy, 1900–1950*, İBB Yayınları, 1988, pp. 96–105.
2   Arif Atılgan, Yeldeğirmeni Öyküsü, 12 January 2017, http://mimdap. org/2017/12/yeldedhirmeni-oykusu-arif-atylgan/, accessed 12/09/22.
3   Irfan Orga, *Portrait of a Turkish Family*, Eland, 2002, ch. 4.
4   Ibid., ch. 6.
5   Yiğit Akın, *When The War Came Home*, Stanford University Press, 2018, ch. 2.
6   Nâzim Hikmet, *Memleketimden İnsan Manzaraları*, YKY, 2002 (first publication 1966), translation by Randy Blasing and Mutlu Konak, *Human Landscapes from My Country*, Persea Books, 2002, p. 49.
7   *Kadıköy Life*, 87, May / June 2019.
8   Blasing and Konak, p. 49.
9   Grigoris Balakian, *Armenian Golgotha*, Knopf, 2009, ch. 6 and 7.
10 Yiğit Akın, ch. 5.
11 Irfan Orga, ch. 15.
12 Giz, pp. 96–105.
13 Cited in Yiğit Akın, ch. 4.
14 Çiğdem Oğuz, *Moral Crisis in the Ottoman Empire*, I. B. Tauris, 2021, ch. 5.
15 Ibid., ch. 3.
16 Gökhan Akçura, *Paris Mahallesi*, 19 June 2021, https://manifold.press/ paris-mahallesi accessed 12/09/22.
17 Akın, ch. 3.
18 Cited in Andrew Mango, *Ataturk*, John Murray, 2004, p. 185.
19 Ibid., p. 190.
20 Daniel-Joseph MacArthur-Seal, *Britain's Levantine Empire, 1914–1923*, Oxford, 2021, ch. 3.

21   Orga, ch. 18.
22   Giz, pp. 96–105.
23   Ryan Gingeras, *The Fall of The Sultanate*, Oxford University Press, 2016, ch. 6.
24   *Kadıköy Life*, 85, January / February 2019.
25   MacArthur-Seal, ch. 4.
26   'Geographical Elements in the Turkish Situation: A Note on the Political Map', *Geographical Review*, vol. 13:1 (Jan., 1923), pp. 122–129.
27   Alexis Alexandris, *The Greek Minority of Istanbul and Greek–Turkish Relations 1918–1974*, Centre for Asia Minor Studies, 1992.
28   Cited in Ronald Grigor Suny, *They Can Live in the Desert But Nowhere Else*, Princeton University Press, 2015, ch. 8.
29   Ibid.
30   Lerna Emekçioğlu, *Recovering Armenia, The Limits of Belonging in post-Genocide Turkey*, Stanford University Press, 2016, ch. 1.
31   Phillip Marshall Brown, 'From Sevres to Lausanne', *American Journal of International Law*, 18:1, 1924.
32   Gingeras, ch. 6.
33   Giz, pp. 96–105.
34   Cited in Akçura.
35   Gingeras, ch. 6.
36   Emekçioğlu, ch. 3
37   Erol Ülker, 'Turkish National Movement, Mass Mobilisation, and Demographic Change in Istanbul, 1922–1923', ch. 12, in M Ersoy and E Ozyurek eds, *Contemporary Turkey at a Glance II*, Springer, 2017.
38   Albert Howe Lybyer, 'Turkey Under the Armistice', *The Journal of International Relations*, 12:4, 1922.
39   Blasing and Konak, 2002, p. 14.
40   Emekçioğlu, ch. 3.
41   Mango, p. 397.

CHAPTER THREE: THE LEGACIES OF HATS

1   Mango, p. 374.
2   Ryan Gingeras, *Eternal Dawn, Turkey in the Age of Ataturk*, Oxford University Press, Oxford, 2019, ch. 3.
3   Mango, p. 404.
4   Gingeras, 2019, ch. 3.

5   Mango, p. 435.
6   Murat Metinsoy, 'Everyday Resistance and Selective Adaptation to the Hat Reform in Early Republican Turkey', *International Journal of Turcologia*, 16:8, 2013.
7   Cited in Camilla Nereid, 'Kemalism on the Catwalk', *Journal of Social History*, 44:4, 2011.
8   Hale Yılmaz, *Becoming Turkish*, Syracuse University Press, 2013, ch. 1.
9   Ibid.
10   Mango, p. 437.
11   Nereid, 2011.
12   Metinsoy, 2013.
13   Gavin Brockett, 'Collective Actino and the Turkish Framework', *Middle Eastern Studies* 34:4, 1998.
14   Michael Meeker, 'The Black Sea Turks', *International Journal of Middle East Studies*, 2:4, Oct. 1971, pp. 318–45.
15   Recep Koyuncu, *Ankara İstiklâl Mahkemesinin Rize Duruşmaları*, Heyamola Yayınları, 2023, pp. 1–60.
16   U. U. Üngör, *Young Turk social engineering: mass violence and the nation state in eastern Turkey, 1913–1950*, University of Amsterdam, 2009.
17   Gingeras, 2019, p. 119.
18   Koyuncu, pp 1–60.
19   Ibid.
20   Yılmaz, ch. 1.
21   John Lonsdale, 'African Pasts in Africa's Future', *Canadian Journal of African Studies*, 23:1, 1989.

CHAPTER FOUR: '38

1   L. Molyneux-Seel, 'A Journey in Dersim', *The Geographical Journal*, 44:1, 1914.
2   Cited in Zeynep Kezer, 'Spatializing Difference: The Making of an Internal Border in Early Republican Elazig, Turkey', *Journal of the Society of Architectural Historians*, 73, no. 4 (December 2014).
3   Soner Çağaptay, 'Reconfiguring the Turkish Nation in the 1930s', *Nationalism and Ethnic Politics*, 8:2, 2002.
4   Erik Zurcher, *Turkey: A Modern History*, I. B. Tauris, 2002, ch. 10.
5   Mango, p. 496.

6   Çağaptay, 2002.
7   Hans-Lukas Kieser, 'Dersim Massacre, 1937–1938, Mass Violence & Resistance', [online], published on 27 July 2011, accessed 17 May 2021, http://bo-k2s.sciences-po.fr/mass-violence-war-massacre-resistance/en/document/dersim-massacre-1937-1938
8   Ibid.
9   David Shankland, *The Alevis in Turkey*, Routledge, London 2003.
10   Michael Benanav, 'Finding Paradise in Turkey's Munzur Valley', NYT, 26 June 2015, accessed 10 October 2022, https://www.nytimes.com/2015/06/28/travel/finding-paradise-in-turkeys-munzur-valley.html
11   Erdal Gezik and Ahmet Kerim Gültekin, eds, *Kurdish Alevis and the Case of Dersim*, Lexington, 2019, introduction.
12   Nicole Watts, 'Relocating Dersim, Turkish State-building and Kurdish Resistance, 1931–1938', *New Perspectives on Turkey*, fall 2000, 23.
13   Kezer, 2014.
14   Watts, 2000.
15   Özlem Göner, *Turkish National Identity and its outsiders: memories of state violence in Dersim*, Routledge, 2017, ch. 2.
16   Mango, p. 500.
17   Kezer, 2014.
18   Cited in Watts, 2000.
19   Martin van Bruinessen, 'Genocide in Kurdistan?', in George J. Andreopoulos, ed., *Conceptual and Historical Dimensions of Genocide*, University of Pennsylvania Press, 1994, pp. 141–70.
20   Kieser, 2011.
21   Robert Olson, 'The Kurdish Rebellions of Sheikh Said, Mt Ararat, and Dersim: Their Impact on the Development of the Turkish Air Force and on Kurdish and Turkish Nationalism', *International Journal for the Study of Modern Islam*, March 2000.
22   Cited in Watts, 2000.
23   Goner, ch. 2.
24   Cited in Watts, 2000.
25   Cited in Kieser, 2011.
26   Goner, ch. 2.
27   Kieser, 2011.
28   Ibid.
29   Translation by Randy Blasing and Mutlu Konak, *Poems of Nazim Hikmet*, Persea, 2003.

CHAPTER FIVE: A TURKISH TINA TURNER

1   Demet Tezcan, Bir Çığır Öyküsü, *Sule Yuksel Senler*, Timas Yayinlari, 2007, p. 58.
2   Şenler interview, 2 March 2012, https://www.timeturk.com/ tr/2012/03/02/sonradan-hidayete-erenler-daha-suurlu.html , accessed 12/06/23.
3   Tezcan, p. 90.
4   Nicholas Danforth, *The Remaking of Republican Turkey*, Cambridge University Press, 2021, ch. 1.
5   Tuba Sarı, 'Changing Urban Pattern of Eminonu', *Athens Journal of Architecture*, January 2018.
6   Tezcan, p. 90.
7   Ibid., p. 33.
8   Zurcher, pp. 237–240.
9   Tezcan, p. 36.
10 *Şule* (magazine), volume 4, October 1962 .
11 Jan-Markus Vomel, 'Global Intellectual Transfers and the Making of Turkish High Islamism', ch. 9 in Deniz Kuru and Hazal Papuççular, eds, *The Turkish Connection*, de Gruyter, 2022.
12 Cited in Emel Çokoğullar and Bakko Bozaslan, '1967–1980 Arası Dönemde Cemiyetin Kurtarılması Misyonu ile Tanımlanmaya Başlanan "İslamcı Kadın" Kimliği', *Ankara Üniversitesi SBF Dergisi*, 69:4 2015, pp. 835–69.
13 Tezcan, p. 40.
14 Şerif Mardin, *Religion and Social Change in Modern Turkey: The Case of Bediüzzaman Said Nursi*, State University of New York Press, 1989.
15 Cited in Ebrar Beşinci, *Şule Yüksel Şenler, Yüksek Lisans Tezi*, TC Marmara Universitesi, 2017, p. 89.
16 Cited in Mardin, p. 178.
17 Tezcan, p. 47.
18 Ayşe Saktanber and Gül Çorbacıoğlu, 'Veiling and Headscarf-Skepticism in Turkey', *Social Politics*, 15:4, 2008.
19 Tezcan, pp. 47–50.
20 Cited in Beşinci, p. 84.
21 Cited in Tezcan, p. 51.
22 Ibid., p. 135.
23 Ibid., pp. 70–100.

24 Jenny B White, 'State Feminism, Modernization, and the Turkish Republican Woman', *NWSA Journal*, 15:3, 2003.
25 Nilüfer Göle, *The Forbidden Modern*, University of Michigan Press, 1996.
26 *Seher Vakti*, issue 10, 1 August 1970.
27 Tezcan, pp. 245–55.
28 Şenler interview, 2 March 2012.

CHAPTER SIX: THE LAST OF THE BANDITS

1 Cited in Ahmet Özcan, 'The Last Kurdish Bandits in Modern Turkey: Analysis of Kurdish "Spontaneous" Individual Uprisings or Banditry Against the Turkish Nation State', *L'homme et la société*, 187, 2013.
2 *Milliyet*, 17 March 1962.
3 Şehmus Kartal, 19 February 2017, http://www.turizmhaberleri.com/koseyazisi.asp?ID=3399, accessed 13 February 2023.
4 Zeynep Oğuz, 'Unintended consequences of Turkey's Quest for Oil', MERIP, 296, 2020.
5 Mehmet Ali Izmir, *Son Eşkıya Kocero*, Birey, 2004, p. 12. (Plus additional information from interview with the author.)
6 Ibid., p. 16.
7 Ibid., p. 45.
8 Serhat Akçan, *Batman'da Petrolün Bulunmasi, Kente Sosyoekonomik Ve Sosyokültürel Etkileri (1940–1970)*, Yüksek LisansTezi, Batman Universitesi, 2018.
9 David McDowall, *Modern History of the Kurds*, I. B. Tauris, 2004, ch. 19.
10 Sinan Yıldırmaz, *Politics and the Peasantry in post-war Turkey*, I. B. Tauris, 2017, ch. 2.
11 *Cumhuriyet*, 25 July 1962.
12 Ali Izmir, p. 75.
13 'Turkey: I Am But a Simple Murderer', *Time Magazine*, 24 July 1964.
14 Ryan Gingeras, *Heroin, Organised Crime and the Making of Modern Turkey*, Oxford University Press, 2014, p. 95.
15 Cited in Özcan, 2013.
16 *Akis Magazine*, issue 423, 5 August 1962.
17 Ali Izmir, p. 57.
18 Cited in Arif Arslan, Yüz Yüze Batman, Berdan Matbaacılık, 2015.

19 Cited in Senem Aslan, 'Everyday forms of state power and the kurds in the early Turkish republic', *Int. J. Middle East Stud.* 43, 2011.
20 Cited in Özcan, 2013.
21 Cited in Akçan, p. 87.
22 Ali Izmir, p. 118.
23 Ibid., p. 138.
24 *Cumhuriyet*, 13 November 1959.
25 *Milliyet*, 28 June 1961, cited in Ozcan, 2013.
26 *Cumhuriyet*, 28 December 1961.
27 *Cumhuriyet*, 30 September 1962.
28 *Siirt Gazete*, 19 July 1962.
29 *Cumhuriyet*, 26 July 1962.
30 *Cumhuriyet*, 11 September 1962.
31 *Cumhuriyet*, 26 December 1961.
32 *Cumhuriyet*, 29 November 1962.
33 *Cumhuriyet*, 4–7 July 1964.
34 *Coventry Evening Telegraph*, 4 August 1964.
35 *Milliyet*, 25 December 1964.
36 Interview, 2005 https://www.haber7.com/yasam/haber/126998-babasi-daglarin-efsaneydi-o-yollarin, accessed 11/02/23.

CHAPTER SEVEN: INTERLUDE

1 Dünden Bugüne İstanbul Ansiklopedisi, Cilt 2, Kültür Bakanlığı ve Tarih Vakfı'nın ortak yayınıdır, 1994, p. 288.
2 Ahmet Topçu, *Anlatımlı Resim Galerisi*, Eskişehir Universitesi, 2016.
3 *Milliyet*, 5 June 1962.
4 Hentry Petroski, 'Bridges of the Mediterranean', *American Scientist*, 2011.
5 *Cumhuriyet*, 21 February 1970.
6 Cited in Jean-Francois Perouse, 'Istanbul Since 1923', in Nicolas Monceau, ed., *Istanbul: Histoire, promenades, anthologie & dictionnaire*, Bouquins, 2010.
7 Murat Gül, *Architecture and the Turkish City, An Urban History of Istanbul Since the Ottomans*, I. B. Tauris, 2017, ch. 4.
8 'Bosporus Bridge, Proc. Brown Parsons and Knox Discussion', *Instn Ciu. Engrs*, Part 1, 1976, 60, Aug., pp. 503–30.
9 *Cumhuriyet*, 27 March 1973.
10 *Cumhuriyet*, 21 February 1970.

11 N. Murat Ersavcı, Bir Anı, 27 June 2021 https://www.tepav.org.tr /tr/blog/s/6935/Bir+Ani_++Bogazici+Koprusunun+Acilis+Toreni+_ 30+Ekim+1973_+___+Kopruden+Ilk+Gecen+Kimdi_, accessed 22/01/24.

12 *Milliyet*, 31 October 1973.

13 *Cumhuriyet*, 1st November 1973.

14 *Milliyet*, 7 December 1973, cited in Topçu, 2016.

15 Cited in Christopher Houston, *Istanbul, City of the Fearless*, University of California Press, 2020, p. 120.

16 Perouse, 2010.

17 *Cumhuriyet*, 15–16 January 1975.

CHAPTER EIGHT: THE END OF THE LEFT

1 Cited in Pertev Aksakal, Bir Yerel Yönetim Deneyi, Simge Yayınevi, 1989.

2 Kerem Morgül, 'A History of the Social Struggles in Fatsa, 1960–80', Master's Thesis, Bogazici University 2007, pp. 75–91.

3 Sumercan Bozkurt, 'The Resistance Committees: *Devrimci Yol* And The Question Of Revolutionary Organization In Turkey In The Late 1970s', Master's Thesis, METU, 2008, p. 46.

4 Dr Atilla Yayla, 'Terrorism in Turkey', *SBF Dergisi: Ankara Universitesi*, 44, 3 (1989).

5 Morgül, pp. 75–91.

6 Ahmet Becioğlu, *Fikri Sönmez*, Su Yayınevi, 2020, p. 13.

7 Peter Schwartzstein, 22 August 2015, https://qz.com/483551/this-small-turkish-town-grows-a-quarter-of-the-worlds-hazelnuts, accessed 03/03/23.

8 Cited in Morgül, p. 49.

9 Ibid., pp. 44–66.

10 Atilla Yayla, 'Terörizm ve Fatsa Örnek Olayı Çerçevesinde Türkiye'de Terör', Doctoral Thesus, Ankara Universitu, 1986, p. 155.

11 Elifcan Karacan, *Remembering the 1980 Turkish Military Coup d'État*, Springer VS, 2016, p. 88.

12 Ibid, p. 90.

13 Hade Türkmen, 'Radicalisation of Politics at the Local Level: The Case of Fatsa During The Late 1970's', Master's Thesis, METU, 2006, p. 60.

14 UNUTTURULANLAR - 1) FATSA GERÇEĞİ, Açılım Belgeleme Filmcilik, 2007.

15 Karacan, p. 77.

16 Altan Yalpat, 'Turkey's Economy Under the Generals', *MERIP*, March/April 1984.

17 Ekin Erdem, '80'lerin Doğuşu: Turk Siyasal Hayatinda 1979–80 AP Azinlik Hukumeti', International Congress on Critical Debates in Social Sciences, Conference Paper, September 2022.

18 Alp Yenen, 'Legitimate Means of Denying: Contentious Politics of Martyrdom in the Turkish Civil War (1968–1982)', *Behemoth, A Journal on Civilisation*, 2019, 12:1.

19 Jenny White, *Turkish Kaleidoscope*, Princeton University Press, 2021, introduction.

20 Morgül, pp. 100–10.

21 Cited in Yayla, 1986, p. 161.

22 Türkmen, pp. 85–95.

23 Cited in Aksakal, 1989.

24 Becioğlu, p. 51.

25 *Cumhuriyet*, 14 October 1979.

26 *Cumhuriyet*, 15 October 1979.

27 Cited in Aksakal, 1989.

28 Cited in Türkmen, p. 99.

29 Morgül, p. 157.

30 Ibid., pp. 150–80.

31 Cited in Türkmen, p. 135.

32 Morgül, p. 182.

33 Metin Munir, 'Turkish Army Moves Against Leftists' "Liberated Zone"', 25 July 1980, https://www.washingtonpost.com/archive/politics/1980/07/25/turkish-army-moves-against-leftists-liberated-zone/6423275f-fb22-4c76-a1f2-c64f3deeb777/, accessed 15/03/2023.

34 *Cumhuriyet*, 4 July 1980.

35 *Cumhuriyet*, 9–10 July 1980.

36 *Cumhuriyet*, 11 July 1980.

37 *Cumhuriyet*, 12 July 1980.

38 *Cumhuriyet*, 12–14 July 1980.

39 *Cumhuriyet*, 15–16 July 1980.

40 Cited in Bianet, 10 September 2011, https://bianet.org/haber/31-yil-onceki-koselerden-80-darbesi-132623, accessed 30/01/2023.

41   Göze Orhon, *The Weight of the Past, Memory and Turkey's 12 September coup*, Cambridge Scholars Publishing, 2015.
42   *Cumhuriyet*, 23 January 1983.
43   Interview in Unutturulanlar - 1) Fatsa Gerçeği, 2007.
44   Morgül, pp. 202–3.

CHAPTER NINE: THE ORCHID ICE CREAM

1   Mary Işın, *Sherbet and Spice*, I. B. Tauris, 2013, p. 234.
2   Ibid., p. 232.
3   Gastro Dergisi, *Metro Yayinlari*, 43, January / February 2008.
4   *Delightland*, Turkish Confection Promotion Group, Issue 1, January 2015.
5   Dergisi, 2008.
6   *Delightland*, 2015.
7   Dergisi, 2008.
8   Ziya Öniş, 'The Evolution of Privatization in Turkey: The Institutional Context of Public-Enterprise Reform', *International Journal of Middle East Studies*, 23, 1991.
9   Ibid.
10   https://www.Anafikir.Gen.Tr/24-Ocak-Kararlari-Ve-Ozellestirmeler/, accessed 14/04/2023.
11   https://Ms.Hmb.Gov.Tr/Uploads/Sites/6/2020/03/%C4%B0%C5%9Fle tme-Sat%C4%B1%C5%9F-Devri.Pdf, accessed 13/04/2023.
12   *Forbes* Interview, 1999, https://www.Forbes.Com/ Consent/?Tourl=https://www.Forbes.Com/Global/1999/1018/058_01. Html, accessed 10/04/2023.
13   Para Dergisi Interview, 2019, http://www.Patronlardunyasi.Com/ Haber/Dunyada-425-Magazasi-Var-Iste-Dondurmanin-Efendisi/227754, accessed 09/04/2023.
14   President of Chamber of Commerce and Industry, Maraş, cited in CNN Turk 2017 - https://www.Cnnturk.Com/Turkiye/Maras-Dondurmasi-Tescilleniyor?Page=1, accessed 31/03/2023.

CHAPTER TEN: THE POCKET HERCULES

1   *The Age*, 8 December 1986.
2   *Sydney Morning Herald*, 10 December 1986.
3   *Sydney Morning Herald*, 13 December 1986.

4   *The Age*, 8 December 1986.

5   *The Age*, 13 December 1986.

6   *The Canberra Times*, 13 December 1986.

7   *LA Times*, 31 May 1987, https://www.Latimes.Com/Archives/La-Xpm-1987-05-31-Sp-9418-Story.Html, accessed 25/01/24.

8   Oğuzhan Keleş, *Examining The 'Pocket Hercules'*, Electronic Thesis And Dissertation Repository, University of Western Ontario, 2021, p. 34.

9   Craig Neff, 'Heroic And Herculean', *Sports Illustrated Vault*, 9 May 1988.

10 Peter Alfano, 'The Seoul Olympics: Weight Lifting; Intrigue On Way To Victory', *New York Times*, 22 September 1988.

11 Tamer Taşpınar, *Naim: Cep Herkulu*, Turkiye Halter Federasyonu, 2019, p. 8.

12 Terry Todd, 'Behold Bulgaria's Vest-Pocket Hercules', *Sports Illustrated Vault*, 11 June 1984.

13 Ibid.

14 Ibid.

15 Ibid.

16 Craig Neff, 'Little Big Man Pound For Pound, Turkey's Naim Suleymanoglu Is The Best', *Sports Illustrated Vault*, 14 September 1988.

17 *LA Times*, 31 May 1987.

18 *Sports Illustrated*, 11 June 1984.

19 Ibid.

20 Gary Smith, 'The Weight Of The World: Having Fled Oppression In Bulgaria, Naim Suleymanoglu Now Strains Under The Adoration Of The Entire Turkish People', *Sports Illustrated Vault*, 22 July 1992.

21 *Sports Illustrated Vault*, 9 May 1988.

22 *LA Times*, 21 September 1988, https://www.Latimes.Com/Archives/La-Xpm-1988-09-21-Sp-2312-Story.Html, accessed 17/02/2023.

23 Victor Bojkov, 'Bulgaria's Turks in the 1980s: a minority endangered', *Journal of Genocide Research*, 6:3, 2004.

24 Ibid.

25 Frederick de Jong, 'The Muslim Minorities in the Balkans on the Eve of the Collapse of Communism', *Islamic Studies*, 36:2/3, 1997.

26 Ibid.

27 Ali Eminov, 'Islam and Muslims in Bulgaria: A Brief History', *Islamic Studies*, 36:2/3, 1997.

28 *The Daily Telegraph*, 20 December 1986.

29 Bojkov, 2004.

30 *LA Times*, 31 May 1987.

31   *Sports Illustrated Vault*, 22 September 1988.
32   Cited in Keleş, p. 47.
33   *Fort Worth Star Telegram*, 2 March 1985.
34   Tufan Türenç, *Naim Süleymanoğlu*, MD Yayıncılık, 2020, pp. 100–40.
35   Ibid.
36   Kemal Kirişci, 'Beyond the Berlin Wall: The forgotten collapse of Bulgaria's "wall"' Brookings Institute, 5 November 2019, https://www. brookings.edu/blog/order-from-chaos/2019/11/05/beyond-the-berlin-wall-the-forgotten-collapse-of-bulgarias-wall/, accessed 10/01/2023.
37   *Sydney Morning Herald*, 16 December 1986.
38   Çınar Yazıcı, *Halter: Temel Ağırlık Çalışmaları ve Güç Geliştirme*, Ertem Basin, 1999, pp. 1–10.
39   *LA Times*, 31 May 1987.
40   *Cumhuriyet*, 21 September 1988.
41   *Cumhuriyet*, 24 September 1988.
42   *Cumhuriyet*, 27 September 1988.
43   Cited in Bojkov, p. 347
44   Darina Vasileva, 'Bulgarian Turkish Emigration and Return', *International Migration Review*, 26:22, 1992.
45   *LA Times*, 18 September 2000, https://www.latimes.com/archives/la-xpm-2000-sep-18-ss-23059-story.html, accessed 10/02/23.
46   *New York Times*, 'Olympic Reign of Pocket Hercules Ends', 17 September 2000.

CHAPTER ELEVEN: AHMET KAYA

1   Gülten Kaya and Emrah Aydoğdu, *Ahmet Kaya*, Gam Yayınları, 2005.
2   Welat Zeydanlıoğlu, 'Turkey's Kurdish Language Policy', *International Journal of the Sociology of Language*, 217, 2012.
3   David McDowall, *A Modern History of the Kurds*, I. B. Tauris, 3rd edn 2004, ch. 20.
4   Zeydanlıoğlu, 2012.
5   Aliza Marcus, *Blood and Belief: The PKK and the Kurdish Fight for Independence*, New York University Press, 2007, ch. 4.
6   Hamit Bozarslan, 'Dark Times: Kurdistan in the Turmoil of the Middle East, 1979–2003', Ch. 10 in Hamit Bozarslan, Cengiz Gunes, and Veli Yadirgi, eds, *The Cambridge History of the Kurds*, Cambridge University Press, 2021.

7   Aliza Marcus, ch. 4.
8   Gülten Kaya and Aydoğdu, 2005.
9   Cited in William Gourlay, *The Kurds in Erdoğan's Turkey: Balancing Identity, Resistance and Citizenship*, Edinburgh University Press, 2020, p. 68.
10 Ozan Aksoy, 'The Soundtrack of Social Movements among Kurdish Alevi Immigrants from Turkey in Germany', *Journal of Ethnic and Cultural Studies*, 6:2, 2019.
11 Ruben Silverman, 'Ahmet Kaya: Witness to the Age', 16 May 2015, https://reubensilverman.wordpress.com/2015/05/16/ahmet-kaya-witness-to-the-age/, accessed 20/02/2023.
12 Ferzende Kaya interview, 12 April 2023.
13 Silverman, 2015.
14 Martin Stokes, 'Music, Fate and State: Turkey's Arabesk Debate', *MERIP*, 160, 1989.
15 Songül Karahasanoğlu, Gabriel Skoog, 'Synthesising Identity: Gestures of Filiation and Affiliation in Turkish Popular Music', *Asian Music*, 40:2, 2009.
16 Martin Stokes, 'The Media and Reform: The Saz and Elektrosaz in Urban Turkish Folk Music', *British Journal of Ethnomusicology*, 1, 1992.
17 Gülten Kaya and Aydoğdu, 2005.
18 Ibid.
19 Cited in McDowall, ch. 20.
20 Ezgi Başaran, *Frontline Turkey: The Conflict at the Heart of the Middle East*, I. B. Tauris 2017, p. 29.
21 Marcus, ch. 6.
22 Cited in Marcus, ch. 7.
23 Ibid., ch. 11.
24 Joost Jongerden, 'Villages of No Return', *MERIP*, 235, 2005.
25 Kevin McKiernan, 'Turkey's War on the Kurds', *Bulletin of the Atomic Scientists*, March 1999.
26 Marcus, ch. 11.
27 Gündem, 1 September 1993, cited in Gülten Kaya and Aydoğdu, 2005.
28 Ferzende Kaya interview, 12 April 2023.
29 Marcus, ch. 20.
30 Ibid.
31 Zeydanlıoğlu, 2012.
32 Gülten Kaya BBC interview, 11 November 2016, https://www.bbc.co.uk/programmes/po4f319d, accessed 05/01/23.

33   Gülten Kaya and Aydoğdu, 2005.
34   Başaran, p. 31.
35   Cited in Gülten Kaya and Aydoğdu, 2005.
36   Başaran, p. 32.

CHAPTER TWELVE: THE PRISON NATION

1   Mustafa Eren, 'Osmanlı'dan Günümüze Türkiye Hapishanelerinin Üç Dönemi', *Toplum ve Kanun*, 8, 2013.
2   *Hürriyet*, 29 March 2008, https://www.hurriyet.com.tr/gundem/ avrupanin-en-buyuk-cezaevi-maalesef-bizde-8573167, accessed 20/09/22.
3   BBC report, 1 April 2008, http://news.bbc.co.uk/1/hi/world/ europe/7322431.stm, accessed 21/09/22.
4   *Hürriyet*, 5 July 2008, https://www.hurriyet.com.tr/gundem/ergenekon- u-bekleyen-ceza-ve-infaz-kampusuna-100-milyon-ytl-yatirildi-9359983, accessed 13/11/22.
5   *Hürriyet*, 10 November 2008, https://www.hurriyet.com.tr/ekonomi/ silivri-nin-nufusu-9-bin-kisi-artti-cezaevi-minibusu-islek-hat- oldu-10320488, accessed 13/11/22.
6   *Hürriyet*, 29 March 2008.
7   BBC, 1 April 2008.
8   Selçuk Kozağaçlı open letter, 3 August 2019, https://tr.euronews. com/2019/08/03/ozel-cezaevinden-mektuplar-yazi-dizisi-6-selcuk- kozagacli, accessed 12/02/23.
9   *Hürriyet*, 19 March 2008 and 5 July 2008.
10   CNN Türk, 14 June 2009, https://web.archive.org/web/20160303183404/ http:/www.cnnturk.com/2009/turkiye/06/14/silivri.cezaevine.yeni. durusma.salonu/530860.0/index.html, accessed 01/02/2023.
11   *Milliyet*, 18 November 2008, https://www.milliyet.com.tr/gundem/ silivri-cezaevi-nin-mecburi-komsulari-1017436, accessed 03/10/22.
12   *Hürriyet*, 10 November 2008.
13   Zeynep Gönen, *The Politics of Crime in Turkey, Neoliberalism, Police and the Urban Poor*, I. B. Tauris 2017, pp. 50–90.
14   Al Jazeera, 12 August 2013, https://www.aljazeera.com/ features/2013/8/12/analysis-turkeys-divisive-ergenekon-trial, accessed 01/03/2023.
15   Dani Rodrik, 'Ergenekon and Sledgehammer: Building or Undermining the Rule of Law', *Turkish Policy Quarterly*, 10:1, 2010.

16   *Middle East Eye*, 30 August 2019, https://www.middleeasteye.net/big-story/ergenekon-trials-turkey-gulen, accessed 11/02/23.

17   Soner Çağaptay, *The New Sultan: Erdogan and the Crisis of Modern Turkey*, I. B. Tauris, 2017, p. 131.

18   *Financial Times*, 12 June 2013, https://www.ft.com/content/2d73a0ca-d382-11e2-95d4-00144feab7de, accessed 27/04/2022.

19   Ihsan Yılmaz, Greg Barton, James Barry, 'The Decline and Resurgence of Turkish Islamism: The Story of Tayyip Erdoğan's AKP', *Journal of Citizenship and Globalisation Studies*, 2017; 1(1).

20   Cited in 'The Gezi Park Case, A Trial Monitoring Report', International Commission of Jurists, 2020.

21   Human Rights Watch, 21 June 2013, https://www.hrw.org/news/2013/06/21/turkish-protests-still-standing.

22   Merve Tahiroğlu, 'How Turkey's Leaders Dismantled the Rule of Law', *The Fletcher Forum of World Affairs*, 44:1, 2020.

23   'Prisons of Turkey Report', Civil Society in the Penal System Association for European Prison Observatory, 2019.

24   Can Dündar, *We Are Arrested: A Journalist's Notes from a Turkish Prison*, Biteback, 2016.

25   Özgün E. Toprak, 'The Authoritarian Surveillant Assemblage: Authoritarian state surveillance in Turkey', *Security Dialogue*, 50:5 2019.

26   Bülent Arınç comments as reported by Reuters 20 November 2020, https://uk.reuters.com/article/us-turkey-security-arinc/ally-of-turkeys-erdogan-calls-for-release-of-two-high-profile-prisoners-idUKKBN2800Y9

27   Amnesty International, 22 July 2019, https://www.amnesty.org/en/latest/news/2019/07/turkey-so-much-space-in-this-courtroom-yet-so-little-room-for-justice/, accessed 28/02/2024.

28   Council of Europe 2021 penal statistics, https://www.coe.int/en/web/portal/-/council-of-europe-s-annual-penal-statistics-covid-19-pandemic-helped-reduce-europe-s-prison-population

29   Noah Blaser, Foreign Policy, 8 August 2021, https://foreignpolicy.com/2021/08/08/turkey-prison-complex-erdogan/, accessed 28/01/2024.

30   Deniz Yonucu, *Police, Provocation and Politics, Counterinsurgency in Istanbul*, Cornell University Press, 2022, p. 108.

31   Human Rights Watch World Report 2019, Turkey Chapter, https://www.hrw.org/world-report/2019/country-chapters/turkey, accessed 28/01/2024.

32   Reuters, 19 October 2021, https://www.reuters.com/world/middle-east/

top-european-court-says-turkey-should-change-law-insulting-president-2021-10-19/, accessed 28/01/2024.

33 Tahiroğlu, 2020.

34 Türkiye Büyük Millet Meclisi İnsan Haklarını İnceleme Komisyonu, Silivri Ceza Infaz Kurumları Incleme Raporu, 2019.

35 Ahmet Altan, *I Will Never See The World Again*, translated by Yasemin Çongar, Granta, 2019.

36 Marmara Bölgesi Hapishaneleri, Hak İhalalleri Raporu, Insan Hakları Derneği, İstanbul Şubesi, Ekim – Kasım – Aralık 2022.

37 Ibid.

38 See the statement, for example, by rights groups on allegations of torture in Silivri in April 2022, https://tihv.org.tr/basin-aciklamalari/silivri-5-nolu-l-tipi-ceza-infaz-kurumunda-gerceklerin-ustu-ortulmeye-calisiliyor/

39 Yasin Doğan, 1970'li Yıllardan Günümüze Türkiye'de Hapishane Tipleri ve Kaza/İlçe Tipi Hapishanelerden Kampüs Tipi Hapishanelere Geçiş. Turkey's Center for Prison Studies, 2015.

40 BBC, 26 April 2022, https://bbc.co.uk/news/world-europe-61218241, accessed 28/01/2024.